Nature Has More Cures

Marie Lasater

Marie Lasater

ISBN:1537156322
ISBN-13:9781537156323

TABLE OF CONTENTS

Marie Lasater

1

FINGER MILLET – FOOD AT YOUR FINGERTIPS

Ezekiel 4:9 Take thou also unto thee wheat, and barley, and beans, and lentiles, and millet, and fitches, and put them in one vessel, and make thee bread thereof, according to the number of the days that thou shalt lie upon thy side, three hundred and ninety days shalt thou eat thereof.

Several months ago, I wrote about a mixed salad that was growing voluntarily in my wheelbarrow. Included in the mix were ground cherries, purslane and finger millet. At this time of year when most of us are feasting, it is appropriate to visit the subsistence diets of those less fortunate.

Locally, finger millet (eleusine Indica) is also called goose grass, and is often overlooked. In Africa, a closely related member of the finger millet family, eleusine coracona, is considered a famine food as the seeds of the plant are fully edible. Finger millet has been cultivated in India for over 4000 years. After being harvested, the seeds store very well for long periods.

Finger millet is especially valuable as it contains methionine, an important amino acid which is lacking in persons on a diet low in protein. Finger millet can be eaten whole, like tiny popcorn, or ground and cooked into breads, cakes or other dishes. As an added plus, it is gluten-free. In fact, it is considered one of the least allergenic and most digestible grains available and it is a warming grain so will help to heat the body in cold or rainy seasons and climates. Millet also contain high amounts of nitrilosides, (vitamin B-17 - laetrile), which helps to combat cancer and many other diseases

Finger millet is very similar to sorghum, and they are often confused. The amino acid and mineral composition of sorghum and millet are quite similar, although unlike sorghum, millet contains no Tyrosine. Finger millet has a sweet, nut-like flavor. 100 mg of finger millet supplies 7.6 gm of protein (nearly 15%), 1.5 gm fat, 88 g carbohydrate, 370 mg calcium, 3 gm of fiber and vitamins A, thiamine, niacin and riboflavin.

Millet is an extremely ancient food, and there is mention in the Bible as being one of the ingredients in the prophet's bread. It is the sixth most important grain in the world, sustaining one third of Earth's population. Millet can grow and flourish in difficult environments, as evidenced by the fact it popped up in my wheelbarrow.

Medicinal Uses

Blood Sugar Regulation

In a 2014 study, the effect of finger millet on high blood sugar levels in Type-2 diabetics (not dependent on insulin) was examined. The test subjects were given a meal with 75 grams of carbohydrates, and those with finger millet included in the meal had significantly lower plasma glucose levels at 2 hours after eating.

Anti-Oxidant and Anti-Inflammatory Effects

In another study this year, the anti-oxidant and anti-inflammatory effects of Eleusine Indica were examined. White blood cells were stressed with hydrogen peroxide, and a series of assays were used to analyze the protection provided by finger millet against antioxidant-induced DNA damage in the cells. The researchers concluded "These results clearly show the antioxidant capacity and anti-inflammatory activities of finger millet extracts."

Teeth and Bones

Finger millet is an excellent source of dietary calcium and fiber for people suffering from calcium deficiencies._Of all the cereals and millets, finger millet has the highest amount of calcium (344mg%) and potassium (408mg%), essential for tooth and bone health.

Other Health Benefits

The seeds are also rich in phytochemicals, including phytic acid, believed to lower cholesterol, and also associated with reduced risk of certain cancers.

Finger millet grows just about anywhere (like my wheelbarrow). Pop off the small seeds, and enjoy a healthy snack.

2

REDBUD (CERCIS CANADENSIS)

Redbud is a beautiful tree that blooms in Missouri in late March to early May, bringing a beautiful splash of color to our Ozark hills. The rose-purple flowers are small, arranged in clusters. Fruit pods containing seeds appear during September and October. Redbuds love to grow on the borders of woods, along rocky bluffs, and sometimes in open woodland. They're small trees in the pea family and among the first to bloom in the spring. They were first cultivated in 1641 and rumor has it that George Washington planted some around Mt. Vernon.

Sold as a wildlife shrub by the George O White Nursery, this is the time order your Redbud seedlings. Only 80 cents each, with a minimum order of 10 plants, you are getting quite a bargain. If you want to recruit various bird species, bees, and even deer to your property, having Redbud trees is quite an attraction. We are lucky to live east of the Rockies, because Redbud is difficult to grow west of Kansas. It must have made its way to Oklahoma though, because it is the state tree (possibly brought there by Native American tribes forced to relocate). It is easy to overlook any Redbuds scattered in your woods unless they are in bloom. Before and after blooming, the tree is so non-descript that it is worthwhile to flag it so it is not accidentally destroyed when clearing brush. We have an advantage in the Ozark Mountains as they often bloom the same time as the dogwoods.

Nutritional Uses

In parts of the Appalachian Mountains, green twigs from the Redbud tree are used as wild game seasoning; for this reason, the Redbud is sometimes called the Spicewood tree.

The seed pods of the Redbud are very edible when green and tender, and can be cooked just like peas, or pickled and used as a substitute for capers. The green seeds are 25% protein, 8% fat and 3% ash and contain the essential fatty acids linolenic, alpha-linolenic, oleic and palmitic.

Redbud flowers are very tasty, and are great raw in salads (the light colored upper part of the blossom is sweet, the darker lower part is slightly sour). Part of the Native American diet, the flowers were eaten raw or boiled; they also ate the roasted seeds. Redbud flower extract contains anthocyanins, powerful antioxidants. The flowers are high in Vitamin C. Redbud roots are also edible.

Medicinal Uses

Herbalists use extracts made from the inner bark and roots to treat colds, flu and fever. There is documentation of the Alabama and Delaware Indians using a similar preparation for fever, congestion and vomiting. The Cherokee used a bark infusion for what we know as whooping cough. Our local Osage used charcoal from the wood for war paint.

Redbud Propagation

Redbud Seeds can be forced to germinate by first dipping them in very hot, but not boiling, water for a minute and then sowing in a pot. Redbud cuttings can be taken 6-8 inches from the tip of a red bud shoot, clipped on an angle. Peel away the bark on 2 sides to allow the new roots to break through as they grow.

Redbud Blossom Muffins
(Courtesy of Green Deane *Eat the Weeds*)

2 cups redbuds blossoms
2 tablespoons minced rosemary
½ cup sugar
Minced zest of 1 lemon
1 ½ cups flour
2 teaspoons baking powder
½ teaspoon baking soda
¼ teaspoon salt
1 large egg
3/4 cup milk
1/2 cup yogurt
2 tablespoons melted butter or oil
1 tablespoon lemon juice

Topping:
1 tablespoon sugar
½ teaspoon ground cinnamon

Preheat oven to 375°F. In bowl #1, combine redbuds, herb, sugar, zest. Let sit 30 minutes. In bowl #2 Sift flour, powder, baking soda, salt large bowl. In bowl #3 Combine egg, yogurt, milk, oil, lemon juice. Pour the content of bowl one in to bowl two and toss. Add the wet ingredients from bowl three, stirring to just moisten. Do not over mix. Fill your muffin tins 3/4 full.

Combine sugar and cinnamon to make the topping. Sprinkle some on each muffin, Bake for 25 minutes, or until tops spring back when lightly touched. Remove from muffin pan and cool on a wire rack.

You can order seedlings online from the George O white nursery at mdc.mo.gov/node/3328. Order early to ensure that the seedlings you want are still available.

The seed pods of the Redbud are very edible and full of nutrients.

Redbud is a beautiful tree that blooms in Missouri in late March to early May

3

HOME MEDICAL KITS

Many folks are getting together a home medical kit, and I frequently get asked what should be included. The good news is, you can equip your home with some great diagnostic tools for about $130, or even less with a little bit of searching.

Why would you want to be able to perform a preliminary diagnosis at home? Often home diagnosis can help you (and your doctor) determine if a doctor visit is needed. It is very helpful to your physician if you have been tracking your blood pressure, and keeping a record. What if your child has an earache? You can inspect the middle ear, and see if there is just excessive wax, or a red, bulging tympanic membrane. While the back of mom's hand is the time-proven method of checking temperature, an accurate thermometer is a little more precise. Has your doctor told you that you may be pre-diabetic, and you are unsure if your diet is working? Does a family member have an upper respiratory infection, and seems to be having trouble breathing? There are inexpensive tools that can be purchased without a prescription that will provide both you and your doctor with valuable information. These tools and their prices are listed below.

Tympanic thermometer 27.99
Otoscope 27.50
Pulse oximeter 19.48
Blood pressure machine 29.99
Comedone extractor/curette 14.99
Glucose meter 10.00

Tympanic Thermometer

Considered the gold standard in temperature taking, second only to a pulmonary artery catheter, a tympanic thermometer measures takes its measurement in the ear, on the ear drum. Grasp the ear lobe, and gently pull back while inserting the thermometer tip snugly into the ear – don't force it! Hold the button until the thermometer beeps (about 2 seconds) and remove the thermometer. A precise, digital reading will be in the window. Obviously, if your child has an earache, you will measure the temperature in the other ear. Most tympanic thermometers have a memory, so you can go back and compare readings.

Otoscope

Now available in several models for home use, otoscopes are even available under the "Dr. Mom" brand, and come with pictures of what to look for when examining the middle ear. Commonly occurring problems concern ear tubes, have they been dislodged? Is there excess cerumen (ear wax) in the ear? Is the eardrum perforated with a visible hole? Are there signs of ear infection – a red, bulging eardrum? Or is there concern there may be a foreign body in the ear? With the exception of excessive ear wax which can be treated at home, these are problems that can be identified early, and followed up in your Doctor's office, often saving an emergency room visit.

Pulse Oximeter

Probably my favorite piece of diagnostic equipment is the pulse oximeter. Small, lightweight, non-invasive and fast, it literally puts NASA technology into your own hands. Pulse oximetry works by bouncing an infrared light off your red blood cells, which either absorb or refract the light. In a healthy person, the blood cells are at least 92% saturated with oxygen, resulting in a pulse ox reading of 92%. If breathing is not adequate, or there is impairment of oxygen delivery to the blood cells, the pulse oximeter reading will fall. We have all heard of people who unexpectedly die of pneumonia, after fighting off a cold at home. With pulse oximetry, you can easily measure your oxygen level, and if your oxygen level is low, immediately seek care. If a family member has a seizure disorder, the pulse oximeter can provide a real-time measurement of oxygen level during a seizure. Often it may look like the person is not breathing, but they are actually getting enough oxygen. What if someone passes out? Getting an oxygen reading is also helpful for the paramedics. The pulse oximeter also provides a pulse reading, so that passing out spell may be due to bradycardia, a very slow heart rate. A pulse oximeter is like a big clothespin that fits gently over a finger, very easy to use.

Continued next week…..

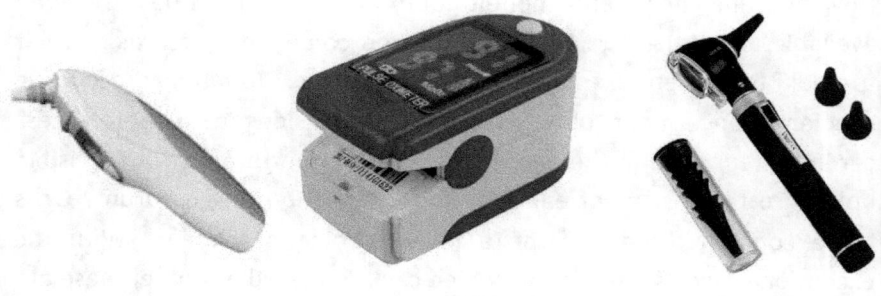

Tympanic thermometer. Pulse oximeter. Otoscope.

4

HOME MEDICAL KITS – PART 2

Last week we discussed preparing our home medical kits to give us the ability to perform some basic diagnostic tests at home. In this week's column we will review three more essential items to add to our kit, a blood pressure machine, glucose meter and a comedone extractor/ear curette.

Blood Pressure Machine

I recommend a semi-automatic blood pressure machine over the manual version for a few reasons. It can be tricky for an untrained person to accurately measure a blood pressure with the traditional cuff/stethoscope. An automatic blood pressure machine provides the pulse at the same time, and perhaps most important, using an automatic blood pressure cuff frees you up to perform other tasks (like checking oxygen saturation with your pulse oximeter) while the machine is cycling.

I see no reason to buy a brand new machine. Used machines can be found at any thrift store or flea market. I prefer the semi-automatic over the fully automatic as the operator controls how high the cuff is inflated. (Fully automatic machines can impede all circulation in your arm!) Textbook normal blood pressure is 120/70-80, and blood pressure greater than 140/90 on repeated readings is cause for concern.

If you are checking a blood pressure on a person with a large upper arm, whether it be due to obesity, or just big biceps, you can get an accurate measurement on the lower arm at the wrist. (Wrist measurements tend to run slightly higher than brachial measurements, those taken in the bend of the arm.) Just be sure that wherever the cuff is placed, the sensor is placed directly over the artery for an accurate measurement. To find the artery, gently palpate with two fingers until you feel a pulse.

If a person appears to be in shock, with a low blood pressure, say 80/40, have them lie on their back and put a pillow under their feet. This will return extra blood volume to the heart, and acts like a short term IV bolus while help is arriving.

Glucose Meter

If you are not a diabetic, you may wonder why I have added a glucose meter to the list. While high blood sugar can definitely cause problems, low blood sugar (hypoglycemia) is the true emergency. Normal, healthy folks can experience hypoglycemia for a variety of reasons. Extreme dieting, certain medications, or reactive hypoglycemia that occurs after eating large amounts of sugary foods provoking a huge insulin response can all cause symptomatic low blood sugar. Symptoms generally occur when blood sugar is 70 mg/dl or lower. Early symptoms of hypoglycemia include a shaky feeling, dizziness, confusion, headaches, irritability, anxiety, and headache.

I worked once with a very competent nurse who had recently lost a great deal of weight by following a low calorie diet. She became very irritable at work, and began arguing with the scheduler regarding her work schedule, and was generally acting irrationally. The astute nurses she worked with recognized the symptoms of low blood sugar, and encouraged her to drink a cup of orange juice with a little added sugar. She adamantly refused to ingest anything with sugar. Her coworkers then persuaded her to allow them to check her blood sugar, which was 40 mg/dl. She finally agreed to drank the orange juice, and within 10 minutes was back to normal. The moral of this story is, if she was not promptly treated, she could have wound up in a coma, and if driving, would likely wreck. More than one person has been arrested for DWI, and was simply experiencing hypoglycemia, as the symptoms are very similar.

Low blood sugar can also mimic a stroke. For this reason, one of the first tests paramedics or ER staff will perform on a suspected stroke victim is a rapid blood sugar test.

You can purchase a brand new glucometer online from eBay or similar sites for about $10. The catch is that the machine only comes with 10-15 testing strips, and they can be expensive. However, as a device to be used only in an emergency situation, a glucometer is certainly an inexpensive and critical piece of equipment to have available.

Comedone extractor/Ear Curette

Unlike the other equipment listed, this piece of equipment is not critical, but is certainly nice to have. In layman's terms, a comedone extractor is a blackhead remover. It is very helpful to extract not only blackheads, but other small objects imbedded in the skin. Using fingers to accomplish the same thing causes increased tissue trauma, but the comedone extractor pushes down on the edges of the object to be removed, and is actually used in dermatology offices.

Included in the $14.99 kit I found on Amazon are not only various sizes of extractors, but also a variety of ear curettes. (See picture). Ear curettes are used to safely remove wax from the ear canal, without pushing it back in as usually happens with Q-tips. Ear curettes can also be used to loop and remove a foreign object in the ear canal, of course using your otoscope to see what you are dealing with.

The maximum price for your entire medical kit should be under $130.00, but can be assembled for much less with careful shopping. You should be familiar with your new tools, and comfortable using them before being faced with an emergency situation. If unsure, ask your health care provider to provide instruction.

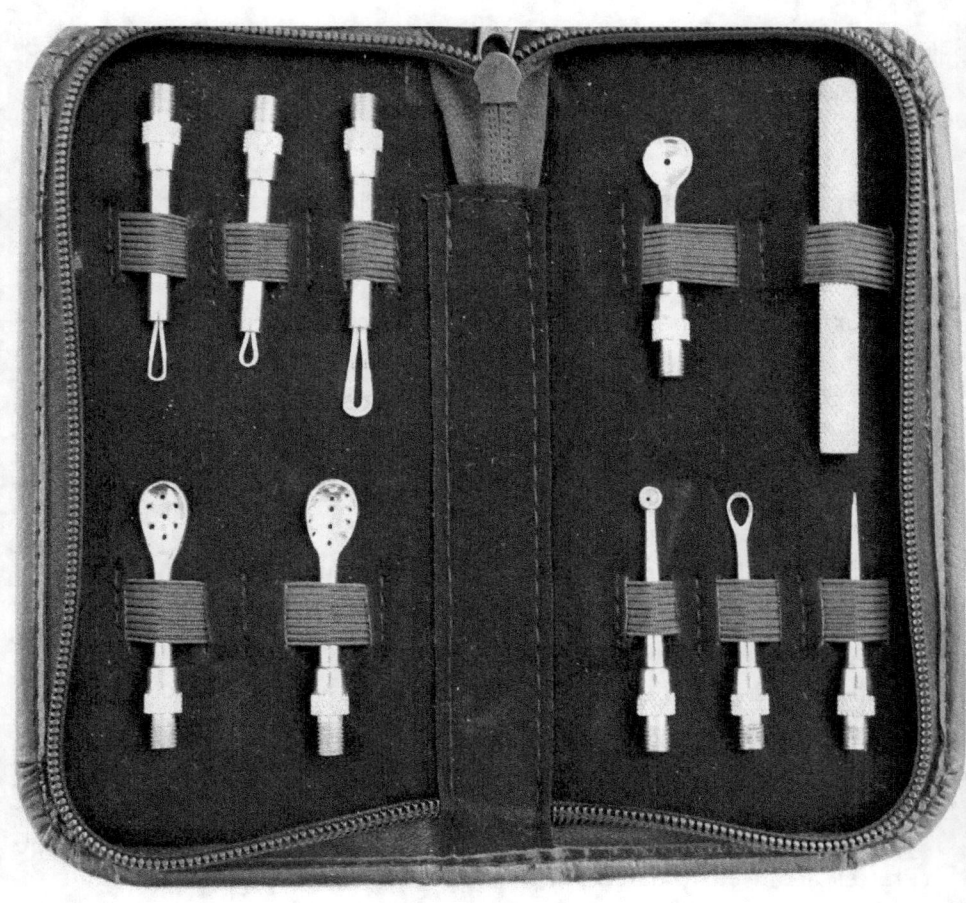

Available in a single kit are a variety of comedone extractors and
ear curettes.

5

HIGH BLOOD PRESSURE? BLACK CHERRY TO THE RESCUE!

Second only to Walnut as the local "money tree," Black Cherry (Prunus serotina), also known as Wild Cherry, has numerous medicinal properties in the bark and fruit, something to keep in mind before harvesting the tree for its beautiful wood.

Black cherry extracts are very popular. One comes from the fruit, one from the bark, and each has their own medicinal properties. Black cherry leaves and the seeds of the cherries should be avoided as they contain compounds, such as amygdalin, that can be converted into hydrogen cyanide. For that reason, black cherry trees should be avoided in pasture with livestock as the wilted leaves can produce enough cyanide to create illness.

Blood Pressure

Black Cherry bark extract has been used in traditional medicine in Korea and Japan to control high blood pressure for thousands of years. In a 2013 study, one mechanism by which cherry bark helps to control blood pressure was identified - a relaxation effect on the blood vessels via activation of nitric oxide and blockage of calcium channels, similar to the effect of blood pressure drugs like captopril. Unlike captopril however, black cherry bark extract inhibits coughing, rather than causing cough. (In some patients taking captopril, the cough is so persistent that the drug dose must be decreased or eliminated altogether.) A cyanide precursor found in cherry bark is also found in Nipride, a common intravenous infusion used in the ICU to treat dangerously high blood pressures. This cyanide precursor is a very potent vasodilator, which relaxes the blood vessels, decreasing the work load of the heart and lowering blood pressure. Although the term "cyanide" is a bit scary, when blood pressures are soaring so high that they cause symptoms like headache, blurred vision, and numbness, a strong medication is definitely indicated. Of note, when patients receive Nipride intravenously in the intensive care unit for several days at a time, thiocyanate levels are monitored via blood work.

The relaxation effect seems to also have a beneficial effect on sufferers of BPH (benign prostatic hypertrophy), and aid in urinary flow.

Cough

Black cherry bark extract has a long history as a cough suppressant, and is a common ingredient in "store-bought" over the counter cough medicines. In addition to suppressing coughs, the extract also helps to dry up mucus and respiratory secretions. After taken by mouth it is metabolized and excreted by the lungs, where it calms the nerves that stimulate coughing. Due to trace amounts of cyanide as discussed above, it shouldn't be used long term, or by pregnant women.

Anti-inflammatory

A 2013 study found that black cherry bark extract had an anti-inflammatory effect similar to decadron, a powerful steroid. In 2014, the Society of Cosmetic Scientists published a study of the anti-inflammatory effect of cherry blossom extract which was used as a soothing ingredient in a skincare product. You have likely noticed a proliferation of these products on the market over the past year.

Depression and anxiety

Black cherry extract acts to inhibit chemicals that can contribute to depression by altering connectivity in the brain, in particular between the anterior cingulate cortex and several other limbic areas, such as the hippocampus,. A 2009 study identified chemicals found in the bark that inhibit monoamine oxidases, enzymes implicated in depression and anxiety. There exists a whole class of these MAO inhibitors available by prescription to treat serious depression.

Fibromyalgia

The juice of the Black Cherry (also called tart cherry) can help reduce fibromyalgia pain via its anti-inflammatory and antioxidant powers. In one study, women with fibromyalgia who drank 10.5 ounces of tart cherry juice twice daily for 10 days had less pain. They also kept up their muscle strength even after researchers had them do challenging arm exercises. The extract from tart cherries appears to be effective in treating the inflammatory reaction seen in both acute and chronic pain syndromes encountered among athletes and non-athletes with chronic inflammatory disease. Tart cherry juice is also very high in melatonin, a natural hormone that regulates your sleep-wake cycle.

Nutritional Benefits

3.5 ounces of black cherries contain the following nutrients: Vitamin C 10 mg; Niacin 0.4 mg; Pantothenic Acid 0.1mg; Vitamin A 1283 IU; Vitamin E (Alpha Tocopherol) 0.1mg; Vitamin B6 2.1 mcg and Beta Carotene 770 mcg. These amounts are roughly double those found in sweet cherries.

Black Cherry Cough Syrup

Ingredients:

2 tablespoons dried wild cherry bark (the inner bark is best)

1 pint water, room temperature

Pour water over bark, and let sit in warm place for at least 4 hours. (Excessive heat can damage the active ingredients). Strain off the liquid, and add ¼ cup of honey. Shake well. Take 1 – 2 tablespoons as needed for cough.

(1 tsp dried slippery elm bark can be added for cough associated with sore throat)

You can also make a cherry bark extract by pouring wine, vodka or other alcoholic beverage over the bark, and letting it sit in a cool dry place for at least a week. Some people take 5 – 12 drops in water 2 -3 times a day for short periods as an anti-inflammatory.

6

FENNEL

Living in California, I would regularly harvest Fennel. It seemed to grow everywhere, and obtaining the seeds was easy – just cut off the top of the plant, put it in a paper bag until dry, then shake the bag until the seeds came loose. At the time, I wasn't interested in medicinal uses, only making the perfect pasta sauce and pizza topping. My neighbor would complain, "Those Italians! They planted that weed!" She may have been right. Fennel seeds are the primary flavor ingredient in Italian sausage, and it makes sense that Italian immigrants would bring the plant from their native land. Although Emperor Charlemagne was known to have encouraged its cultivation in Central Europe, in the USA , Fennel is sometimes considered a nuisance plant after escaping gardens and becoming entrenched in many parts of North America, especially Florida, California and Washington. In Missouri, it has been spotted growing in Boone, Jackson and St. Louis counties. The flowers are very attractive to butterflies, and it serves as a larval plant for certain swallowtail butterflies.

A perennial plant, fennel is easy to grow. It is definitely worth having a few plants in your garden. Dried fennel seed is a flavorful spice that tastes like anise, and is one of the ingredients in Chinese Five Spice Powder. The bulb is also edible, and can be eaten raw, or prepared in a variety of ways. The young leaves can be used for a flavorful garnish, or to add flavor to sauces.

Fennel possibly has more medicinal uses than any other plant. To describe all of the ways in which fennel is used in health would take a small book, so we will examine the most common uses.

Abdominal Pain

Like many plants, extremely effective pharmaceutical products have been formulated from Fennel. A very popular prescription drug in Germany made from fennel is Lomatol®. An early 1996 study compared Lomatol® with commonly prescribed metoclopramide (Reglan). Over 2 weeks, the medication containing fennel had a significant impact on the symptoms of pain, nausea, heartburn, retching and stomach spasms as compared with Reglan. As a board-certified neuroscience nurse, I am wary of Reglan in any event, due to the high incidence of tremor associated with the drug, especially at high doses.

Menstrual cramps

Menstrual cramps are no joke. In some girls, they can be almost incapacitating, causing missed school and sports participation. A 2002 study in Iran compared 110 high school girls, median age 13 years, divided into two groups. In the group receiving fennel extract over 2 months, there was an 80% incidence of pain relief, often complete.

Colic in Infants

A report published in 2012, looking at effective treatment for colic, did a comprehensive review of all the major journals. One measurement of colic was excessive crying in the infant. The most validated treatments for infantile colic was the substitution of cows' milk by a hydrolyzed formula, the use of L. reuteri (a probiotic) and use of fennel extracts.

Pregnant and Nursing Mothers

The aerial parts, (those above the ground, such as the leaf, stem, and seed) of the fennel plant are used extensively in several countries as *galactagogues,* not only for increasing the quantity and quality of breast milk, but also for improving the milk flow of breastfeeding mothers. In India, women prone to repeated miscarriages take a mixture of 50 gram of fennel seed powder mixed with 50 grams of power from trapa natans (a type of water chestnut) daily to protect the fetus.

Mouth ulcers and gum disorder

From ancient times, fennel seeds have been used as an ingredient for removing any foul odors in the mouth. Roasted fennel seeds are used as a mouth freshener in India and Pakistan. In Italy, mouth ulcers are treated with the tender leaves that are chewed and stuck on the ulcer, and a mouthwash made from the fruit and seed is used for gum disease.

Glaucoma

Water extract of fennel seeds has shown significant lowering of the ocular pressure in glaucoma. The extract exhibited 17.49, 21.16, and 22.03% reduction of intraocular pressure in healthy rabbits. (Rabbits are often used for eye research). Fennel extract lowered the intraocular pressure by an average of 31.20%, which was found to be as good as that of reference standard glaucoma drug Timolol.

Anxiety

Anxiety is the unpleasant feeling of fear and concern. Fennel is a drug used for the treatment of anxiety and its related psychological and physical symptoms. In a 2014 study with mice placed in anxiety extract at a 100 to 200 mg/kg showed significant activity when compared to the common anxiety drug diazepam Valium. As a side note, in the 1970's, I recall a Mennonite father telling me that it was frequent practice to give the children 1 fennel seed to suck on to keep them quiet in church!

Medicinal uses of Fennel could easily fill a small book.

7

COFFEE – THE UNIVERSAL BEVERAGE

There is a lot of debate about coffee. Is it good for you, or bad? It can't be grown in Missouri, right? What is all the hype about green coffee beans?

A Brief History

Coffee (*Coffee Arabica*) is originally from Ethiopia, despite the name. The name coffee comes from an old Arabic word for wine – kahwah. It was first brought to Arabia around 1450. The first bag of coffee made its way to Europe in 1652, and was considered a luxury, available only to the privileged. In 1774, a Franciscan monk introduced coffee to Brazil, which is now the greatest producing coffee country in the world, supplying over 5 and a half billion pounds per year. In comparison, Hawaii produces 6 million pounds per year. In early years, coffee consumption was equated with affluence, and the poorer citizens diluted their coffee with chicory. Coffee has proven to "the universal beverage," enjoyed in some form by virtually every culture.

Cultivation

Coffee plants require climates over 40 degrees. A hardy plant, it grows best on a hillside, at 1000 – 3000 feet above sea level. The Ozarks have 2 out of 3 requirements. Easy to grow, coffee should be planted in large pots that can be brought inside during the winter months. For those impatient to brew their first cup of coffee from their home-grown bean, you won't have to wait long. The coffee tree yields fruit at 2 years old, and is full bearing from 4 until 20 years old. As a teenager, I grew a beautiful coffee tree from a seed in my living room in Illinois.

Unfortunately, our local Kentucky Coffee Tree is not the same, and its raw seeds are actually toxic.

Alertness

Most of us have used coffee to "get us going" in the morning. The effect of coffee on levels of alertness have been well documented, but a 2015 study in the International Journal of Surgery looked at the effect coffee had on learning certain surgical skills. The researchers noted that "Coffee is consumed almost ubiquitously by surgeons not just as a stimulant but also socially in the well-rested individual. It's therefore worth investigating its potentially negative effect on performance of surgical skills as it is known that coffee has psychomotor effects."

In this interesting study, students learning surgical skills were tested under three different conditions: decaffeinated, 100mg caffeine and 200mg caffeine. Surgery was performed with a simulator, and outcomes measured were completion time, accuracy, and number of movements. The candidates were crossed over to the other caffeine doses on a different day. They found that caffeine intake did not affect accuracy at any dose, but did result in slower task completion time, which may be due to increased concentration and focus.

Anti-depressant effects

In a 2014 study, it was noted that depressed persons tend to drink a lot of coffee or tea. This may be a form of self-medication, because the study found that coffee intake increased levels of norepinephrine, dopamine, and serotonin levels, the so-called "feel good" chemicals. When taken with the antidepressants Cymbalta or Wellbutrin, caffeine increased their effectiveness.

Blood Pressure

In hypertensive individuals (those with high blood pressure), coffee intake produces a short term increase in blood pressure for about 3 hours. However, current evidence does not support an association between longer-term coffee consumption and a continued increase in blood pressure, or between habitual coffee consumption and a higher risk of heart disease in hypertensive subjects. In other words, coffee makes your blood pressure go up for about 3 hours, but the effect is short-term, and most evidence suggests that regular intake of caffeinated coffee does not increase the risk of hypertension.

That being said, coffee intake can trigger rupture of a brain aneurysm. During a 3-year period, 250 patients with aneurysmal subarachnoid hemorrhage completed a structured questionnaire regarding exposure to 30 potential trigger factors in the period soon before the aneurysm ruptured. 8 trigger factors were identified, all of which caused a sudden and short increase in blood pressure. Of the 8 eight risk factors, the most prevalent were coffee consumption (10.6%) and vigorous physical exercise (7.9%).

Next week we will cover some astounding research about coffee and gout, discuss the role of coffee in headache treatment, and delve into the green coffee bean phenomena.

8

COFFEE – PART 2

Last week we talked about some of the common effects of coffee on alertness, mood and blood pressure. This week will cover some astounding research about coffee and gout, discuss the role of coffee in headache treatment, and delve into the green coffee bean phenomena.

Gout

One doesn't usually think about coffee in the treatment of gout, in fact, some gout sufferers avoid it altogether, fearing the mild diuretic effect may lead to dehydration, aggravating symptoms. This is not validated by science, however, and in fact there is a staggering amount of research available showing that coffee intake actually decreases the incidence of gout.

Gout is the most prevalent inflammatory arthritis in men, with a much higher incidence than occurs in women, although rates in women are rising. The findings of several epidemiologic studies from a diverse range of countries suggest that the prevalence of gout has risen over the past few decades. Dietary factors can contribute to gout, but low-fat dairy products, coffee, and vitamin C have a protective effect.

One huge long term study that took place over 26 years prospectively examined the relation between coffee intake and risk of gout in 89,433 participants in the Nurses' Health Study. The results were significant. The risk of gout was 22% lower with a coffee intake of 1–3 cups/d and 57% lower with a coffee intake of ≥4 cups/d compared with the risk of gout in individuals with no coffee consumption. The effect of coffee on gout was independent of other risk factors such as obesity, age, alcohol consumption, diuretic use, hypertension, and intakes of dairy, meat, seafood, and sugar-sweetened soft drinks.

So why is coffee helpful in preventing gout? Another study from Japan that included 2240 men receiving pre-retirement physicals found that coffee had a profound effect on uric acid levels in the blood, dropping levels an average of 4 points. Elevated uric acid is responsible for the excruciatingly painful symptoms of gout. Green tea, another major source of caffeine in Japan, was not found to have the same effect.

Glaucoma

Many ophthalmologists instruct patients with all forms of glaucoma to avoid coffee. The amount of caffeine intake appears to be the problem. In one study researchers looks at intake of regular and decaffeinated coffee in patients with both normal pressure and hypertensive glaucoma and found that intra-ocular pressure (IOP) was increased slightly in those drinking more than 180 mg caffeine. (There is about 100 mg of caffeine in a cup of regular coffee)

The Blue Mountains Eye Study examined 3654 participants aged 49+ years in an area west of Sydney, Australia. Participants with open-angle glaucoma (OAG) who reported regular coffee drinking had a 3 point higher IOP than non – coffee drinkers. No association between coffee or caffeine consumption and higher IOP was found in participants with ocular hypertension (OH) and those without open-angle glaucoma. Open angle glaucoma is the most common type, caused when the aqueous fluid in the eye doesn't drain well, causing a build-up in pressure.

Coffee and Headaches

Working in neurology, the greatest portion of our practice is treatment of headache. Some severe headaches can last for months, requiring hospitalization, and one treatment is caffeine, given intravenously.

There are many forms of headache, and while overuse of caffeine can certainly cause a headache, drinking a cup of coffee will also help to relieve headache. Hypnic headache is a form of headache that is characterized by strictly sleep-related headache attacks. Mainly elderly patients are affected, but younger patients and even children might also be affected. Headache attacks can last up to 10 hours. A strong cup of strong coffee seems to be the best acute and preventive treatment option.

Coffee Use in Pregnancy

Study after study has looked at the influence of maternal coffee consumption on the child, particularly as it relates to inattention and over activity. No relation was found between coffee drinking in the mother and subsequent behavioral problems in the child. In fact, intrauterine exposure to soft drinks rather than coffee, the traditional focus, was associated with maternal reports of overactive behavior in children aged 18 months. Present results give no indication to advise pregnant women to reduce their caffeine intake to prevent behavior problems in their children.

Green Coffee Beans

Green coffee beans are simply unroasted beans. They contain an active ingredient *chlorogenic acid* (CGA) that is destroyed in the roasting process. High in antioxidants, CGAs boost metabolism and aid in weight loss, in part by breaking down fatty tissue. Green coffee beans have caffeine, but in lesser amounts than roasted beans. Green coffee beans can lower cholesterol and improve glucose tolerance.

9

POPCORN

We've all heard about GMOs (genetically modified organisms), and many of us are trying to avoid these products. Approximately 90% of corn grown in the US today is genetically modified to be herbicide resistant (Roundup Ready) and to produce its own insecticide (Bt Toxin). Unfortunately, GMO corn is toxic to milkweed, necessary for the Monarch Butterfly population, and is killing off the bees. Popcorn has escaped genetic medication at this point, perhaps because it doesn't have the cross uses of field corn, such as fuel, and isn't included in thousands of food products in some form.

Today, popcorn is grown mainly in the United States and consumed around the world. Here in Missouri, we are in the Corn Belt, and can easily grow all types of corn. Popcorn is one the earliest races of corn, probably developed 7,000 to 10,000 years ago in Mexico and Central America. As a healthy snack, popcorn is hard to beat. Very filling, 1 cup of air-popped popcorn has only 31 calories with 1.2 gm of fiber and 1 gm. of protein.

Hazards of Microwave Popcorn

In May 2000, the Missouri Department of Health and Senior Services investigated eight cases of fixed obstructive lung disease in former workers of a microwave popcorn factory. Four of the workers were on lung transplant lists. All eight had a respiratory illness with symptoms of cough and dyspnea on exertion, and had worked at the same popcorn factory at some time during 1992-2000 for periods ranging from 8 months to 9 years. The epidemiologist investigating the illnesses found that workers exposed to flavorings at microwave popcorn factories are at risk for developing fixed obstructive lung disease, which is due to coating of the workers' lungs with airborne particles of the artificial flavoring. If that's not enough reason to avoid artificially flavored microwave popcorn, the diacetyl chemical that is contains has been linked to amyloid plaque, an abnormal brain protein linked to Alzheimer's.

Popcorn's Role in Health

Popcorn has even higher levels of antioxidants, in the form of polyphenols, than fruits or vegetables. As readers recall, antioxidants are anti-aging and cancer-preventive. Unlike fruits and vegetables, popcorn provides a very concentrated form of polyphenols, with popcorn hulls having the highest concentration of both polyphenols and fiber.

Popcorn is 100 percent unprocessed whole grain, and one serving of popcorn will provide more than 70 percent of the daily intake of whole grain. The average person only gets about half a serving of whole grains a day, and popcorn can easily fill that gap.

Popcorn Cautions

While popcorn can remove plaque from your teeth, biting an unpopped kernel can also crack a tooth, or the husk can slip under your tooth and be trapped next to the gum. Both of these situations can be avoided by eating popcorn carefully, avoiding unpopped kernels, and flossing your teeth after eating,

Make Your Own Kettle Corn

Who doesn't love kettle corn? With this recipe you can make your own at home, and rival anything you can buy at the State Fair.

Using a stove-top popcorn maker (a large skillet with cover will also work), heat 1/8 cup oil (healthy olive oil works great!), ¼ cup sugar, and ½ cup popcorn, stirring or shaking the cooking utensil until the kernels are popped. Pour the kettle corn into a large bowl, let sit for a few minutes, and then gently stir to break up the clumps after the popcorn cools. No salt is needed with this recipe.

You can also make caramel corn by substituting brown sugar for cane sugar – but add the brown sugar just after the corn starts to pop so that it doesn't burn.

It's easy to make delicious kettle corn in your own kitchen.

10

ANOTHER LOOK AT FLUORIDE

In a previous discussion on toothpaste, we looked at the hazards of fluoride – dental fluorosis, bone fractures, thyroid toxicity and negative effects on IQ in children, Switching to non-fluoridated toothpaste is not enough, as an even more hazardous form of fluoride is being added to our drinking water in some areas close to home.

The purported beneficial effects of fluoride on dental decay have largely been refuted. Fluoride makes bones and teeth more brittle. Strong teeth in those of us who grew up on well water can be attributed to the high amounts of calcium in the water, not naturally occurring fluoride, which is occasionally found in small amounts, but not here in the Ozarks.

Although the American Dental Association continues to adamantly defend fluoride, at least 17 prominent organizations have withdrawn their support since 1990, including the American Academy of Diabetes, the American Cancer Society, American Nurses Association, American Psychiatric Association, National Kidney Foundation, and the Society of Toxicology. The reversal of these organizations in their former support of water fluoridation is in response to new research, and to increased toxicity in the type of fluoride being added.

New studies have been published; including one from the New Jersey Department of Health documents males under the age of 50 had 5 – 7 times the incidence of bone cancer in fluoridated areas, with teen males ages 10-19 with highest levels.

Another study of cancer rates in the ten largest fluoridated US cities found 10% more cancer deaths than the non-fluoridated cities, especially tumors of tongue, mouth, pharynx, esophagus, stomach, colon, rectum, pancreas, larynx, bronchi and lungs.

Hip fractures in 2 Utah cities were compared: fluoridated Brigham City and non-fluoridated Cedar City. Hip fracture rates were double in elderly men and women in the city with fluoridated water.

A study published in 2008 conducted over a 20 year period looked at effects of fluoride in children. 16 different studies were included in the analysis, and found "Children who live in a fluorosis area have five times higher odds of developing low IQ than those who live in a non-fluorosis area."

A 2011 article actually quantified the decrease in IQ as related to fluoride levels. Looking at excreted fluoride in the urine, researchers found that each increase in 1 mg/L of urine fluoride was associated with 0.59-point decrease in IQ, and concluded that even low levels of fluoride exposure in drinking water had negative effects on children's intelligence and dental health.

On the basis of new research, Hardy Limback, DDS, President of the Canadian Association for Dental Research reversed his position on water fluoridation stating "children under 3 should NEVER use fluoridated toothpaste and baby formula must never be made up using tap water."

Fluorosilicic Acid

One thing that happened in 1989 and 1990 concerned the switch from fluoride to fluorosilicic acid, which is gathered by removing the residues in smokestack scrubbers left behind from the treatment of phosphate ores with sulfuric acid, and would be considered a toxic waste, if it wasn't added to our water supply. When the hurricanes hit Florida in 1989 – 1990, the supplies of flurosilicic acid were depleted in the holding tanks, so supplies were imported from countries such as China, who likely thought that putting their hazardous waste in our drinking water was a pretty good idea. Fluorosilicic acid contains variable amounts of lead, arsenic, and mercury, which you will see identified on your annual water quality report.

What exactly is fluorosilicic acid? I spoke with a long-term employee of a local water system who actually was the one to add it to the drinking supply. It comes in large barrels from a chemical company, marked "Poison," and has an acid pH similar to battery acid. Per first hand report, it is corrosive to the pipes, especially close to the points where it is added. It gradually disperses, but the homes closest to the treatment plant get the highest doses. Taxpayers actually pay for the privilege of having China's industrial waste added to their water, a cost of about $2.00 per person per year, in addition to the significant cost of replacing pipes.

Filters do not work to remove fluoride, because of the small diameter of the fluoride ion. It can only be removed by reverse osmosis or distillation.

Legislation

The FDA designated fluoride "not generally recognized as safe" in 1985, and permitted no fluoride to be added to food or dietary supplements. The Department of Health and Human Services exempted fluoridated water from the ban, including water used to make food. Even the World health Organization says fluoride levels should be around 0.7 mg/L, and in 2011 the federal government adopted this standard. Unfortunately, fluoride levels in Houston, Missouri are as high as 1.13 mg/L and 1.1 mg/L in Cabool as of their 2012 reports. Fluoride has been added to Cabool's water supply since March 1, 1962, and in 2013 they received an award from the ADA for "50 Years of Water Fluoridation." I saw the award first hand, but it was not publicized. Fluoride was first added to the city water supply Houston, Mo in 2002 by a vote of the City Council, following a comment period, creating a new ordinance.

How to Help

First, the town of Licking and all of Dent County do NOT have fluoridated water. The only towns in Texas County adding fluoride are Cabool and Houston. Cabool's addition of fluoride is documented on the CDC webpage, but Houston is erroneously listed as having zero fluoride, with none added. I called the CDC, and was told that they "hadn't updated the website in a while." It must have been quite a while, as fluoride has been added for the past 13 years. I challenged them to update their website, as this is false information for those searching on their own. I pulled my own samples from the Houston water supply, confirming the presence of significant levels of fluoride. I then contacted Missouri DNR who established that the city of Houston does indeed add fluoride, and directed me to the location of some obscure reports.

If you live in an area still adding fluoride to your water, contact your city council, or attend a meeting, requesting that fluorosilicic acid be removed. When fluoride was added, no public vote was required. Fluoride can be taken out the same way – by a vote of your city council. Dozens of surrounding cities are removing fluoride from their water, including most recently Waynesville and Bolivar, let's not be the last.

(Article originally published 2/13/2015. Since that time the CDC website has been corrected to adequately reflect the addition of artificial fluoride in the form of hydrosilicic acid to Houston's water supply.)

11

LAMB'S QUARTERS

With a foot of snow on the ground, it is not too soon to talk about Lamb's Quarters - *Chenopodium album.* The time to gather and eat the leaves and stems is in early spring when this annual plant first appears in areas of disturbed ground throughout the Ozarks.

Often referred to as "the second most nutritious plant," with Amaranth coming in first, Lamb's quarters has edible leaves, shoots and seeds. It is so nutritious that in Great Britain it is referred to as "Fat-Hen." A relative of both beets and spinach, it has a crude protein content of 26.4% and is a tremendous source of beta-carotene, calcium, potassium and iron, in addition to multiple vitamins, including Vitamin C, and has been used to prevent Scurvy. Foods can be high in certain vitamins, but often those vitamins just flush through our system. Calcium is one vitamin that can be difficult to absorb. In a just published 2015 study, the bioavailability of calcium obtained from Sheep's Quarters was found to be twice that of other green, leafy vegetables.

Considered a weed in the US, it is cultivated and grown as a food crop in India. The leaves are very tasty, often considered better than spinach, which they can replace in any recipe. In many parts of the world, such as Tibet, Lamb's quarters is a staple food, and practically all families collect the plant and either dry or lacto-ferment it for later consumption. In the Western Hemisphere, Lamb's Quarters are a part of the New Nordic Diet, a spin on the Mediterranean Diet, which includes wild plants from the countryside.

Medicinal Properties

In addition to nutritional benefits, antioxidant and antibacterial properties have earned Lamb's Quarters the designation of "great medicinal value." Traditionally, the plant has been used as a laxative, diuretic, sedative, and treatment for rheumatism.

A 2014 study looking at the anti-arthritic potential of Lamb's Quarters found significant reduction in inflammation at dose level s of 200 mg/kg, similar to the drug Indomethacin, at least partially due to its capacity to inhibit the NFκB protein that has been linked to cancer, inflammation, autoimmune disease, and viral infections, among others.

Another study looked at the antibacterial, antioxidant and DNA protective capacity of leaf extract from Lamb's Quarters, and found strong antibacterial activity against certain types of bacteria. Anti-oxidant properties were dose dependent, and there was statistically significant correlation between dose of Lamb's Quarter leaf extract and genotoxicity, the property of chemical agents that damages the genetic information within a cell causing mutations, which may lead to cancer.

Breast Cancer

A 2009 study entitled "Chenopodium album prevents progression of cell growth and enhances cell toxicity in human breast cancer cell lines" examined the effects of Lamb's Quarter on the growth of estrogen dependent and estrogen independent human breast cancer cell lines. The study concluded Lamb's Quarter leaf extract has potential for possible clinical use to counteract malignancy development as an anti-breast cancer agent.

Vitiligo

Vitiligo is an autoimmune skin disease destroying the pigments of the skin, causing large white patches on the body. It is very distressing, as is first presents on the hands, face and neck. It is very difficult to treat, but there is some anecdotal evidence that Lamb's Quarters may help, and it is a component of some proprietary ointments. No scientific studies have been done to document its effectiveness, and the use of Lamb's Quarter's is considered a folk remedy at this time.

Harvesting and Preparing Lamb's Quarters

Lamb's Quarters leaves are diamond-shaped with a light green color. The top leaves may look like they've been dusted with powder due to pollen. Stems of mature plants may be streaked with purplish-red lines running the length of the plant. Early leaves from a plant less than a foot tall are the most tender, but can be harvested throughout the summer. You can also harvest a type of quinoa by collecting seeds from the plant in the fall. Leaves can be eaten raw or cooked, and are a wonderful free substitute for spinach. The seeds can be ground into flour, or eaten whole. Lamb's Quarters are usually available in abundance, and can be preserved for several months by lacto-fermentation.

Lacto Fermentation

Before electricity, canning and refrigeration, folks knew how to preserve vegetables for long periods through a process known as lacto-fermentation. Lactobacilli are found on all living things, and especially numerous on leaves and roots of plants growing near the ground. Vegetables are washed and cut up, mixed with salt, crushed to release juices, then packed into an air-tight container. The lactobacillus species feed on natural sugars found in the vegetables. The resulting mix of salt and lactic acid is a hostile environment for other microbes, and the vegetables are thus preserved -- remaining edible for long periods. *Lactobacillus* bacteria may possess potential therapeutic properties including anti-inflammatory and anti-cancer activities. Lactic acid, the main byproduct keeps vegetables and fruits in perfect preservation for long periods, but also promotes healthy bacteria in the intestine. For the first week, fermented vegetables may be kept at room temperature, and afterwards must be kept in a cool dark place.

Lamb's Quarters are an excellent spinach substitute.

12

BLACK COHOSH – REAL HELP FOR MENOPAUSE SYMPTOMS

Black Cohosh, also known as cimicifuga recemosa or actaea racemosa, is a highly valuable plant, native to our area. A perennial herb in the buttercup family, Black Cohosh has been catalogued in 30 Missouri counties, all south of the Missouri River. It grows everywhere, but loves growing in the forest under deciduous trees. It is a brisk seller on-line for those interested in harvesting native plants for profit.

Black Cohosh has a long history of traditional use and effectiveness for symptoms of menopause, and new applications are being discovered. For younger women that have had a hysterectomy or ovary removal, Black Cohosh helps to correct the hormonal deficit. A proprietary extract of Black cohosh called Remifemin is available on the market, and is commonly prescribed as a safe and effective alternative to hormone replacement therapy. The dried root and rhizome are the medicinal parts of the plant, and are black in color, hence part of the name. Cohosh is a word from the Algonquin dialect, meaning "rough" in reference to the root structure. Native Americans used the plant for conditions ranging from female problems to snake bites. Black Cohosh was commonly prescribed in the 19th century for fever, menstrual cramps, insomnia, and arthritis.

Menopause

Black Cohosh has reliable and consistent scientific data showing a substantial benefit in the treatment of menopause. It has been shown to also be safe, without the hazards of traditional hormone replacement therapy with estrogen that can trigger certain cancers. One of the most disconcerting symptoms of menopause is hot flashes. Despite the jokes, hot flashes are very uncomfortable, and interrupt daily activities, and even sleep. Hot flashes are due to a slowing of signals between the ovaries and the pituitary gland, slowing estrogen production and an increase in luteinizing hormone levels. Black Cohosh can also relieve symptoms of insomnia and depression in menopausal women, and recent data has demonstrated that Black Cohosh may have an effect on dopaminergic and serotoninergic systems – the "feel good chemicals."

Breast Cancer

Any hormone replacement therapy is considered a risk for increased incidence of breast cancer. Black cohosh has been thoroughly studied, and no association has been found to date. Premarin, a common hormone replacement drug, is made from Pregnant Mare Urine, hence the name. In addition to the implications for animal abuse, Premarin has long been linked to breast cancer. Premarin also brings an increased risk of strokes, blood clots and dementia. Black Cohosh has none of these side effects, in fact, some early studies show that it may actually inhibit tumor growth, and may be safely used by patients with existing breast cancers who should never be prescribed Premarin. The only concern at this time is that Black Cohosh may delay the breakdown of Tamoxifen, a drug commonly prescribed for breast cancer.

Prostate Cancer

While mainly used by women, Black Cohosh has been show to kill human prostate cancer cells, both androgen responsive and non-responsive. A 2006 study found black cohosh that compounds in Black Cohosh inhibit prostate tumor development, with no significant effect on serum testosterone levels. Researchers concluded that Black Cohosh extract "may prove to be efficient in preventing and treatment of prostate cancer."

Osteoporosis

Osteoporosis is a process that demineralizes the bone, leading to increased bone frailty and possibility of fracture. There are three types of osteoporosis, with post-menopausal being the most common. Actein, a compound in Black Cohosh, causes a significant elevation of alkaline phosphatase activity, collagen synthesis, osteocalcin production, mineralization, and glutathione content in bone cells, resulting in a stimulatory effect on new bone formation, helpful in preventing osteoporosis. A 2013 study looking at the effect of Remifemin (Black Cohosh extract) compared with the drug estradiol in post-menopausal subjects or those who had removal of the ovaries found that both drugs prevented bone density loss in the distal end of the femur in the legs and preserved the bone structure in the lumbar vertebra in the back following ovary removal. They concluded that with adequate treatment duration, Remifemin is as effective as prescription estradiol in preventing post-menopausal osteoporosis.

Dosage and Precautions

Black cohosh can be taken in several forms, including a dry powdered extract of the root, or as a tincture. The recommended amount is 20–40 mg twice per day. Black cohosh can be taken for up to six months, and then it should be discontinued, Remifemin can be purchased online for $19 for 120 tablets (20 mg of root per tablet), or you can pick your own. It should not be used by pregnant or breast feeding women.

Black cohosh (Cimicifuga racemosa)

13

BEEFSTEAK PLANT – WILD BASIL

Definitely nutritious, and a favorite of sushi chefs, beefsteak plant, *Perilla frutescens*, grows naturally throughout Missouri, south of the Missouri River. It is an annual plant, found almost everywhere in the Ozarks, and was likely brought to North America by Asian immigrants in the middle 1800's. Beefsteak plant is a traditional crop of several countries in East Asia, and has been present in China since records were kept. It was introduced to Japan in the 8th or 9th century, so there is a great deal of research available on both the nutritional and medicinal uses.

Cultivation

Beefsteak plant is very easy to grow. It prefers well-drained soil in the full sun. It has a minty smell, and is attractive to butterflies. It blooms from July to October, but the edible tender leaves can be harvested at any time, and used in place of traditional basil. The leaves are used in making sushi, where they are called shiso. The entire plant can be harvested while in bloom, and dried to prepare seasonings and medicinals.

Nutrition

3 ounces of leaves from the beefsteak plant contain 37 calories, 500 mg of potassium, 230 mg of calcium, 1.7 mg of iron, a whopping 11,000 micrograms of Vitamin A, 690 mcg. of Vitamin K, small amounts of thiamine and riboflavin, 110 micrograms of folic acid, and 26 mg of Vitamin C. Oil derived from the plant is a rich source of omega-3 fatty acids.

Medicinal Uses

Cancer

A 2015 study looked at the effect of beefsteak plant leaf extract against the growth, migration and adhesion of human cancer cells and found that it exerts anti-cancer activity against colon and lung cancers, completely abolishing cancer cells in the laboratory setting. Tests in humans have not yet been published, but the results are encouraging.

A 2014 study found that an extract from the beefsteak plant increased the effectiveness of a new treatment protocol for primary prostate cancer, abbreviated TRAIL, that has previously had limited effectiveness due to resistance and poor uptake in the body. They concluded that supplementation with a chemical obtained from the beefsteak plant has potential for increasing the effectiveness of prostate cancer therapy with the TRAIL protocol.

Stroke Recovery

Perillaldehyde (PAH), one of the major oil components in Beefsteak plant, has strong anti-inflammatory effects. A 2014 study examined the neuroprotective effect of PAH on stroke. The extract was taken by mouth for 7 days, and researchers found PAH decreased cerebral ischemia and reperfusion injury in the brain cortex following stroke.

Another study published just last week found that extracts from the beefsteak plant protect from neurotoxicity, and slow the development of Alzheimer's disease.

Anti-Inflammatory

Beefsteak plant leaves have shown therapeutic efficacy in the treatment of inflammatory disorders, allergies, and bronchial asthma. In order to validate the effectiveness, in 2014 researchers isolated a chemical called luteolin, which significantly reduces histamine release from mast cells. The administration of luteolin markedly decreased scratching behavior of the skin. These results suggested that luteolin "has potential as a therapeutic agent against inflammation and itch-related skin diseases."

Antidepressant Effects

A 2014 study on the antidepressant effect of a diet rich in seed oil from the beefsteak plant found that levels of serotonin were significantly higher in stressed animals that received the oil, and concluded that a diet rich is oils from the beefsteak plant exhibited antidepressant-like properties through modulation of fatty acid profiles and chemical expression in the brain.

Another study in Oct. 2014 found that administration of essential oil extracted from the leaves of the beefsteak plant also produced significant antidepressant-like effects, which may be related to the relation between alteration of serotonergic responses and anti-inflammatory effects.

Gastrointestinal Disorders

Beefsteak plant extract combines prokinetic (keeping the intestines working), antispasmodic and anti-inflammatory effects on the intestinal system. A recent study investigated the effects of the proprietary Perilla extract on GI discomfort in healthy subjects with gastrointestinal discomfort and reduced bowel movements in comparison to a placebo product. In a double-blind study with 50 subjects with gastrointestinal discomfort, he beefsteak plant extract was found to decrease bloating, abdominal discomfort, feeling of fullness and passage of gas.

In a 2013 study looking at reflex esophagitis, beefsteak plant oil significantly decreased the gross volume of gastric juice secretion, total acidity, and esophagitis index and raised the gastric pH in comparison to controls.

Other Uses

Beefsteak plant is a good companion plant for tomatoes, and the leaves can be rubbed on your clothing during nature hikes to ward off ticks. Cooking oil can be made from the seeds. Oil made from the plant is also used as a food flavoring, and has been used as one of the main ingredients in sarsaparilla, hence the name. Perilla seed extract tablets sell briskly online as an allergy medication, a homegrown product that receives excellent reviews.

Perilla (Beefsteak Plant) Tea

To ½ cup dried beefsteak plant leaves, add 1 pint boiling water, and let steep for 10 minutes. Helpful for allergies, colds, sore throat, and congestion. Can be boiled and the steam inhaled to clear the sinuses.

Beefsteak plant grows up to 3 feet tall and has dark burgundy stems and burgundy or olive green leaves with a wrinkled upper surface. The flowers are small, light purple, and bloom on long, spike-like clusters up to 6 inches long, making it a distinctive plant.

14

SHEPHERD'S PURSE – CAPSELLA BURSA-PASTORIS

As Spring approaches, it is time to make a list of our "most-wanted" native plants, then go out and gather them as they are at their freshest and most potent, both in terms of nutrition and medicinal properties. One plant that is definitely on my list (along with dandelion root, purslane, lamb's quarters, sassafras root, prickly pear, beefsteak plant and dittany) is Shepherd's purse, (*Capsella bursa-pastoris*).

An annual plant with leaves that resemble a dandelion and heart-shaped seed pods, Shepherd's Purse blooms early, from March through November, a longer period than most plants.

Nutrition

A tasty salad ingredient, Shepherd's purse is used in China in stir-fry dishes and wonton fillings. One cup of leaves contain 36 calories, and is extremely high in Vitamin K, with double the recommended daily requirement, and respectable amounts of Vitamin A, C, E and Folate. It also contains several essential amino acids, and Omega-3 fatty acids. Chickens also love the plant, and after stripping the leaves, will demolish any leftover stems that you throw to them.

Medicinal Uses

Bleeding

Shepherd's Purse has been used in traditional medication for heart problems, including heart failure and low blood pressure. It has been used for urinary tract infections and inflammation. It stands out as one of the best herbal products for stopping bleeding, both internal and external. During WWI, when the typical preparations (ergot and goldeneal) to stop hemorrhage were in short supply, Shepherd's purse was used as a substitute. In 1939, a patent was filed by Arthur Steinberg for the use of Shepherd's Purse to stop bleeding by either IV or injection. Johnson and Johnson followed up with a patent in 1946 for a similar product that could be placed in a wound, causing the blood to clot, thereby stopping hemorrhage. I've used the most modern application, a product called Surgicel ®, and it works beautifully to stop mild hemorrhage, including nosebleeds. No wonder that traditional medicine promotes applying Shepherd's purse directly to the area for nose bleeds or superficial injuries.

The plant works via two ways for stopping bleeding. When taken internally, the high content of Vitamin K (the coagulation vitamin) stops bleeding by helping the liver to make four clotting factors (II, VII, IX and X). When applied externally to a wound, leaves from the plant cause blood to clot by mechanical means, as the plant fibers help form a natural clot, acting to prevent the wound from bleeding.

Anti-Bacterial and Cancer Prevention

In 2014, researchers isolated sulforaphane (SCS) from Shepherd's Purse, a substance that is effective against super bacteria like VRE and *B. anthracis (Anthrax)*. They also noted its potent chemopreventive activity. Shepherd's purse extract was not only effective in preventing chemically induced cancers in animals in the lab setting, but also effective in inhibiting the growth of established tumors. Older studies have reported antimicrobial effects against *Helicobacter pylori* (that causes stomach ulcers) and fungus infections, and noted an anticancer activity to stomach tumors. The study authors noted: "our present findings clearly indicate that SCS is a novel candidate for a functional food or therapeutic agent for control of inflammation and multi-drug resistant bacteria."

In a 2013 study, Shepherd's Purse extract both slowed growth of oral cancer cells, and contributed to apoptosis (programmed cell death) in cancer cells, making it an attractive drug candidate for oral cancer.

Alzheimer's Disease

Alzheimer's disease is the most common cause of dementia in the elderly. It is assumed that the dysfunction of cholinergic neurotransmission in the brain contributes to the disease process. The loss of cholinergic cells is accompanied by the loss of the neurotransmitter acetylcholine, thus, one of the most accepted strategies in AD treatment is the use of cholinesterase inhibitors like Aricept or Exelon. Shepherd's Purse extract is a cholinergic agent, and is being explored for the treatment of Alzheimer's.

Infusion of Shepherd's Purse

Per folk lore, a medicinal infusion can be made with 1 ounce of plant to 12 oz. of water, reduced by boiling to 1/2 pint, strained and taken cold.

Precautions

Shepherds Purse should be used with care in persons with any clotting disorders, those on Coumadin or other blood thinners, those with low blood pressure or slow heart rate due to its cholinergic effects, or in pregnancy, as it can cause uterine contractions by stimulating oxytocin.

Shepherd's Purse. Note the heart-shaped seed pods and dandelion-like leaves

15

OSTRICH FERN - FIDDLEHEADS

As you start your springtime nature walks, be on the lookout for a most wonderful Ozark delicacy, the fiddlehead. Considered the first vegetable of the growing season, you will have about one month to harvest them after they appear. There are over 10,000 species of ferns, and only 69 of them are found in Missouri, fortunately, one of those is the Ostrich Fern (*Matteucia struthiopteris*). Fiddleheads are an early shoot from the Ostrich Fern, a feathery fern, resembling an ostrich tail that grows 2- 6 feet tall. You will most likely find them growing in moist soil adjacent to rivers and streams. All ferns have a fiddlehead stage, and none will kill you, but those of the Ostrich Fern are the most edible. Ferns are unique in that they reproduce without flowers or seeds, and instead grow from spores.

Harvesting

NorCliff farms in Ontario Canada has the distinction as a certified fiddlehead plant, and is the largest commercial distributor of fiddleheads, with a record 27,000 kg. handled in a single day. They host an annual culinary competition, and have generated some amazing recipes (see below) using the fiddlehead. In general, the fiddlehead harvest is a cottage industry, much like the morel mushroom harvest, and gatherers make note of where the plants grow, so they can return each spring to gather the annual delicacy.

If you are gathering your own fiddleheads, harvest them while they are still curled at the top, usually about 8 inches long. You will likely see a brown papery substance at the base of the shoots. As this is a perennial plant, leave the base of the fiddlehead intact to insure the fern's survival for next year.

Nutrition

Great as a side dish for fish, fiddleheads have the qualities of both asparagus and artichokes, but don't turn mushy with cooking. Unsaturated fatty acids contribute 65% of their lipid content. They are also high in niacin, riboflavin, thiamin, vitamins C and A, and minerals potassium, phosphorus, magnesium and calcium. Fiddleheads have very low sodium content, and are also a good non-fish source of Omega-3 fatty acids.

Medicinal Uses

Lupus

A 2010 study looked at the effect of polysaccharides found in Ostrich Fern on symptoms of systemic lupus erythematosus (SLE). Compared with the SLE control group, treatment with Ostrich Fern extract at 15 mg per kilogram doses reduced weight loss and spleen swelling in affected subjects. Increased production of autoantibodies and total immunoglobulin G (IgG) were also significantly inhibited. The Ostrich Fern components also protected the kidney against glomerular injury and lowered the level of protein in the urine. In all six compounds shown to have a protective effect on lupus-like syndrome were identified in the Ostrich Fern.

Precautions

Some common ferns can be poisonous or cancer-causing. Ostrich Fern is considered non-toxic, with one caveat. In 1994, several diners became ill eating either raw or lightly cooked fiddlehead in New York and Western Canada. Diners who consumed the same product from the same distributor at other restaurants where the fiddleheads were fully cooked did not become ill. It is recommended that you boil the fiddleheads for about 15 minutes until tender with a fork before eating.

Another similar fern that grows mostly in the southern portion of Missouri is the bracken fern *(Pterdidium aquilinum)*. This fern should not be eaten as is contains harmful compounds that have been associated with intestinal tumors. Bracken ferns also contain thiaminase, a compound that removes Vitamin B1 from the body. I had first-hand experience with this in the mid 1980's when one of my horses had a grand mal seizure. The cause of the seizure was determined on a weed walk with my veterinarian who found that the horse in question had been eating the bracken ferns in a wooded part of the pasture. I eradicated all of the bracken ferns, and my horse recovered.

Coconut Curry Fiddleheads and Chicken

(Courtesy NorCliff Farms, 2012)

<u>Ingredients</u>

3 tbsp. olive oil

4 tbsp. curry powder

4 boneless chicken breasts; cut in thick slices

8oz. fresh fiddleheads

1-1/2oz. carrots julienne

2 cloves of minced garlic

1/2 onion

4 Tbs. sweetened coconut

salt and pepper to taste

<u>Preparation</u>
1. Boil fiddleheads for approximately 10 minutes.
2. In large saucepan, heat oil. While heating, add 2 tsp of curry powder to hot oil.
3. In separate saucepan sauté onion, carrots and garlic until tender
4. When the oil is heated, turn down the heat to medium-high, add chicken and cook for 2 minutes.
5. When the chicken is perfectly seared and has taken the color of the curry (yellowish green), add fiddleheads and carrots.

6. Then add rest of curry powder and sweetened coconut flakes, stir well and cook for an additional 5 minutes. Finish off with salt and pepper to taste.
7. Serve Immediately.

Fiddlehead sprouts. These are still too early to harvest; they should grow to about 6-10 inches tall.

16

SPICEBUSH (WILD ALLSPICE)

Spicebush, *Lindera Benzoin*, is found in the eastern half of the United States, as far west as Kansas, making it perfectly at home here in the Ozarks. It is a medium sized deciduous shrub that grows up to 6 feet tall, usually found in moist woods and marshes. The leaves have a strong aroma when crushed, and smell similar to sassafras; not surprising as it is in the same family as both sassafras and cinnamon. The fruit-like red berry on the tree (called a *Drupe)* is full of oils, tastes a bit like turpentine, and is loved by birds. The plant itself is a favorite food plant of the spicebush swallowtail butterfly. Early settlers used the presence of spicebush to indicate rich, fertile soil, as that is where the plant thrives, and often planted their crops there.

Native Americans, primarily the Ojibwa and Iroquois, brewed the leaves and twigs for tea, and used it to season meats. The Cherokee, Creek and Delaware tribes were also familiar with the plant, and used it in a variety of medical applications. The oil of the berries of the spicebush, called *drupes,* was used in the late 1800's to treat rheumatism and nerve pain. As far back as the Revolutionary war, the ground drupes were used as a substitute for Allspice. There are many accounts of the use of the plant during the Civil War era as both a tea and for medicinal purposes. Tea made from the plant was used as a diuretic, fever reducer, tonic, stimulant, anti-arthritic, and anthelminthic (worm killer). A chemical analysis of the bark shows that it contains over 39 active compounds, including beneficial limonine that is found in the rind of citrus fruit, terpinene camphene, zingiberene and curcumene. Many of the compounds found in spicebush have been used as food additives, both to enhance flavor and smell, and have been classified as GRAS (generally recognized as safe) by the FDA.

Spicebush has some insect predators, and its numbers are declining in the northeast. Seedlings are readily available at the George O. White nursery, and cuttings of the plant are also easy to grow. In addition to the spicebush swallowtail butterfly, several forms of wildlife, including deer, are attracted to the plant. If you plant it, or locate a patch, you will always have a source of allspice that is less pungent with fewer nutmeg overtones.

Medicinal Uses

Expectorant

In 2010, Spicebush was reviewed in an article on treatments for cough by the International Journal for Pharmaceutical Sciences. 3 different chemicals in the plant were found to help raise secretions from the breathing passages. Although it doesn't suppress cough, it loosens and thins sputum, making it easier to expectorate.

Measles and other viruses

There is documentation in several sources that the Cherokee Indians used an infusion made from Spicebush bark to speed recovery from Measles. In 1996, McWhorter investigated this scientifically, and his research was published in the North Carolina Medical Journal. He found components in spicebush bark with antiviral properties. In 2013, another shrub in the same family as spicebush was studied and found to contain a chemical called lucidone that stops the hepatitis C virus from replicating. The incidence of Hepatitis C is greatly expanding, and conventional treatment costs are astronomical, but with herbal medications providing a rich resource for antiviral drug development, we can expect to see a new more affordable treatment in the near future. (Note that 100 percent of the active ingredients in Tamiflu come from the fruit of the Sweet Gum tree.)

Preparation

The leaves, buds, and new growth twigs can also be made into a pleasant tea with a hint of sassafras and cinnamon. To make your own allspice, wash and dry the drupes, and grind them in a coffee grinder. You can remove the seeds if you wish, but it's not necessary. The old timers recommend laying the meat of old roosters on fresh spicebush branches to tenderize and season them.

17

WILD GINSENG (PANAX QUINQUEFOLIUS L.)

Think of it as the Missouri Money plant. At approximately $40 per ounce, the name Forest Gold is well-earned. Ginseng has been hunted in Missouri since the mid-1800's, and is unfortunately becoming scarcer due to poaching and over harvesting. Ginseng can be grown commercially, but the roots differ from the wild plant which is highly preferred. In 2001, almost $60 million dollars of wild Ginseng was exported from the United States. It is a little strange that most of the ginseng consumed in the US is imported from Asia, while the bulk of our Ginseng is sent overseas, and has been for over 300 years. There are strict laws and even a "hunting season" for wild ginseng in Missouri in order to protect and maintain this most valuable resource. We are fortunate, because only 19 states allow harvest of ginseng.

A rare plant found only in certain areas, wild Ginseng likes the Ozarks, with naturally growing ginseng in 13 counties. You can find it in hardwood forests on north and east facing slopes in rich soil, and also in ravines. Generally, the more mature the forest, the better for ginseng, which can live up to 50 years. It has 3-5 leaflets, and can look a little bit like poison ivy to the untrained eye. Mature plants produce a cluster of red berries in late summer and early fall, making it easy to identify. When you harvest the plant, seeds from those berries must be planted within 100 feet of the parent plant in order to prevent eventual complete eradication. If you harvest ginseng too early it will not have viable seeds, so it is important to adhere to the harvest rules. Seed germination studies done in Missouri show that seed sown at 1" − 1 ¼" germinates the most readily.

Missouri Rules

1. No license needed to gather on private land. Of course, you must have permission.
2. The harvest season in September 1st through December 31st, and the plant can only be sold from Sept. 1 to March 15.
3. Seeds from each harvested plan must be planted within 100 feet of the parent plant.
4. All harvested plans must have a least 3 prongs (3 leaves with 3-5 leaflets each), and must be kept with the plant until you get it home.
5. You cannot harvest ginseng on conservation land or state land, but it can be harvested in the Mark Twain National Forest with a permit.
6. There are laws regarding buying and selling ginseng, and the Missouri Dept. of Conservation acts as ginseng coordinator.

Medicinal Uses

Wild ginseng is particularly prized in Asia, where it is usually consumed as a tea. The medicinal properties of ginseng are contained in the root, and include use in cancer treatment, cognitive function and memory, blood glucose regulation, cholesterol regulation and fertility in males.

Blood Sugar Regulation

A study published in the April, 2000 edition of the prestigious JAMA (Journal of the American Medical Association) looked at effect of wild ginseng on blood sugar levels in both diabetic and non-diabetic subjects after eating a high glucose meal. They found that wild ginseng lowered postprandial (after eating) blood sugar levels in both groups by 18 – 49% when ginseng was taken before the meal. The effect was so dramatic that the researchers cautioned that diabetic persons should always take ginseng with a meal in order to prevent dangerously low blood sugar levels.

18

WILD GINSENG – PART 2

Last week we looked at the effect of wild ginseng on lowering post-prandial (after eating) blood sugar levels. As one of the most pharmacologically active plants, ginseng also shows promise in treating several forms of cancer, impaired cognitive function, male infertility and elevated cholesterol.

Cancer

Wild Ginseng has also been found to have promise in treating gastric, liver and colon cancer, and has also been found to extend the life span of both adult and juvenile test animals with leukemia. It is thought that wild ginseng works by enhancing cells that act as the first line of defense in combatting tumors, so-called "natural killer" cells. Five anticancer compounds have been isolated in wild American ginseng, and unlike many other plants, the anti-cancer activities of the root are increased when the root is heat-processed. The effect against cancer appears to be dose-related.

A 2013 article in Oncology Case Reports documents the dramatic effect of wild ginseng on a Stage IV Non-small cell lung cancer. The patient received no surgery, chemotherapy or radiation. A series of CT scans from December 2013 to September 2014 showed the tumor decreased from 54 mm to 11 mm over that period, and remained stable at 11 mm. *(Images available upon request.)*

A 2014 study by the National Cancer Institute looked at the role of wild ginseng in preventing cancer-related fatigue (CRF). The study was deemed important because "safe, effective interventions to improve cancer-related fatigue are needed because it remains a prevalent, distressing and activity-limiting symptom." 364 patients from 40 hospitals were enrolled in the study. A multisite, double-blind trial randomized fatigued cancer survivors to 2000 mg of American ginseng vs. a placebo for 8 weeks, and decrease in fatigue was significant. Greater benefit was reported in patients receiving active cancer treatment vs. those who had already finished treatment. The researchers concluded that data support the benefit of American ginseng, 2000 mg daily, on CRF over an 8-week period. There were no complications associated with the treatment.

Memory

In a 2015 study published in Human Psychopharmacology, researchers looked a working memory performance after a single dose of American ginseng. In this double-blind study of 52 volunteers between 40 – 60 years old, there was significant improvement in working memory at 3 hours after a 200 mg dose. This recent study validated the findings of an earlier study in 2010 that tested 19 measures of memory and cognitive function in volunteers given 100 – 400 mg of wild ginseng. In the earlier study, subjects had increased memory speed and recall, and also reported an increased feeling of calmness. (Working memory is short-term storage and processing of memory – like doing a math problem in your head.)

The mechanism by which ginseng helps memory is still being investigated, but loss of nicotinic receptors in the brain is associated with age-related decline in cognitive function. Ginseng stimulates these receptors, reversing some of the effects of aging.

Male Infertility

In laboratory animals treated with powdered ginseng root for six weeks, there was an increase in both number and quality of sperm. In a study conducted in 1996 with human subjects, 66 male subjects with infertility were matched with healthy volunteers used as controls. The infertile subjects were treated with wild ginseng extract. Use of ginseng showed an increase in spermatozoa number and increased motility, an increase in plasma total and free testosterone, DHT, FSH and LH levels.

Cholesterol Lowering

Components in wild ginseng activates an enzyme that breaks down very low-density lipoproteins (the bad ones), resulting in a decrease in both triglycerides and cholesterol.

Grow Your Own
If your ginseng hunt doesn't pay off, ginseng roots can be purchased and will grow with very little effort when planted here in the Ozarks. Keep in mind that there are regulations on when Ginseng can be sold. If you purchase roots now, they likely won't be shipped until September.

Wild ginseng that has not yet produced its signature cluster of red berries can be confused with poison ivy.

19

YELLOW ROCKET

Yellow rocket (Barbarea vulgaris) is the first member of the Mustard family to bloom in the spring. It is in the same family with many other crop plants, including broccoli and cauliflower, and it even looks like broccoli to the casual observer. A native of North America and Eurasia, Yellow Rocket grows abundantly throughout the Ozarks, south into Arkansas, and north into Canada, and it is found in hayfields as well as along roadsides.

Although food plants are rarely found year round, Yellow Rocket remains hardy throughout the winter. In fact, the flavor is best when leaves are covered with snow, or early in the spring, before the plant flowers. Also called winter cress, the basal leaves (at the base of the plant) can be eaten raw or boiled, and taste similar to turnip greens with a peppery taste. Rich in Vitamins C and A, Yellow Rocket is considered an anti-scurvy plant. Three ounces have about 5,000 IU of Vitamin A and 150 mg of vitamin C. The yellow flower buds can also be eaten, but after flowering both the leaves and buds should be boiled in two changes of water to prevent bitterness.

The history of yellow rocket goes back to medieval times, where it was used as a wound poultice. The genus name Barbarea comes from *Barbara*, the patron saint of artillerymen and soldiers.

Insect resistance

Anyone who has ever grown broccoli knows what an insect magnet it appears to be. Yellow Rocket has been heavily studied because of its insect resistance, and the fact it can protect nearby plants from insect activity by virtue of being what is called a "trap crop." Trap crops attract insects away from other plants. The insect repellent properties of Yellow Rocket are thought to be due to the presence of saponins, which are natural insecticides. Yellow Rocket is the only plant in the crucifer family known to produce saponins, and in one study where yellow rocket was planted in the bed with cabbage plants, insect activity was decreased by 11.3 percent.

Health Benefits

Many of the health benefits of Yellow Rocket are due to its saponin content, including decreased blood cholesterol, cancer prevention and immune system support.

Cholesterol Reduction

Saponins in yellow rocket bind with bile salt and cholesterol in the intestinal tract, blocking the reabsorption of cholesterol, and decreasing levels in the blood stream.

Cancer Prevention

Saponins lower the risk of cancer by preventing mutant cells from growing. They seem to do this by reacting with the cholesterol-rich membranes of cancer cells. A 1995 study in the Journal of Nutrition found that saponins found in yellow rocket were particularly helpful against colon cancer. Other studies show that they can stop leukemia cells from dividing and multiplying. Saponins also have a direct antioxidant effect, which also helps to prevent cancer and heart disease.

Immune Defense

Just like saponins in yellow rocket fight off insect pests in the garden, they also fight viruses and bacteria in the human body. This may explain the traditional use of juice from the leaves in treating warts, which as we know, are caused by viruses. A 1952 study documented the effectiveness of Yellow Rocket against Mycobacterium tuberculosis (the causative organism in most forms of tuberculosis.)

Yellow Rocket Potato Patties

1 cup cooked, mashed potato
1 cup chopped yellow rocket leaves, boiled in 2 sets of water and drained
2 tbsp milk
1 egg
1 tbsp. Butter
¼ cup bread crumbs
2 Tbsp chopped fresh wild onion and garlic, including green tops
Salt and Pepper to taste.
Mix all ingredients and fry until brown and crispy in butter or oil.

Yellow Rocket looks very similar to broccoli, and is in the same family.

20

MAY APPLE – THE FORGOTTEN FRUIT

Anyone who has ever walked in a Missouri forest in early spring has surely noticed the carpeting of little green umbrella plants. Those cute little plants hold some important secrets. As the name implies, they produce a flower in early May that only lasts a day or two, and a little known tasty apple-like fruit in early summer that ripens slowly and is ready to eat in early August. Be warned - if you aren't on the ball, the forest animals will steal the fruit right out from under you!

The other secret of the May Apple is its importance in treating certain forms of cancer. The roots and rhizomes of the plant contain Podophyllotoxin (PTOX), used to treat all kinds of warts, including plantar warts, genital warts, and HPV. Derivatives of the May Apple include etoposide and teniposide that have been heavily studied for their anticancer activity and used in various chemotherapies, including treatment of lung cancer, lymphomas, and genital tumors. The plant was used by Native Americans to treat warts, parasites and syphilis.

Some of us remember "Carter's Little Liver Pills." You likely didn't know that May Apple was a main ingredient.

Drug Resistant Cancer

Certain tumor cell lines have been found multi-drug resistant, and are hard to treat. Chemicals found in May Apple are immune to classical drug resistance and are considered valuable in the treatment of drug-resistant cancers. Some of the most effective anti-cancer agents, such as paclitaxel (Taxus brevifolia) were originally discovered through extensive National Cancer Institute plant research. They also discovered one of the most potent natural products for human breast cancer is derived from May Apple root.

May Apple is so important that a great deal of study has been done on domesticating the plant in North America and developing sustainable harvest procedures. The extensive use of these anticancer drugs and high demand in the international market for the past three decades has caused plants in the May Apple species to be endangered overseas. Since synthesizing PTOX in the lab is an expensive process, availability of the compound from natural renewable resources is an important issue for pharmaceutical companies that manufacture these drugs, and cultivation of May Apple in the US has the potential to become profitable.

Etoposide and Teniposide

PTOX derived from May Apple is used to produce anticancer pharmaceuticals such as etoposide and teniposide. The National Cancer Institute publishes a list of 167 clinical trials using etoposide in cancer cocktails. Etoposide (Vepsid) comes exclusively from the May apple and is used as a treatment for cancers such as Kaposi's sarcoma, Ewing's sarcoma, lung cancer, testicular cancer, lymphoma, non-lymphocytic leukemia, and glioblastoma multiforme.

Teniposide (Vumon, VM-26) is mainly used in the treatment of childhood acute lymphocytic leukemia (ALL). It works by slowing the growth of cancer cells in the body.

Other applications

PTOX is also the precursor to a new derivative CPH 82 that is being tested for rheumatoid arthritis in Europe, and it also used for the treatment of psoriasis and malaria. Several PTOX preparations are on the market for dermatological use to treat genital warts. In 1988, May Apple extract was assigned US Patent 4788216 in the treatment of malaria, psoriasis and arthritis. A study published in the Dec. 2013

Journal of Cosmetics found Podophyllin 10% ointment more effective than clobetasole 0.05% at the end of 8 weeks, with no side effects and a lower relapse rate in treatment of mild plaque-like psoriasis, and the journal posts stunning photographs of almost full resolution of psoriatic lesions.

Emetic

In a publication from 1883, entitled "The American Eclectic Materia Medica and Therapeutics," John Scudder, MD talks about the use of May Apple root tincture, and states even a fraction of a drop works as a cathartic, causing great nausea and protracted vomiting." Although it sounds awful, there is a use for medications that induce vomiting, as in drug overdoses, or ingestion of toxic substances. Syrup of Ipecac, which comes from the root of a plant found in Central America, is the emetic familiar in American Medicine. (Interesting note: Karen Carpenter was using Syrup of Ipecac to induce vomiting in an attempt to lose weight, a fact that lead to her death in 1983.)

Precautions

The leaves, stem and rhizome are toxic, and shouldn't be eaten. It is recommended that you wear gloves when handling these parts of the plant, as many people are allergic. The fruit is fully edible when ripe, and can be eaten raw, but is commonly consumed as a jam or jelly.

Mayapple in bloom.

21

CHICKWEED – NOT JUST FOR CHICKS

As I was putting in my garden this week, my almost 4 year old grand-daughter and foraging companion was seeking out and gorging herself on chickweed. With every bite, she would exclaim "This is good!" Because it is a small plant, and so abundant, it is easy to overlook and I have been guilty of that myself. The first mention of chickweed (Stellaria media) is found in a British herb publication from 1538 where Turner writes "It growth on olde houses and in all places, all most in summer." Although most consider chickweed a pesky weed, it is beneficial to adjacent plants because it has significant defense mechanisms, and helps protect against fungal diseases. Chickweed is also attractive to members of the Lepidoptera order of insects, including the Monarch butterfly.

Nutrition

A very tasty plant, chickweed is also high in nutrition. Chickweed has the singular ability to accumulate mineral nutrients in higher quantities than crop plants. Nitrogen, phosphorus, potassium and magnesium have been found to be at much higher levels in chickweed than vegetables that grow in the same area. In addition to the minerals mentioned above, chickweed is also an excellent source of Vitamin A, C, B complex, and D, and contains 75 mg of ascorbic acid per cup. It also provides iron, calcium, zinc, manganese, and small amounts of sodium.

Medicinal Uses

Chickweed has been used in traditional medicine as an astringent, carminative (gets rid of gas and bloating), anti-asthmatic, demulcent, depurative, diuretic, and expectorant, It is also used for bronchitis, rheumatic pains and kidney diseases. A poultice of chickweed can be applied to cuts, burns, ulcers and bruises for enhanced healing.

Obesity

Several studies have documented the effect of chickweed on treating obesity. It appears to work by several mechanisms. A 2011 study looked at the effect of the plant against drug-induced obesity caused by progesterone. The effect on food consumption pattern, change in body weight, thermogenesis, and fat metabolism were examined specifically. Progesterone is a female reproductive hormone that waxes and wanes during the menstrual cycle, and is also used in contraceptives and hormone replacement therapy. Progesterone is felt to cause weight gain by causing hyperphagia (excessive eating) and increased fat deposition in the body. Researchers found that oral administration of chickweed extracts reduced the level of circulating lipids as well as the size of fat cell diameter, resulting in decreased body weight. Chickweed appears to show such activities by causing an anorexic effect (not feeling hungry) and through delaying the intestinal absorption of dietary fat and carbohydrates by inhibiting digestive enzymes.

A 2012 study published in the International Journal of Nutrition examined the practice of local people in the Assam State in India who use chickweed extract as an aid for obesity. The researchers found that chickweed has both thermogenic and appetite-suppressant properties and concluded "With this study we conclude that MESM (extract of Stellaria media) is beneficial for the suppression of obesity and its associated complications."

A New Protein

In 2011, a novel antiviral protein, designated as Stellarmedin A, was purified from chickweed. This protein inhibited herpes simplex virus type 2 (HSV-2) replication and was also able to inhibit the proliferation of promyelocytic leukemia HL-60 and colon carcinoma LoVo .

Hepatitis B (HBV)

A 2102 study published in *Molecules* takes a close look at chickweed juice, a traditional Chinese medicine that has been used for over 200 years, mainly for the treatment of dermatitis and other skin diseases. It has also been used as an anti-viral agent. Researchers specifically looked at its anti-hepatitis B virus activity. They found chickweed possesses potential anti-HBV activity in the laboratory setting. Chickweed extract is currently under early development as a potential anti-HBV drug candidate.

Preparation

Chickweed can be used raw in a salad, or as a substitute for spinach in recipes. The leaves, stems and flowers are all edible and tasty. Chopped chickweed makes a great substitute for zucchini in zucchini bread. You can also drink it as a tea.

Precautions

Although chickweed is very safe, it does have a poisonous look-alike, spotted spurge. Like chickweed, spotted spurge grows close to the ground with paired leaves, but has different flowers, and all parts of the spurge produce a milky sap when broken (chickweed has no milky sap.) The sap from spurge can also be a skin and eye irritant, so handle with care.

Chickweed is a tiny powerhouse of nutrients.

22

CINQUEFOIL

Cinquefoil may likely be the most amusing plant. Visitors from the city often inquire if it is a form of cannabis. The answer is "no," because other than its appearance, there are no other similarities. Now considered an invasive weed, cinquefoil was brought over from Europe and introduced to North America. In Missouri, we have 7 species of Cinquefoil; all with the Latin prefix Potentilla, which means "little potent one." The most commonly found Cinquefoil plant is Potentilla Simplex, but Potentilla Canadensis also abounds in the Ozarks.

A noble looking plant, Cinquefoil has 5 leaflets, and the name is literally translated from the French to mean "five leaf." The cinquefoil emblem is found on many family crests, with the 5 leaflets symbolizing the 5 senses. In medieval times the right to use the emblem was an honor, and only granted to knights who had proven mastery over self. Fishermen attached the plant to their nets in a belief they would catch more fish.

Cinquefoil was recognized and written about in ancient Greece. A student of Aristotle named Theophrastus was the first to describe the medicinal uses of the plant.

Traditional uses have included use as an astringent, an aid to stop bleeding, and an effective treatment for healing sores in the mouth and stopping the pain of toothaches. It has the nickname "cramp weed," because of its effectiveness in treating menstrual cramps.

In 2009, an extensive review of the pharmacological properties of Cinquefoil was published in Ethnopharmacology. Cinquefoil was found to have a role in treating diarrhea, stomach ulcers, and certain types of cancers and diabetes. It has antiviral, antimicrobial, anti-inflammatory, spasmolytic, liver protective and antioxidant properties.

Nutritional Uses

In parts of Europe, Cinquefoil is eaten as a vegetable. It contains starches, amino acids, calcium, iron, sulfate, magnesium potassium sodium and Vitamin C. The leaves can be eaten raw or cooked, and are often added to soups. The best time to harvest cinquefoil is the month of June, as the plant is at its tastiest and most nutritious. It blooms from May through August, producing a yellow flower that attracts several types of bees and other insects seeking nectar. Rabbits and groundhogs eat the plant, as do livestock. The plant is non-toxic.

Medicinal Uses

Pain and Fever

A 2014 study investigated the fever and pain reducing properties of Cinquefoil. Although the plant has been used as a fever reducer for centuries, this was the first study that found a strong antipyretic effect. This same study documented a decrease in pain perception of up to 67.29%. It is often used for abdominal cramping and painful periods, but is usually mixed with chamomile for this purpose.

Thyroid Disease

Cinquefoil has been discussed as an effective treatment for thyroid gland disease since mid-1970. A 2014 study looked at the role of Cinquefoil root extract in treating thyroid disease in children and teenagers. The findings confirmed visible reduction of size of the thyroid gland and normalization of thyroid function following oral ingestion.

Peptic Ulcer

Extract from the cinquefoil rhizome has been found helpful in treating gastric ulcers, and effect has been compared to the common drug Ranitidine. Cinquefoil extracts have strong antifungal and antibacterial activity, and in one study showed the strongest antimicrobial activity against H. pylori – the bacteria associated with ulcers, thereby treating the cause of the underlying condition.

Anti-inflammatory

A study earlier this year looked at the anti-oxidant and anti-inflammatory effect of both the stem and root of the cinquefoil plant. While both had significant activity, the root was more effective than the stem (aerial part) of the plant, and was found to be 89% as effective as the steroid Decadron.

Astringent

An astringent works to constrict body tissues, which is helpful in controlling bleeding. It is thought that the astringent activity in cinquefoil is due to the high level of tannins. When used as a mouth wash, it is useful for decreasing swelling in the mouth and throat, and healing bleeding gums. Extract can be added to bath water to ease pain and swelling and stop bleeding from hemorrhoids, boils, and ulcers.

Anti-diarrheal

Cinquefoil is listed as an effective treatment for diarrhea in the PDR for Herbal Medicines, and is also approved by Commission E - a committee of researchers, physicians, toxicologists and pharmacists that determines the safety and effectiveness of herbs sold in Germany,

Preparation

For pain or diarrhea, boil 1 tsp. of fresh leaves per 1 cup of water. You can drink the tea, add it to bath water, or use it to make a moist compress. Since there are no side effects associated with the use of the cinquefoil, you can drink one cup of tea up to three to four times a day.

Cinquefoil has a distinctive appearance and a long and noble history.

23

BUTTERBUR FOR SEASONAL ALLERGIES AND MIGRAINE

Just about everyone is suffering with allergies to some extent. The pollen seems to be exceptionally heavy, and runny nose, constant sneezing and watery eyes affect both our work and leisure. Most of the traditional allergy medications have side effects, such as drowsiness, and Benadryl has recently been linked to dementia.

Butterbur, of the Petasites genus, was recommended for the prevention of episodic migraine in the 2012 Guidelines published by the American Academy of Neurology. Even more remarkable is its effect on seasonal allergies. Also known as Sweet Coltsfoot, butterbur grows well in Missouri, mostly in the areas of Ballwin, Columbia and Piedmont. A perennial plant, it is considered invasive, so if you wish to introduce it to your garden it would be wise to plant it in a container. Butterbur is in the sunflower family, and has large, rhubarb-like leaves. In fact, it has the largest leaves of all native plants. It likes to grow in moist places like riverbanks and ditches.

Medicinal Uses

Butterbur has over a 2000 year history of use in treating lung problems, pain and fever. It is listed in the Herbal PDR as a treatment for urinary spasms in the presence of kidney and bladder stones.

Headache Prevention

Headaches comprise about 30 percent of any neurology practice. Episodic migraine can be particularly debilitating, and sufferers pretty much have to stop everything and lay down in a dark room. Pain medication is not effective for migraine, and actually causes rebound headache, so prevention is the goal. In a previous article feverfew for headache was reviewed. Since that time, feverfew was rated Level B in effectiveness for migraine prevention, while Butterbur was rated Level A, with the following recommendation: "Petasites (butterbur) is effective for migraine prevention and should be offered to patients with migraine to reduce the frequency and severity of migraine attacks." The chemicals petasin and isopetasin found in butterbur are thought to be the active ingredients that prevent migraine, possibly by preventing blood vessel inflammation. The highest concentration of active ingredients is found in the root of the plant, although the leaves also contain the compounds, Controlled studies show a decrease in migraines by 48 – 77%

Anti-Allergy

The beneficial effect of extract from butterbur has been demonstrated many times over. In a 2013 study, researchers found a dramatic effect on mast cells with extract from the leaves. Mast cells play a huge role in allergies. When they are activated, they cause an allergic response – sneezing, runny nose, watery eyes. Mast cells remain inactive until stimulated by an allergen, such as pollen. Bakkenolide B, a major component of butterbur leaves, blocks the activation of mast cells. The researchers concluded that butterbur has "suppressive properties for allergic and inflammatory responses and may be utilized as a potent agent for the treatment of asthma."

A 2011 study used extract from the entire butterbur plant. They found it inhibited interleukin, TNF α, and eosinophils – all chemicals involved in allergic response in asthmatic patients, resulting in the suppression of airway inflammation and mucus production.

Treatment for simple allergic rhinitis was the focus of a 2006 study that examined safety and efficacy of butterbur extract. The extract was made into 8 mg tablets, and subjects with severe allergic rhinitis were given 2 tablets daily for 2 weeks. Symptoms of rhinorrhea (runny nose), sneezing, nasal congestion, itchy eyes and nose, red eyes, and skin irritation improved in 90% of the patients. Another study in 2004 found butterbur extract to be as effective as the Fexofenadine (Loratidine) in treating allergic rhinitis. Butterbur extract has been proven in post marketing surveillance trials to be safe and efficacious in the treatment of patients with seasonal allergic rhinitis, and is readily available for purchase online.

Dosage and Precautions

Per Web MD: Butterbur extract has been used in doses of 50 to 100 mg twice daily with meals. Higher doses seem to be work better. Lower doses of 50 mg twice daily may not be effective in adults. Some researchers suggest taking the extract for 4-6 months, then lowering the dose over time until the number of migraines begins to increase again. In 6-9 year-old children with migraine, a dose of 25 mg twice daily has been used; 50 mg twice daily has been used in older children. Three times daily dosing has been used in children who don't respond to the twice daily dose. Burping and other mild gastrointestinal complaints have been the main side effect of butterbur extract.

Butterbur is broken down by the liver, so should be used cautiously in persons with liver disease. Safety in pregnant and nursing mothers and children under the age of 6 has not been evaluated and should be avoided.

Butterbur has large leaves and rhubarb like stalks.

24

WALKING ON EGGSHELLS

The word is out on fluoride, and just last month the government admitted permissible fluoride levels have been way too high. According to the CDC, 41% of American Children have dental fluorosis due to excessive fluoride. Most of us realize ingested fluoride is toxic at any level, prompting a brisk cottage industry in home-made toothpaste. I have several recipes for home-made toothpaste, but often they involve baking soda that can adversely affect blood pressure due to the sodium level.

There is a new kid in town on the toothpaste front, and that is chicken egg shell powder! A great replacement for baking soda, it is a mild abrasive, prevents cavities, and has even been proven to remineralize the teeth. Cavities are a process, and a tooth goes through several cycles of demineralization and remineralization before a cavity appears, so it is possible to repair a cavity in the early stages by increasing the net mineral gain of the tooth. This can be accomplished with a healthy diet and the simple addition of eggshell powder to our toothpaste and diet.

Chicken eggshell powder has been investigated in various fields regarding its potential use, and is a well-known source of calcium. One whole medium sized eggshell makes about one teaspoon of powder, which yields about 750-800 mg. of elemental calcium, plus other micro elements including phosphorus and magnesium and trace amounts of trace amounts of sodium, potassium, zinc, manganese, iron and copper. The calcium in eggshells is highly bio-available, and increases bone mineral density, preventing osteoporosis. Eggshells also stimulate cartilage growth and reduce pain and bone resorption in older women. The composition of an eggshell is very similar to that of our bones and teeth. I remember both my mother and grandmother adding crushed eggshells to coffee grounds when brewing coffee and I've learned this now forgotten practice used to be the norm. Eggshells are especially beneficial for small children with the formation of their bone structure, which requires calcium. In so-called "third world countries" shells are often added to baby food to help prevent rickets and anemia.

Cavity Prevention

Research published in March of this year in the Journal of Clinical Diagnostics looked at how eggshells can remineralize tooth enamel. Your toothbrush acts as a drug delivery device, and brushing action assists the introduction of calcium from the eggshells into the enamel of the tooth. The researchers concluded that the high pH of the of chicken egg shells along with their rich bioavailable calcium content returned minerals to the teeth. Bacteria in the mouth and certain foods, esp. those high in sugar are acidic, working to dissolve enamel. Saliva is important in the process. When the pH goes below 5.5, enamel is dissolved, allowing cavities to start. Your saliva normally helps to neutralize the acid, and protect your teeth, but sometimes the process is overwhelmed.

Bone Density

A 2002 study looked at the impact of chicken eggshell powder on bone mineral density in the lumbar spine and hip. Biochemical markers of bone and calcium metabolism were also examined. 85 healthy Caucasian women between the ages of 50 and 70 were either given placebo or eggshell powder. At the end of 12 months measureable increases in bone density were found in the subjects receiving supplementation with chicken eggshell power. This is extremely important as it decreases the risk of hip fracture in post-menopausal women.

Osteoporosis

In a 2003 study looking at the effect of eggshell extract on osteoporosis, researchers found that eggshell powder stimulates chondrocyte differentiation and cartilage growth. Clinical studies in postmenopausal women and women with senile osteoporosis showed that eggshell powder reduces pain and bone resorption and increases mobility and bone density or arrests its loss. They concluded that "Clinical and experimental studies showed that eggshell powder has positive effects on bone and cartilage and that it is suitable in the prevention and treatment of osteoporosis."

How to use

Before adding eggshells to coffee or toothpaste, they should be thoroughly cleaned. Boil shells for 5 minutes and remove residual egg matter. (Keep the membrane, as it is high in collagen, and very beneficial for joints.) Let the shells dry. I like to grind mine to a powder in my coffee grinder. You can then add the powder to milkshakes, soups, stews, or grounds when you are brewing coffee. Nature Has The Cure/Facebook has a video pictorial on making homemade toothpaste with eggshells and coconut oil, or email Marie Lasater at calhorselover@yahoo.com for detailed instructions.

Tip: You can also add eggshells to your garden. They provide a wide range of valuable nutrients, and their high pH is beneficial to the soil, acting much like lime.

25

CRYPTO GARDENS

Crypto: Secret, hidden
Garden: a fertile and beautiful region.

Some of us have lavish gardens, and some of us have a few pots on the porch. All of us can have a crypto garden: a private space known only to ourselves and God. My neighbor who passed away a couple of years ago had such a place. Every summer, he would take off on a meandering path into the woods, and return with a basket of wild raspberries from his secret patch. Only he knew its location, and he wasn't giving it up. That patch, likely there for decades, has now resumed complete secrecy, until another woods walker happens upon its bounty.

Sometimes crypto gardens are happened-upon, sometimes they are created. The miracle seems to be that they are largely left alone by wildlife. I have a patch of Mayapple staked out – just waiting for the fruit to fully ripen. I spotted it from the back of my horse, and frequent it regularly to be sure I get to the fruit before the squirrels. I know where the sassafras trees are located when I need a root to make root beer, and also where the best patch of dittany (wild garlic) is located.

In the past month, I was fortunate to visit crypto gardens in both Phelps and Texas counties. My friend Judith has a lovely home in Phelps County, with a beautifully manicured lawn. On one corner of her property, she has piled brush for wildlife refuge, and we giggled at her hidden garden, with poke, butterbur, henbit, chickweed, purslane and even a small persimmon tree – a virtually salad storage cabinet that can only be appreciated by the initiated.

In Texas County, a colleague invited me over to pick lettuce. On first glance, there was no lettuce to be found. It was hidden beneath the lamb's quarters and other invasives, but when the "weeds" were brushed aside, there was a large variety of perfect salad greens, untouched by squirrels, rabbits or other critters, and I took home a week's worth of salad fixings.

Likely the most popular crypto gardens are the areas where the morel mushroom is found. The king of mushrooms, the morel can often be found in consecutive years at the same location. Usually a closely guarded secret, the location of the morel mushroom patch is the stuff a Last Will and Testament is made of.

You too, can plant a crypto garden, even if you have no land. Since man first started gathering food, the forest has provided an abundance of food in the form of perennials that return year after year, unlike the annuals planted in a cultivated garden. The forest is a very stable plant environment, and resists rapid change, which is one reason that one of the most valuable plants, ginseng, can grow for up to 50 years in the same place. Plants that grow in the forest are considered part of the permaculture – a self-contained habitat, and are very low maintenance, usually fairly well established after the first year. There is no weeding, watering, fertilizing, pest control or mulching with a crypto garden. Shade tolerant plants that grow well in the forest include wild raspberries, green onion, horse radish, lettuce, mustard greens, cabbage, ginger, beats, bush beans, garlic, parsley, grapes, rosemary and mint.

When you develop your hidden garden, it works best in a circular formation, not a row. Nature has its own rules. Starting with your taller plants, such as an existing hickory or a paw paw tree, plant your perennials in a circular formation from larger to smaller plants. If you pile brush around your garden, you can camouflage it to safeguard your private food stash.

Now go out and find your perfect hidden garden!

26

ALL AROUND THE MULBERRY BUSH

The fruit of the Mulberry tree is a delicious ingredient in home-made jam, but the native Ozark red mulberry tree *Morus Rubra* offers much more than a tasty treat. The roots, bark and leaves have antioxidant, antiviral, antibacterial, anti-inflammatory, cholesterol lowering, blood sugar regulation and neuro protective qualities. The leaves are popular in Korea and Japan for diabetic patients and are also used as nutritional supplements.

In addition to the native American red mulberry, there are over 150 species of Mulberry trees worldwide, and most familiar to Ozarkians is the white mulberry *Morus Alba*, an introduced plant from Asia, used for silkworm cultivation. Mulberry trees are very strong and adaptable, resistant to drought, and stable below 0 degrees centigrade. Our native red mulberry can live up to 75 years. White mulberry is named for the color of its flowers, not its fruit, that can be either red or black. White mulberry is considered an escaped invasive, and is found in urban areas. The native red mulberry is found in natural settings, scattered throughout the forest. Even if you don't want to reap the health benefits of mulberry, having a tree on your place will protect other fruit trees from birds and squirrels, as they greater prefer mulberries over any other fruit!

Nutrition

The different species of Mulberry offer significant nutritional benefits in varying amounts. Our native Red Mulberry is highest in protein with 2 grams of protein. At just 60 calories per cup, it also contains 2 grams of fiber, and 85% of the RDA for Vitamin C and 14% for Iron.

Atherosclerosis

A 2010 study examined the effect of a water extract of the leaves from the Red Mulberry plant on atherosclerosis (hardening of the arteries with plaque.) Treatment with the extract for just 5 consecutive days showed significant improvement in body weight and blood cholesterol levels. Factors adversely affecting the lining of blood vessels were reversed to near normal. The researchers concluded "our study show that aqueous leaf extract of *Morus rubra*, (400 mg/g) significantly improves glucose and fat metabolism and possesses significant anti-atherosclerotic activity."

Obesity

What I find the most exciting is the effect of Mulberry leaf extract on obesity. A 2014 study looked at the effect of mulberry leaf extract on fat cells. They found that without any apparent toxic effects, mulberry leaf extract prevented fat accumulation in the cells, concluding it is has potential as an anti-obesity drug, with no side effects.

The fruit of the mulberry also aids in weight loss. A study published in February of this year examined the effect of mulberry juice on brown fat. Brown fat generates body heat by burning calories – resulting in weight loss. Infants have very high levels of brown fat, which is why they don't shiver when it's cold. We tend to lose brown fat as we age, and it is largely absent in obese people. Mulberry juice supports the production of beneficial brown fat.

A 2013 study found that mulberry juice prevents diet-induced obesity through increases in adiponectin, a protein hormone that regulates glucose regulation and fat metabolism. Higher levels of adiponectin are seen with lower body fat percentages, and are elevated in patients with anorexia nervosa.

Blood sugar stabilization

A study from January of this year looked at the effect of mulberry tea in the reduction of abnormally high postprandial (after-eating) blood glucose levels in Type 2 diabetic patients.

Fasting blood sugar levels were recorded, then after the consumption of plain tea or mulberry tea, post-meal blood glucose levels were measured, showing a highly significant decrease in the glucose level in response to mulberry tea in all the test patients compared with the subjects that drank plain tea. The effect on blood sugar level was also found to be very large.

In a 2010 animal study, red mulberry leaf extract was orally administered to diabetic rats daily for 21 days. Blood samples were drawn to measure glucose tolerance and lipid parameters. The extract showed a dose-dependent fall in fasting blood glucose with an increase in plasma insulin levels. Examination of pancreatic tissue revealed an increased number of islets and beta-cells in extract-treated diabetic rats. This is extremely important, because these cells are where insulin is produced, and they are either absent or decreased in diabetic patients.

Oral Health

The mulberry fruit itself has excellent anti-microbial activity against many forms of bacteria, yeasts, and fungi, including the common oral pathogen that causes cavities - Streptococcus mutans. A few studies have studied the used of red mulberry juice in oral health, and it was found to be an excellent "temporary storage medium for the maintenance of periodontal ligament cell viability in avulsed teeth." In other words, if your tooth is knocked out, save it in red mulberry juice until you get to the dentist and it can likely be re-implanted.

27

MULLEIN – HELP FOR CHRONIC COUGH

Commonly found in Missouri with the descriptive nicknames of Flannel Plant, Beggar's Blanket and Blanket Herb, American Mullein is actually native to Europe, but was one of the first plants introduced to North America due to its medicinal properties.

Mullein has a permanent place in history, because in Carravaggio's 1604 painting of St. John the Baptist in the wilderness, the mullein plant is included prominently in the foreground, and is considered a symbol of protection and courage. (You can see the painting at the Nelson-Atkins Museum of Art in Kansas City.) In the field, the plant is easy to spot with its blanket-like soft leaves and tall spikes with yellow flowers.

There are roughly 250 species of mullein, but the one we are most likely to see is the common mullein, (Verbascum Thapsus). The leaves are blue-green in color, soft and flannel-like and have been used as diapers, cushioning inserts for shoes, lamp wicks, and fire starters. In its first year, the mullein plant has low-growing leaves, but as it matures, it sends up tall flower stalks that are usually bright yellow and hard to miss. The flowers of the mullein plant have been used in hair dyes.

Although it is largely forgotten today, mullein has been a traditional remedy in many cultures, going back to ancient Greece where it was used for lung problems. Mullein contains powerful expectorants, and is often made into teas, and even a steam inhalation.

Tuberculosis

Because of its long history in successfully treating lung diseases, researchers are taking a closer look at mullein. In an article entitled *"What's in a Name? Can Mullein Weed Beat TB Where Modern Drugs Are Failing?"*, researchers looked at the traditional use of mullein in treating tuberculosis, formerly called "consumption." Although the use of mullein in many forms of lung diseases with chronic cough is found in the literature, the mechanism hasn't been well-defined, but is thought to be due to the effect of mullein on mycobacterum – an organism that causes tuberculosis and some forms of pneumonia characterized by a severe chronic cough. In an era of drug-resistant organisms, mullein may present a viable alternative to traditional antibiotics.

A study published in August, 2014 looked extensively at the antibacterial action of a water extract of mullein and found good effects against both Gram-positive and Gram-negative bacteria. Their results have been replicated, and mullein is found to have activity against *Klebsiella* pneumonia equal with that of erythromycin.

Earache

In Europe today, mullein flower oil is used as a remedy for earache, and clinical trials show improvement in acute otitis media when the oil is applied to the eardrum, due to both the anti-inflammatory and antimicrobial action.

Anti-inflammatory

One of the reasons mullein is so useful for lung diseases is its soothing effect on the mucous membranes that line the respiratory tract. It does this by several means, including reducing the activity of irritating chemicals that form in the lung during the disease process. It also helps to mobilize secretions so they can be coughed up, and is used to treat symptoms of asthma, chronic bronchitis and chronic cough.

Lung Cancer

As scientists looked closer at Mullein, a new substance called verbathasin-A was discovered. In 2011, this chemical was found to have "an obvious effect of inducing apoptosis (death) of A549 lung cancer cells."

Hair Rinse

In addition to making a world class cough medicine from the leaves, a water extract of mullein flowers can be used as a rinse to brighten light colored hair

Cough syrup

Mullein is especially effective for dry cough. In addition to being antimicrobial, in contains demulcents – soothing chemicals that are rich in mucilage. To make your own cough syrup, boil 1 cup of dried or fresh leaves in 2 cups of water. (If using fresh leaves, crinkle them a little to release the oils.) Boil gently for about 5 minutes, and let stand for 15 minutes. Strain the mixture, and add in 1 -2 Tbs. of local honey and mix well. Store in a dark glass container in the refrigerator. Shake well before use – 1 tablespoon as needed for cough.

Precautions

Mullein contains coumarins, blood thinning substances, so should be used with care in those with bleeding problems or who are currently taking blood thinners. It is considered safe, but herbs should always be used with caution in pregnant women, or those wishing to conceive.

Mullein has soft, blanket-like leaves and tall shoots with bright yellow flowers.

28

PURPLE CORNFLOWER – ECHINACEA PURPUREA

Adding to the storehouse of medicinal plants found here in the Ozarks is the Eastern Purple Cornflower, also known as the widely popular Echinacea. The Plains Indians used the plant as a pain killer, cold remedy, and snakebite treatment. Today, Echinacea is extremely popular as an herbal remedy. Although the root is widely gathered for the herbal medicine market, the aerial parts (those above the ground) also contain active ingredients. Chemicals in purple cornflower enable body cells to be up to 80% resistant against a variety of viruses, including influenza. There is also some evidence that it stimulates the immune system. A member of the daisy family, it has slightly drooping daisy-like purple petals, and blooms from May to October across Missouri, with the exception of the Bootheel and the northwest part of the state.

Purple cornflower is also safe and useful in animals. Traditionally the plant was added to feed for horses or cows that were eating poorly. New studies have shown that it improves the immune system in dogs.

Harvesting

The above ground parts of the plant are most potent when the plant is flowering, and the root is best gathered in the fall.

Common Cold

Hundreds of products used to treat colds include the ingredient

Echinacea. The studies are mixed on the effectiveness, with the ability of the herb to prevent the common cold in doubt, but there does seem to be scientific evidence that Echinacea will shorten the duration of illness.

Recurrent Respiratory Infections

Despite the mixed reviews on the effectiveness of Echinacea in the common cold, in March of this year, a huge meta-analysis, including 6 clinical studies with a total of 2458 participants was published that showed the use of purple cornflower extract was "associated with reduced risk of recurrent respiratory infections." Increased doses during acute episodes further enhanced the beneficial effect, and in individuals with higher susceptibility, stress or a state of immunological weakness, Echinacea cut in half the risk of recurrent respiratory infections. Complications including pneumonia, ear infection, and tonsillitis were also less frequent with Echinacea treatment.

Anxiety and Pain

The effect of extract from the purple cornflower root on anxiety and pain may be explained by its action on cannabinoid receptors in the body, which we all have. Cannabinoids are the beneficial compounds also found in marijuana, one of which is the controversial THC, which is NOT found in purple cornflower. There are several other types of cannabinoids in purple cornflower that have been shown to have positive effects on both anxiety and pain, and even improving appetite. Echinacea has been used successfully to treat the pain of arthritis.

Treatment of Warts

Warts on the skin are known to be recurrent and often resistant to therapy. There are dozens of treatments for warts, including cauterization and laser removal that can cause scarring, and patient-applied treatments like mayapple root extract that is effective, but has the risk of a reaction at the application site due to its toxicity. Medical researchers have been looking for an effective wart treatment that would not cause scarring and prevent reoccurrence of the wart. Extract from the purple cornflower has been studied due its influence on immune function. In a 2011 study from Italy, patients were given an oral supplement containing two forms of Echinacea with other additive that resulted in a 9% decrease in the development of new warts.

Numbing properties

Most of the studies of purple cornflower have been done on the root, but the petals contain many of the same compounds. Pinch off a couple of petals and chew on them, and you will be surprised at the numbing properties. In the early 20th century, physicians prescribed Echinacea routinely for toothache, and the numbing properties are due to alkamides contained in the plant.

Precautions

As purple cornflower contains so many different chemicals, several side effects have been reported, including abdominal pain, angioedema (dangerous swelling of the face, throat and tongue), shortness of breath, nausea, itchiness, and rash. There is limited evidence that purple cornflower extract at highly concentrated doses impairs sperm motility, an effect that might impair conception.

Purple Coneflower has slightly droopy purple daisy petals.

29

BLACK RASPBERRY

Not 2 weeks after writing about crypto gardens, I discovered a patch of wild black raspberries (*Rubus Occidentalis*) 150 feet from my house! I'm not the only one; several readers now have patches of their own.

In addition to being delicious, and exceeding easy to turn into jam, black raspberries have many medicinal properties, and are much more potent than their store-bought cousins.

Cervical Cancer

As the second leading cause of cancer in women, methods to prevent and treat cervical cancer are a top priority. Black raspberries have shown a marked ability to slow cancer cell growth and tumor formation in the cervix. In 2011, researchers studied the effect of black raspberry extract on 3 different cervical cancer cell lines, and found a decrease in growth of cervical cancer cells by up to 67%, dependent on dose and length of therapy. Even after therapy was stopped, inhibition of cancer cell growth remained halted in laboratory studies.

Ulcerative Colitis and Colon Cancer

Ulcerative colitis is an inflammatory disease of the colon that dramatically increases the chance of colon cancer. A 2011 study published in *Carcinogenesis* looked at a dietary intervention with freeze-dried black raspberries and found that treatment for just 7 days suppressed inflammation in the colon.

In another study published just last month, the seeds of the black raspberry were examined and found to stop the growth of human colon cancer cell. Black raspberry seeds are abundant in a class of tannins that are bioavailable to the colon and the prostate.

Black Raspberry Suppositories?

Familial adenomatous polyposis is a hereditary disease that has early onset of polyps in the colon. Patients with this disease usually have their colon removed to prevent colon cancer, and have to return for repeat surgeries to remove polyps in the colon. A phase 1b study published last year looked at the effect of Black Raspberry in suppository form to regress rectal polyps. While no benefit was seen for this disease with oral intake, the suppository form of black raspberry significant reduced rectal polyps.

Esophageal Cancer

In a 2014 study funded by the American Association for Cancer Research, black raspberries were found to significantly reduce esophageal tumors, and also decrease inflammation in the esophagus.

Effect on Triglycerides

A 2011 study published in the Journal of Medicinal Food looked at the effect of Black Raspberry seed oil on cholesterol and triglyceride levels. Raspberry seed oil "dramatically" reduced triglyceride levels, likely due to enrichment in α-linoleic acid, leading researchers to conclude that black raspberry seed oil provides a promising alternative to fish oil supplementation in management of hypertriglyceridemia."

Oral Cancer

Oral squamous cell is cancer that occurs in the mouth, and is one of the hardest to treat cancers. Before there is actual squamous cell cancer present, pre-cancerous cells can form in affected persons; in fact 30% of these lesions do progress. Even when lesions are removed surgically, they tend to reoccur. A variety of preparations have been tried to prevent progression of these pre-cancerous cells to actual cancer, and to prevent the recurrence of lesions after they are removed. In a study involving 3 major universities and 40 adult subjects, a new preparation of a bio adhesive gel containing 10% freshly harvested black raspberries applied to oral lesions 4 times a day for 6 weeks was shown to result in significant reduction in size and progression of oral lesions, with no toxic side effects.

Skin Cancer

Sunlight in the UVB spectrum causes changes in the epidermis of the skin that can lead to cancer. In a 2009 study, a topical cream containing black raspberry extract significantly reduced edema, oxidative DNA damage, and neutrophil activation in the skin that can lead to the development of cancer, leading researchers to conclude that there is "compelling evidence to explore the clinical efficacy of black raspberry extract in the prevention of human skin cancers."

Black Raspberry Jam

While many jam recipes have directions for removing the seeds, the benefits of black raspberry seeds are clear, so be sure to keep the seeds in your finished product!

Take 2 cups of fresh black raspberries that have been washed. In a stock pot, mash them with a potato masher to release the juice. Add 6 cups of sugar, and stir well. Heat to boiling, stirring constantly, then add 1 package of liquid pectin. Bring back to boil and stir for one minute. (If you add ¼ tbs. of butter, your jam will not foam.) Ladle hot jam into sanitized jars, and water bath can for 10 minutes, or for a small batch, you can just refrigerate.

30

NOT SO NICE NATIVES

Over the past two years, we've examined hundreds of beneficial native plants, and other natural materials like eggshells that can greatly enhance our lives. There are some not so nice non-natives out there, but there are ways to manage them. Today we are going to talk about are Japanese Honeysuckle, Bush Honeysuckle, American nightshade, and the recurrent problem of Japanese Beetles.

Non-Native Honeysuckles

On the top 10 kill list of several botanists I know is the Japanese honeysuckle. As the name indicates, Japanese Honeysuckle is native to Japan. It was introduced to the US in 1806 for landscaping, but has since escaped cultivation, and is popping up all over in the Eastern US thanks to birds that spread the seeds. The plant can be a nightmare, because it climbs over native vegetation and smothers it. The best way to get rid of the plant is to dig it up and burn it. You don't want to cut it, because it will just grow back stronger. Bush Honeysuckle, from another family isn't much better, and should be kept out of your yard. Bush Honeysuckle is another plant from Asia that competes with native plants and steals the pollinators. It also produces juicy red berries that are horrible to taste and mildly poisonous in children (diarrhea and vomiting) and the plant emits a chemical into the soil that hinders the growth of native plants.

American Nightshade

Another plant that looks tempting to eat is American Nightshade,

Solanum_americanum that produces deceptively tasty-looking little green tomatoes. Unfortunately, this is a very common plant that is very toxic. The green fruit, that eventually turns black, is especially poisonous, and eating them raw has caused death in children and pets. Even eating the ripe berries can be toxic if they are eaten raw. There are almost 2 dozen toxic substances in this plant, including atropine, scopolomine and hyoscyamine. Some countries find the plant edible; the ripe fruit is cooked and made into jams or preserves, and the greens are cooked to remove the toxins, but it is still linked with a high rate of cancer of the esophagus. With so many safe edible herbs to choose from, I'd leave this one alone.

Japanese Beetles

Every year, around the beginning of July, Japanese Beetles invade our gardens. This year the beetles were 3 weeks early, with larger than expected numbers. They love young fruit trees, and can completely devour the leaves, leaving only a skeleton. They can devastate a corn crop, feeding on corn silk, disrupting pollination and leaving ears with just a couple of kernels. Their numbers are on the rise, but with some work, they can be kept in check. The beetles can travel up to 5 miles, but usually stay in a 1- 2 mile area, and are usually gone by early August. While there are many pesticides to help curb the beetle invasion, I prefer natural methods. You can use pheromone traps, but they can actually attract more beetles, so I don't recommend them. Food grade diatomaceous earth will destroy the exoskeleton of the beetle, and can be sprinkled at the base of affected plants where the female beetles have laid their eggs. My favorite method is to hand pick the beetles off my plants. I go through twice a day, and easily knock them off affected plants into a coffee can half full of water. I then set the coffee can in front of the chickens. I've been able to keep them manageable that way with no pesticide, and happy chickens. Over the past 3 years, I have definitely seen a decrease in the beetle population on my place, even though their numbers are rising elsewhere. I have a friend who actually freezes the beetles to give to her chickens in the winter, and another otherwise normal friend who is an entomophagist (insect eater) who collects the beetles and kills them by freezing. He then rinses them, and boils for 5 minutes, marinates in a tangy sauce, and dehydrates to crispy crunch.

It is always wise to teach small children toxic plants to avoid. Unfortunately, pets and livestock can also consume these plants and cause illness, so it is wise to destroy these plants in the yard or pasture to avert later problems.

Bush Honeysuckle has juicy red berries that taste horrible and are mildly poisonous.

American Nightshade has attractive fruit that looks like a little green tomato, but contains 2 dozen toxic substances.

31

WILD LEEKS (ALLIUM TRICOCCUM)

A member of the garlic and onion family, wild leeks are plentiful in the Ozarks, growing in forested areas and on wooded bluffs. A perennial, leeks return year after year and are recognized by wide green leaves with purple tints on the lower stems and an onion like stalk and bulb. During the summer months a single stalk appears with a 2 inch diameter cluster of tiny white flowers that smell like onions. The entire plant is edible, but some people harvest only the leaves, a good idea to prevent eradication of the plant. Wild leeks are a delicacy in Canada, causing them to be placed on the protected plant list, but poachers still illegally gather and sell the plant. Leeks grow in close groups rather than being scattered, added to the ease of harvest. They are available year round, but they are best in the fall through early spring, so now is the time to start scouting for plants!

Nutritional Value

Wild leeks taste like a combination of onion and garlic with a more subtle and sweeter flavor, and are a great addition to many recipes. 1 cup of cooked leeks has only 32 calories, a nutrient dense food packed with Vitamins K, B6, C, A, E and folate, in addition to a rich blend of minerals including calcium, manganese, iron and magnesium. Leeks also contain important Omega-3 fatty acids, and flavonoids that protect blood vessels from damage.

Medicinal Use

The majority of studies on leeks deal with how to prevent their eradication by over harvesting. In the Smoky Mountain National Park in Tennessee and North Carolina, areas where they are considered a delicacy and reason for celebration, leek harvesting has been banned since 2002. Efforts are being made to restore the plant population with literally hundreds of studies looking at how to best accomplish this goal.

Cancer Prevention

In 2000, a signature study on the role of leeks grown in selenium-rich soil in preventing cancer was published. Levels as high as 784 mg of selenium/kg were obtained in the leek bulbs when grown by this method. There was an approximately 43% reduction in chemically induced mammary tumors in laboratory animals fed a diet with Selenium enriched leeks. Selenium in leeks was found to be 15-28% more biologically available than that obtained from supplements. Researchers concluded that selenium enriched leeks "appear to have potential for the reduction of cancer in humans."

Multiple studies of all plants in the allium family, including leeks, garlic and onions have shown a relationship between intake of these vegetables and decreased risk of cancer, particularly cancers of the gastrointestinal tract, and certain types of breast cancer. The beneficial effect is thought to be due to its sulfur-containing compounds, especially allicin. Allicin is not only anti-bacterial, anti-viral and anti-fungal, but research has revealed that allicin produces sulfenic acid, a compound that neutralizes free-radicals that can result in cancer. In addition to cancer prevention, sulfur has been found particularly helpful in ulcerative colitis and arthritis, and improving resistance to illness.

Sulfur

Leeks are one in only a handful of vegetables that are considered high in sulfur, i.e. containing at least 80 mcg. Sulfur is an essential element for life and is found in two amino acids, the building blocks for proteins. Sulfur is vital for proper health, but most of us fail to get enough of it in our diet. Before the change to petro-chemical fertilizers, farmers fertilized their crops with animal manure, naturally high in sulfur. Modern farming methods have pretty much eliminated sulfur from the soil, and also from the vegetables grown there. MSM, An organic form of sulfur, is quite popular and available as a supplement, but including 1 cup of leeks, onions, or garlic in your daily diet will ensure an adequate level in your body.

Precautions

Leeks are among a small number of foods that contain measurable amounts of oxalates, naturally occurring substances found in some plants. In persons prone to kidney stones, especially those that are oxalate based, leeks should probably be eaten sparingly, and consumed with adequate water to prevent crystallization. .

Preparation

Leeks can be chopped and then frozen for future use. The green leaves are usually chopped in and added along with the bulbs.

Bacon Leek Potato Soup

4 to 6 slices bacon
4 cups chopped leeks (green parts and bulbs)
4 cups diced potatoes
3 tablespoons flour
4 cups chicken broth
1 cup heavy cream

In a large skillet or Dutch oven, fry bacon until crispy; set bacon aside. Add leeks and potatoes to the skillet; fry on medium-low heat until leeks are tender. Sprinkle with flour; stir until flour is absorbed. Stir in chicken broth; simmer until potatoes are tender. Stir in the cream and heat thoroughly. Add salt and pepper to taste.

32

SPIDER BITES

"I got bit by a spider, and it hurts like crazy!" In truth, it is much more likely you have contracted a Staph infection of the methicillin-resistant type – MRSA. Incredibly misdiagnosed, MRSA infections are becoming an epidemic. Due to the fact they start as a very painful red bump, with no known injury, folks assume they are caused by a spider. In general, the only time you can verify a spider bite is if you actually *see* the spider.

Only 2 spiders warrant medical concern – the black widow and brown recluse. Black widows have distinctive red spots on their bodies. Only the female spider will bite, and then only if provoked by having her territory invaded. The bite is not known to be deadly, but requires medical attention. The spider's venom contains a neurotoxin that works systemically, not locally, producing pain and spasm in large muscle groups within 30 minutes to 3 hours. Symptoms include muscle cramps, high blood pressure, stomach cramps, headache and nausea. There can be swelling in the hands and feet, but not at the actual area of the bite. Symptoms can last for up to a week, and are usually treated with muscle relaxants and pain medication.

The brown recluse spider is a little more aggressive. It is also called the violin spider because of a violin shaped patch on its back. They are more active than the black widow, making an encounter much more likely as they seem to love to hide in clothes, towels and bedding. A brown recluse bite is almost never fatal, but in the frail elderly, diabetics and persons with impaired immune systems, there can be disfiguring tissue loss in the area of the bite. I recently experienced a brown recluse bite, and my symptoms were typical. While asleep, I was awakened by itching on the back of my left hand. I scratched at my hand and fell back asleep.

In the morning, the back of my hand was swollen and a little tender. I found the dead spider lying in the bed. Over the course of the next few hours, my hand swelled some more, and felt vaguely itchy. I washed the area thoroughly, and the wound never ulcerated. The swelling resolved in a couple of days. In one study, the average healing time from a brown recluse spider bite was 17 days, and only 21% had any permanent scarring. The good thing about brown recluses that may be hiding out in your home is the fact they eat other bugs.

It is important to note that a bite from either of the "problem spiders" doesn't produce the characteristic painful, red, swollen bump of a MRSA infection. Previously contracted mostly in the hospital, MRSA can now be community acquired. I've personally seen several cases in young men who work out in the gym, as the bacteria likes to hang out on the gym mats and equipment. Frequent areas for eruption of a MRSA infection include the axillae (armpits), buttocks, and thighs. If left untreated, a MRSA infection can develop into a huge, exquisitely painful boil. Lancing the boil and letting it drain brings immediate pain relief, but often must be repeated several days in a row. Simply applying warm, moist soaks to the area will hasten the drainage process. Applying ice, while helpful in relieving the pain, can lead to tissue death due to decrease in blood flow to the area. While the boil can be resolved with home treatment, and eventually heal, medical treatment is recommended if the condition reoccurs as people can become colonized with MRSA, and have flare ups of the condition. The most commonly prescribed antibiotic for community acquired MRSA is Bactrim DS 1-2 tablets every 12 hours. Of course, family members, especially children, should be protected from contracting the bacteria through careful disinfection, and keeping lesions covered with an occlusive dressing.

If unsure about any of these conditions, contact your health care provider. If you think you have been bitten by a spider, attempt to locate it and take it with you to the doctor's office for identification.

33

BLOODROOT (SANGUINARIA CANADENSIS)

Bloodroot is a beautiful plant in the poppy family without a stem, but rather a flower stalk with a single white flower that blooms between March and April. The distinctive flower has 8-16 white petals that last only 1-2 days. This beneficial plant improves the soil, provides food for wildlife, and supplies pollen during the brief time flowers are present. Blood root extract has been used to treat skin growths since the mid-1800's, and its ability to kill cancer cells has been increasingly reported in a range of studies investigating new cancer therapies. Like many things that are beautiful, bloodroot can have a dangerous side if used improperly.

Although the roots contain the highest concentration of the active ingredient sanguinarine, every part of the plant can be harvested and made into extracts, salves, and even powders. It is a very powerful topical agent when used to treat skin tags and moles.

Black Salve

One of the main applications of bloodroot is the preparation of black salve, used for skin cancers, skin tags, warts, eczema and removal of moles. When bloodroot is added to any salve, it makes it corrosive. In 2013, the Journal of Pathology published a series of 16 cases involving 11 patients who used blood root salve for skin lesions. While the salve was effective in removing lesions, residual skin cancers were present in 2 of the 16 cases, including a basal cell carcinoma and a melanocytic mole. Caution should be taken when applying black salve, as it can mask a malignant tumor due to excessive scarring, and at the very least cause permanent scars on the skin.

Melanoma and other cancers

Blood root extract is one of a handful of plants with very strong tumoricidal effects on cancer. The medicinal properties of bloodroot come from sanguinarine. A 2013 European study showed "a remarkably rapid killing activity against human melanoma cells."

A 2012 study documented the effect of blood root extract against HT-29 human colon cancer cells. Treatment with the extract induced a dose dependent increase in cancer cell death, and also triggered activation of the body's own defenses in eradicating cancer cells. Researchers concluded that blood root extract may have a potential therapeutic use in the treatment of human colon cancer.

In the past 2 years, there have been several reports on the effectiveness of blood root extract in the treatment of prostate cancer. It has been found to suppress prostate cancer growth, migration, and invasion into surrounding tissues.

Blood root is also showing promise in treating human gastric adenocarcinoma, especially with drug-resistant cancers that are not responding to other medications.

Veterinary Medicine

Blood root extract has been successfully used in treating sarcoids in horses, the most common equine skin tumor. Sarcoids don't spread, but their size and location can be painful for the horse, and affect the ability to saddle and bridle the animal. In a study with 49 horses with 125 sarcoids, 66 lesions responded to externally applied salve, and only 6 of those reoccurred. Adverse effects were reported in 16 horses and consisted mainly of hair loss and soreness.

Because of its anti-tumor effects, blood root extract has also been used as an intra-tumor injection. This can have disastrous effects (see the Tragedy of Thomas Crawford below). Blood root extract is still used in limited fashion to treat skin tumors in dogs. While sometimes successful, the Journal of the American Veterinary Association details the effects of intra tumor injections on 2 dogs. One of the dogs had severe tissue death and inflammation following the injection, and the other dog had similar adverse effects, but to a lesser extent. You can purchase blood root paste online for veterinary use, and user reports are very positive, especially when used on sarcoids in horses.

Precautions

Blood root works by creating a scab, also called eschar, that can leave a permanent scar. It can also mask malignant cancers. A published case study describes this well. A 53 year old man developed a small lump on his chest that turned black. He looked on the internet, and found bloodroot salve as a treatment for skin lesions. He applied the salve for 10 days, which worked initially, but then the lesion began growing again. Despite being in intense pain, he resumed the blood root treatments, and in 6 weeks the lesion doubled in size and became ulcerated and draining. When he was finally seen by a physician, he was found to have malignant melanoma.

The Tragedy of Thomas Crawford

Thomas Crawford was a famous sculptor in the middle 1880's, well known for sculpting the Statue of Freedom that sits atop the Capitol dome in Washington, DC. Sadly, he developed double vision, and was incorrectly diagnosed with a cancerous tumor in the orbit of his eye, for which he underwent an experimental injection containing blood root extract that completely destroyed his eye and orbital contents. (He actually had a brain tumor). He died 5 months later.

Application

Blood root extract seems to work best for skin tags, moles and warts, and possibly some skin cancers. The user should leave the paste only 12 hours, then wash off thoroughly, applying vitamin E to the area and waiting 24 hours before reapplication. In the case of skin cancer, medical supervision should be relied upon to verify destruction of all of the cancerous cells.

34

PARTRIDGE PEA

One of the things I love to do is room the land around my house, looking for native plants I haven't yet discovered. The funny thing about plant identification is the way it works like a magic-eye picture: once you spot a plant that was previously overlooked, you begin to see it everywhere.

One of the most overlooked, but a tremendously important native plant in our region is the Partridge Pea. As the name implies, it is a member of the legume family. High in protein (nearly 30 percent) and phosphorus, it is a major food source for bobwhite and other quail species, turkeys, pheasants and mallards. Deer like it too, and it can be a critical winter food source. The plant is attractive to the common sulfur butterfly that lays its eggs on the leaves. It is also an important honey plant, with nectar found in glands at the base of the leaves. The plant fixes nitrogen in the soil where it grows, improving soil fertility and preventing erosion, so it is often added to seed mixes when attempting to establish or refresh a mixed prairie. It is also a beautiful ornament plant with bright yellow flowers that produces pods with multiple black seeds.

Medicinal Uses

Partridge Pea (chamaecrista-fasciculata) has a long history of medicinal use in several Native American tribes, who valued the leaves and roots as a tonic for endurance. It had early usage in sports medicine, and was used by tribal runners and before long hunts. Sadly, there are reports of the plant being used along the Trail of Tears where the root was chewed to prevent fainting from exhaustion. The leaves can also be used to make a tea.

Skin Problems

A poultice made from bruised and moistened leaves of the plant can be used to treat skin problems, such as burns, boils, ringworm and other minor infections. The plant contains chrysophanic acid-9-anthrone which is an important fungicide. There are reports in the literature that eating the seeds can cure skin itch and psoriasis, but no scientific evidence exists to date.

Demulcent

Several Native American tribes and the early Shakers made a cough syrup from Partridge Pea pods. Soaking the pods in cold water releases the mucilage and the resulting solution can be added to honey to treat sore throat. The solution was also used for nausea.

Infections

Partridge Pea has a long history in treating infections. There is evidence an extract from the seeds inhibits the growth of several strains of bacteria, including diphtheria, shigella, salmonella, bacillus, E.coli, and fungal infections candida and aspergillus.

Liver Protection

Whole plant extract of Partridge Pea has been shown to cause decrease in the levels of serum markers SGOT, SGPT, bilirubin and alkaline phosphatase that occur with liver damage. There is a significant dose dependent protection against Tylenol induced liver injury. (Note: Tylenol usage should never exceed 2000 mg per day due to its impact on the liver.)

Lipid Lowering

Alcohol and water extracts of Partridge Pea seeds have been found to decrease serum levels of total cholesterol by up to 71%, LDL (bad) cholesterol up to 76%, and increase the serum HDL (good) cholesterol level by up to 19%. Triglyceride levels were decreased by up to 35%.

Other Uses

Native Americans hastened the ripening of Persimmons by placing them in a pit and covering them with Partridge Pea plants.

Precautions

Partridge Pea should be used in only small amounts as it is both a purgative in high doses. Pregnant and nursing women should avoid the plant. Due to these effects, Partridge pea can't be considered a a source of food in humans, despite the high protein content. Deer and other wildlife can eat the plant freely, but there are reports of livestock poisoning, so cattle and horses should be prevented from grazing the plant in large amounts.

Partridge Pea is easy to identify by its bright yellow flowers and fern-like leaves.

Look carefully to find the long, slender pea pods that contain multiple black seeds.

35

POTATO BEAN

Flowering now through September is the native Potato Bean, (*Apios Americana Medikus*). Also known as American Ground Nut or Indian Potato, the rhizome of the Potato Bean was prized by early Americans and Indian tribes due to its nutrition and versatility — it can be fried, boiled or roasted, just like a potato, but has over double the protein, and while usually bean-sized, can grow to the size of an egg. We are pretty lucky in the Ozarks, because this plant is becoming rare in many other states, and is almost extinct in Iowa, Colorado and North Carolina. In Colorado, there are significant efforts to reestablish the plant in that state. It loves to grow in woodlands, and along lakes and streams.

The Potato Bean has been an extremely valuable plant to in North America for thousands of years. The seeds and tuberous roots have been important food sources among many Native American tribes and it is widely credited as having saved the pilgrims at Plymouth Rock from starvation in the tough winter of 1623. The Pilgrims were taught to find and prepare American groundnut by the Wampanoag people. Later, explorers Lewis and Clark wrote about the potato bean in their journals that it "is the true pomme de terre of the French and wild potato of the Sioux Indians, and is extensively used as an article of diet. They boil with meat or pound and make agreeable bread. It may be used in its green or undried state without danger provided it be well roasted or boiled."

About Rhizomes

A rhizome is like a root that grows horizontally to the ground, and if they are separated, or even branch out, each piece can produce a new plant. Rhizomes are super-nutritious, because it is where the plant stores starches, protein and other nutrients to form new shoots or to rejuvenate after the winter freeze. Common examples of rhizomes are ginger, arrowroot and asparagus. The Potato Bean is one of the few species that can fix atmospheric nitrogen in its root nodules and produce an edible tuber. In fact, the potato beans, or tubers, contain 13 − 17 percent protein, nearly 3 times that of potatoes. As we will see, the potato bean also contains anti-cancer and other beneficial compounds.

High Blood Pressure

In a 2007 study published in Nutrition Research, hypertensive lab animals fed powdered potato bean as 5% of their diet for 3 weeks had a 10% decrease in blood pressure and also a reduction in cholesterol and triglycerides. The researchers concluded that "It is suggested that Apios Americana is a healthy food material for prevention of hypertension and hyperlipidemia."

Cancer

Potato Bean tubers also have been shown to have anti-cancer properties against breast, colon and prostate cancer.

Prostate

In 2013, new isoflavones were isolated from the plant, and found to have anti-androgen properties that block the spread of prostate cancer. Androgens stimulate the growth of prostate cancer cells, and lowering their levels often makes prostate cancer cells shrink, or grow more slowly.

Breast

The isoflavones found in potato bean aren't only beneficial in treating prostate cancer; they are also showing some benefit in preventing the growth of breast cancer cells, without harming surrounding tissue. In another 2013 study, 100 µg/mL groundnut extract prevented the depletion of glutathione. Glutathione, often called "the body's most powerful protector against many forms of cancer," restores antioxidant defenses, repairs DNS, and helps to detoxify carcinogens in the body.

Leukemia

Extract of potato bean can also help decrease the proliferation of leukemia cells through a protein called AATI (Apios Americana Trypsin Inhibitor). AATI has 59 amino acids (the building blocks of protein) and a high heat stability that keeps it in active form despite boiling or cooking. Blocking trypsin is important, because Cancer-associated trypsin has been identified in cancers such as ovarian carcinoma, pancreatic cancer, hepatocellular and cholangiocarcinomas, lung neoplasms, colorectal cancers, fibrosarcoma, leukemia, gastric cancer, and oral cancer.

Now is the time to identify the flowering Potato Bean for later harvest. Look in moist areas and around creeks and ponds. The plant grows in clusters, and the purplish maroon flower clusters are easy to spot, but like other potato plants, they will die off before the root is ready to be harvested.

Look for the Potato Bean when it flowers between June and September. Its flowers are deep purplish maroon internally with deep brownish purple wings. It likes to twine around other plants and grasses.

36

WILD LICORICE

Wild Licorice is found in 26 states, Missouri included, where it is identified as a native species. The role of wild licorice in Native American medicine is manifold. It has been used as to treat fever, and as a treatment for earache and sore throats. The sweet roots are edible, and can be eaten for nourishment. Birds and wildlife, including deer, love this member of the pea family, as do we humans when we are able to find it. A common companion plant is poison ivy, so beware.

There are at least 20 species of licorice, with Europe and China having their own varieties. The Chinese variety is what is found most abundantly on the market. The only species native to the United States is *Glycyrrhiza lepidota*.

When you chew raw licorice root, it has an initial strong, bitter taste that becomes sweet. The taste we associate with licorice is actually anise, to which licorice has been added as a sweetener. The medicinal properties are concentrated in the root, which contains up to 6% glycyrrhizin, a glycoside that is 50 to 200 times sweeter than sugar. Glycyrrhizin stimulates the release of adrenal cortex hormones, which increases metabolism and theoretically can result in higher blood pressure, water retention and loss of potassium.

Liver Protection

Protective effects provided by licorice root are well documented. Glycyrrhizin isolated from the licorice root is a prescription drug used in Japan to treat liver and allergic disease. For over 60 years, it has been available in injectable and tablet form and is used to treat viral Hepatitis B and Hepatitis C in at least 7 Asian countries.

Peptic Ulcers

One of the most common uses of licorice root is use as an antacid. Licorice has been used to treat ulcers in Europe for over 75 years due to its protective effects on the stomach lining. It has been specifically found to decrease stomach ulcers caused by aspirin. An infusion made from the root is also an effect treatment for diarrhea.

Chronic Fatigue

There are anecdotal reports in the medical literature of licorice root being used to treat chronic fatigue syndrome. In a case published in a 1995 issue of the New Zealand Medical Journal, a person suffering with chronic fatigue started taking daily doses of licorice root extract in milk. In less than a week he had improvement in both physical and mental stamina, thought to be due to the effect of licorice on the hormones of the adrenal cortex.

Cough, Cold and Sore Throat

Wild Licorice is "one stop shopping" to treat all of the above. As an anti-inflammatory and anti-spasmodic, it is helpful for dry coughs with wheezing. It acts as an expectorant to loosen and thin mucus, and the mucilage in licorice helps to soothe sore throats. Its antimicrobial properties help to protect against infections. It is even more powerful for chronic cough when combined with mullein. To treat sore throat or cough, simply chew on a root, or make a hot tea (recipe below).

Anti-viral

Licorice root has been found to be effective against several viruses, including influenza A, spurring research into use to the plant against HIV. A study published in 2001 isolated a previously unknown compound from licorice root after a study by the US National Cancer Institute showed moderate activity against the HIV virus.

External Applications

A poultice can be made from the leaves and applied externally to treat sores. Native Americans treated earache by applying a poultice externally over the ear.

Preparation

Wild licorice roots can be eaten raw or cooked. When slow roasted, they resemble a sweet potato. The roots are used as flavoring in many foods. Teething children can safely chew the roots as well. The new shoots of the plant can be eaten raw in the springtime, and added to salads. According to one source, one "dose" of licorice consists of 1 teaspoon of cut and sifted root in a cup of boiling water that is allowed to steep for 5 minutes daily.

Precautions

Since I first studied licorice in nursing school in the 1970's, it has always been associated with the warning it can cause high blood pressure, even hypertensive crisis. I love licorice, and eat it all the time, so I have had the opportunity to do a little study on myself over the years. I have never found that is increased my blood pressure. New research is showing protective effects of licorice on the heart via its component Glycyrrhetinic Acid that has been shown to improve palpitations and arrhythmias by regulating potassium channels in the heart. Cases of high blood pressure due to licorice in the literature are always associated with licorice abuse with very high consumption! Licorice root can interact with certain heart medications such as digitalis, so should be taken with care by these persons.

Identification

Wild licorice is found on low ground and along streams. It grows about 1- 4 feet tall, has alternating green leaves and yellowish-white flowers in clusters that bloom from May through August. It produces small brown seed pods, helpful in collecting seeds! The plant grows from deep, extensive woody rhizomes, so is found in clusters and can regrow after an area is burned off.

Wild licorice is native to Missouri, but is becoming scarce. Photo credit Barry Breckling (Breckling@garlic.com)

37

STALKING THE WILD CARROT

It's late in the season, and the wild carrots are about 2 feet tall with browning tops that look like bird nests. It's the perfect time to harvest the seeds!

Wild carrot, *Daucus carota*, is commonly known as Queen Anne's Lace. Originating in Europe, it came to the United States in flour sacks with the early settlers. As the legend goes, Queen Anne was tatting white lace, representing the lacy white flowers of the wild carrot, when she pricked her finger and lost a drop of blood that became the single dark red floret in the middle of the umbrella-shaped flower cluster.

Wild carrot flowers between June and September, and the white flowers are beautiful, but before they appear, the entire plant is much more tender and edible. As the predecessor to the selectively bred domesticated carrot, the green shoots of the wild carrot are identical, and are often found in dry fields. Unlike the modern version, the taproot is smaller and somewhat woody textured, but contains most of the same nutrients and medicinal properties. The early greens are excellent in stir fry and salads, but the main nutrients are found in the root, best harvested before flowers appear. First year plants of this biennial are tastiest and most nutritious.

Nutrition

Wild carrot provides 3 forms of carotenes, but is very low in beta-carotene that provides the orange color to the domestic version. Carotenes are important, because they are metabolized into Vitamin A, an important vitamin for night vision and healthy eyes. In fact, 1 serving of carrots provides over 100% of the daily requirement. Carrots also provide significant amounts of B vitamins, vitamin K, and essential minerals. Unfortunately, "store bought" carrots also contain fluoride as they have high uptake from fluoridated irrigating water and fluoride based pesticides.

Medicinal Properties

There are dozens of medicinal uses of wild carrot: treatment of urinary tract problems, including kidney stones; treatment of gout, diarrhea, heart disease, cancer, worm infestations, and even as an aphrodisiac!

Cancer

A 2014 study published in Chemotherapy found potent anti-cancer activity of wild carrot on lung, skin, breast and glioblastoma (brain) cancer cells. Upon treatment, a pronounced decrease in cancer cell motility was observed in all 4 cell lines. The treatment also led to a decrease in cancer cell invasion, making it a potential candidate for cancer therapy specifically targeting metastasis.

A 2015 study published in the Journal of Cancer Prevention showed that wild carrot oil extract is selectively cytotoxic to human acute myeloid leukemia cells

Kidney Stones

Wild Carrot is one of the top ten natural treatments for kidney stones. In addition to being a natural diuretic which helps flush the kidneys, there is some evidence a tea made from wild carrot leaves and seeds helps prevent kidney stone formation and is also reported to help break up existing stones. As the seeds are high in oils, they ease the pain of cystitis and the passage of kidney stones.

Gout

Wild carrot diminishes uric acid in the blood that can lead to crystal formation, causing gout. A 2013 study with wild carrot root extract showed a significant improvement in kidney function, and a decrease of up to 3.5 mg/dl in uric acid levels. A recent article from Purdue University states the carrot root is "indicated in the diet of gout-prone people."

Hormonal Effects

Wild carrot belongs to a group of plants in the *Umbelliferae* family that have been shown to increase libido in both men and women. Wild Carrot leaves contain significant amounts of porphyrins, which stimulate the pituitary gland and lead to the release of increased levels of sex hormones.

The seeds of the wild carrot have been shown to block Progesterone causing a decrease in fertility, likely due to disruption in implantation of the fertilized egg in the uterus. The anti-fertility effects are temporary and reversible, but seeds of the wild carrot should obviously be avoided if you are contemplating or already pregnant. Wild carrot seeds have also been used for birth control in small animals, such as cats.

Precautions

Wild carrot has a deadly look-alike – hemlock. Hemlock, *C. maculate,* is also common in Missouri. Hemlock is toxic, and if you handle it you should wash your hands thoroughly. If eaten by mistake, you should seek medical treatment.

The legend of Queen Anne's lace helps to distinguish wild carrot from hemlock. Although the white flowers look very similar, if the small crimson colored flower is present in the center of the bloom, it is surely wild carrot. Unfortunately, that small crimson flower isn't always present. The greenery of the hemlock plant is also different, but similar to that of the carrot. The stem of poison hemlock is smooth, and has purple or black spots, while wild carrot has a hairy, completely green stem. As wild carrot matures, the flowers fold up into a bird-nest like configuration, but hemlock flowers just turn brown. A final test is the smell of the stem or the root. If it smells like carrot, it is a carrot! If it doesn't, wash your hands right away, as it may be hemlock.

The Wild Carrot is going dormant for the season, perfect time to harvest seeds from its bird nest -like umbrel.

38

NUT SEDGES – THE GOOD, THE BAD AND THE UGLY

Sedges are plants that resemble grasses or rushes. Sedges differ in the fact that the stems are a perfect triangle. There is a little rhyme to help identify the plant: Sedges have edges. More tough and fibrous than a grass, the leaves are arranged in spirals of 3 vertical rows, while grasses have alternate leaves. Sedge flowers are unique and spiky. Sometimes called "one of the 5 worst weeds in the world," sedges have a very bad reputation. They can be invasive and are hard to eradicate, mostly because of what may be their best feature, their underground tubers, or root nutlets.

In Missouri, there are two type of nut sedges of interest in food and medicine. One is Cyperus esculentus, the yellow nutsedge, and the other is purple nutsedge, *Cyperus rotundus. We are all familiar with Chinese water chestnuts , the root nutlet found on a foreign sedge variety.*

Yellow Nutsedge

The yellow nutsedge, also called Chufa, has a yellow top with spiky flowers that appear between August and November. The roots can get the size of hazel nuts, and are fully edible either raw or cooked at all stages of development. A staple plant in North Africa and Spain, the yellow nutsedge is considered a noxious plant here in the US. It is so prolific that in a single growing season, one plant can produce 1900 new plants with 7000 nutlets. With a taste like almonds, and nutrients similar to olives, the root nutlets have a high content of oleic acid, and are also high in sugars, proteins, vitamins B1, E and C, plus essential minerals, including phosphorus, potatssium, calcium, magnesium and iron. When eaten with other grains, it can combine to make a complete protein. In Spain, a popular drink called Horchata is made from the root nutlets. In Europe, dry roasted tubers have been used as nutritive extenders in chocolate and coffee products.

While all sedge nutlets are edible, those from the yellow nutsedge are the tastiest, and the species name esculentus actually means edible. They have a husk, which can easily be rubbed off if desired. (It provides a good source of fiber, though.) They can be eaten raw, but soaking them in water will make them softer.

Purple nutsedge

Purple nutsedge (C. rotundus) is also edible, but not as tasty. The fact it can also be used as mosquito repellant gives that away. If used for food, it should be dried a few days, then consumed raw or cooked. As the name implies, it has purplish tops. The true value of purple nutsedge does not lie in its use as a source of nutrition, but rather its medicinal properties. Almost all of the pharmaceutical studies concerning sedge plants have been conducted on the purple nutsedge. Compared to the yellow variety, purple nutsedge is smaller, darker and has reddish purple seed heads. In addition, the underground tubers of purple nut sedge form in chains along the roots, while yellow nut sedge produces only one tuber at the end of each runner.

Medicinal properties of Purple Nutsedge

Purple Nutsedge has a long history in Chinese medicine where it is valued for stomach ache, diarrhea, pain associated with menstruation, and even impotence. It has been used as a diuretic and to treat high blood pressure. An antiseptic ointment can be made from the plant to apply to wounds to prevent infection. The plant has also been found to have anti-malarial properties. Literature dating back to the medieval age talks about the anti-inflammatory, fever reducing, antibacterial and anti-diarrheal properties of the plant. It has also been used in the treatment of obesity.

In next week's column we will look at the many medicinal properties of

Purple nutsedge.

The yellow nutsedge has a firm, triangular stem and yellow spiky flowers. Pull it up by the root, and you will find edible nutlets at the base.

39

NUT SEDGES – PART 2

In August, 2013, the Journal of Ethnopharmacology reviewed dozens of published reports on the use of purple nut sedge, *Cyperus rotundus*, in atherosclerosis, aging, cancer, cystitis, epilepsy, excessive hair growth, pain, prostatitis, and other disorders. The authors concluded that "phytochemical and pharmacological activities of C. rotundus have supported its traditional as well as prospective uses as a valuable plant. Furthermore, future study should aim at confirming the clinical activities and safety of this plant before being used for the development of new therapeutic agent in human subjects."

Anti-Ulcer

A 2015 study looked at the effect of an extract from purple nutsedge on stomach ulcers due to aspirin. It already has a long history as a traditional ulcer cure. It was found that oral administration of different doses of root extract at 250 mg/kg and 500 mg/kg doses significantly inhibited aspirin-induced gastric ulceration in a dose-dependent manner up to 53%, comparable with the standard gastric ulcer drug ranitidine (Zantac).

Another study in 2014 assessed the anti-inflammatory, anti-ulcer and neurological activities of a crude extract of purple nutsedge. The plant exhibited significant anti-inflammatory effects. Anti-ulcer effects were seen at a 30mg/kg. In this study, a slight muscle relaxant effect was also seen.

Cancer

A 2015 study investigated the anti-tumor effect of Purple nutsedge on ovarian cancer. Research found an extract of the roots inhibited cell growth in 3 cell lines of ovarian cancer and two types of endometrial cancer cells. They concluded that a chemical isolated from C. rotundus rhizome is an anti-tumor compound that causes apoptosis (cell death) in ovarian cancer cells.

Anti-obesity

A 2007 obesity study examined the biological efficacy of C. rotundus tubers extract on weight control in obese rats. It was demonstrated that administration of 45 or 220 mg/kg/day of extract from purple nutsedge tubers for 60 days induced a significant reduction in weight gain without affecting food consumption or causing side effects. Effects were partially due to increased metabolism. Researchers conclude that an extract of purple nut sedge tubers may prove to be effective as an herbal supplement for controlling body weight .

Lactation Support

In animal studies, oral administration of 300 and 600 mg of purple nutsedge root extract induced about 23% and 40% more milk in experimental group of animals as compared to the control group of animals. Weight gain in offspring was significant higher in the experimental as compared to that of control group. Purple nutsedge was found to stimulate the synthesis of prolactin significantly, and did not cause any signs or symptoms of toxicity which implied that Cyperus rotundus is safe. Used for centuries in humans, horchata, a Spanish drink made from the roots of the nutsedge is very popular in nursing mothers, due to its effect on breast milk production.

Anti-oxidant effect

Several studies this year have investigated the anti-oxidant effects of Purple nut sedge. One study found not only significant anti-oxidant effects (think anti-aging and cancer protective qualities), but also metal chelating effects. We can accumulate unwanted heavy metals in our blood, such as lead, arsenic, and mercury. Chelation agents bind these metals where they can be excreted from the body. Purple nutsedge was also found to have a protective effect on red blood cells, keeping them from breaking down prematurely.

A second study found flavonoids in the leaves of yellow nut sedge had pronounced antioxidant activity. This extract also inhibited the growth of both Gram positive and Gram negative bacteria. No obvious effects on fungi or mold were seen. The researchers concluded "Our studies indicate that flavonoids from C. esculentus (Yellow nutsedge) leaves can be taken as a natural antioxidant and bacteriostatic substance in food and pharmaceutical industry.

Anti-inflammatory

Another 2015 study explains how purple nut sedge may work against inflammation. Purple nutsedge contains a chemical called fulgidic acid in its rhizomes.   Fulgidic acid reduces the production of nitric oxide, prostaglandin E2 (compounds that sensitize nerves to pain), and tumor necrosis factor-α (TNF-α), These effects work in a manner similar to Cox2 inhibitor drugs, commonly known as Celebrex.

Precautions

There are no known published or toxic effects of our native nut sedges. That being said, they are widely regarded as an unwanted invasive plant. Difficult to eradicate by usual methods, there is a product called Sedgehammer exclusively designed to eliminate sedges. Farmers use swine to control the nutsedges. Pigs love to eat the tubers and root out the buried nutlets, eradicating the weed in short order.

Nutlets at the base of the Yellow Nutsedge (shown here) are most edible, while those from the Purple Nutsedge are used most often in medicine.

40

MELATONIN MATTERS

Melatonin, first discovered in 1958, is an often forgotten, but extremely important hormone. Mostly known for its role in helping people get to sleep, it has even more important qualities. As a sleep aid, melatonin is actually *good* for you, unlike addicting prescription medications, or over the counter Benadryl that has been linked to dementia. Ambien is downright scary. There are reports of people sleep-eating and even sleep-driving after taking Ambien, and there is even an FDA warning to this effect.

Melatonin is a natural hormone produced by the pineal gland, mostly at night. Melatonin regulates sleep and wake cycles, and production slows when the body is exposed to light. Children have naturally higher levels of melatonin than adults and levels drop with age, which may explain why we sleep less as we get older. Other roles that melatonin plays include the regulation of female menstrual cycles, energy metabolism, antioxidant effects, and boosting the immune system. It also has a role in preventing cancer and arthritis, and protecting against fatty liver.
What is the Pineal Gland?

The Pineal Gland is a tiny endocrine gland located in the center of the brain. It gets its name from the pine cone, which it resembles. It is about 10 mm in diameter, the size of a small pea. Normally the pineal gland is not visible on x-ray unless it is calcified, which is most often due to fluoride deposits. Calcification of the pineal gland can occur at any age, but is most prevalent in the elderly, and is much higher in patients with Alzheimer's Disease. The primary function of the pineal gland is the production of melatonin.

Food Sources

Although ideally our pituitary gland supplies us with the necessary melatonin to adequately function, melatonin supplements can also be purchased over the counter. Natural melatonin is also present in some plants and foods; including tart cherries, St. John's Wort flower, fever few, purslane (an abundant source!) and the seeds of the following plants: white and black mustard, fenugreek, sunflower, fennel, cardamom and flax.

Medical Uses

Insomnia

Melatonin is a very helpful and safe sleep aid in those with disrupted circadian rhythms (like night shift workers), and those with low melatonin levels, especially seniors and people with Alzheimer's or schizophrenia. Melatonin can also help prevent jet lag.

Immune Response

Melatonin is a strong anti-oxidant that serves as a free radical scavenger. Free radicals are organic molecules in the body associated with aging, tissue damage, inflammation and some diseases including cancer, kidney disease, fibromyalgia and others. Melatonin also functions in the immune system and provides protection against radiation. With the recent Ebola scare, Melatonin in fairly high doses (15 mg per day) was found to provide some immunity against the disease.

Cancer

Melatonin also has anti-tumor effects. Multiple studies suggest that melatonin may protect against some types of cancers, especially breast and prostate cancer. Women with breast cancer tend to have lower levels of melatonin, and prostate cancer has also been linked to low melatonin levels. In the laboratory setting, adding melatonin to the cell lines of some breast cancer cells slowed their growth, and another study showed melatonin also blocked the growth of prostate cancer cells. There is some evidence that melatonin may also enhance the effect of some chemotherapy drugs used to treat breast cancer, and prevent a decrease in blood platelets that can lead to an interruption in therapy.

Fatty Liver

In people with elevated cholesterol levels due to a high fat diet, melatonin treatment for just three months can significantly reduce serum total cholesterol and LDL (bad) and remarkably increase HDL (good) cholesterol. A 2006 study by Kadmin et al reported that lipid levels were improved in patients with type 2 diabetes after treatment with melatonin. Fat in the liver, a condition known as steatosis, can lead to insulin resistance and impairment of glucose and lipid metabolism. Melatonin seems to be particularly effective in treating this disease, but works best in prevention.

Diabetes

Melatonin plays an important role in the regulation of insulin secretion and glucose/lipid metabolism. There are melatonin receptors on human pancreatic islets where insulin is produced. A recent 2015 study showed that melatonin supports the production of insulin and its receptors. In addition, glucose intolerance and insulin resistance triggered by disturbances in our circadian rhythm can also be helped with melatonin treatment.

Making the change

Melatonin is safe and non-toxic. Always talk with your health care provider when switching from prescription sleeping pills to melatonin, as abruptly stopping benzodiazepines can have serious consequences. In general 1-3 mg of melatonin will help you get a good night's sleep with no drowsiness the next day.

Photo Caption: Our native friend Purslane is an abundant source of natural melatonin with 19,000 pg/gm.

41

MOUNTAIN MINT

While digging up some Spotted Knapweed on my place, I was met with the captivating aroma of a rich peppermint. Much to my surprise, I was in the middle of a small patch of Whiteleaf Mountain Mint, *Pycnanthemum albescens*, sometimes known as wild basil.

Native to the Eastern United States, there are 6 species of Mountain Mint in Missouri. If you can find it, the Hairy Mountain Mint is the most minty of them all. It gets its name because of "hairy" feel of the leaves. Whiteleaf Mountain Mint actually has green leaves that start to turn white as the plant matures. Like all mints, every variety of Mountain Mint has a smooth, square stem. A perennial, native mint blooms from June through September, and now is the time to gather seeds. The entire plant has a strong, unmistakable pleasing mint smell. Pollinators love the plant, but deer and other wildlife (except minks) are not attracted. It is found in dry, open areas on the edges of wooded areas (where I found mine), along roads and streams, and in other areas where it gets the full sun. As it has a rhizome, it grows in clumps. Be nice to this plant if you find it, because it is highly localized, and is becoming critically imperiled in several states. The variety I found here in Licking, Whiteleaf Mountain Mint, is endangered in Kentucky, and completely extinguished in Illinois where it was last seen in the wild in 1973.

Nutritional Properties

The flower buds and leaves of Mountain Mint are edible raw or cooked. It contains small amounts of the sugar fructose, and markedly high amounts of sucrose. It also contains considerable amounts of Vitamin A.

Native American Uses

Mountain Mint has been used for headache relief, to cure laziness, arouse unconscious people and to stop nosebleeds by wetting the leaves and packing the nostrils. Native Americans also used mountain mint as a meat tenderizer and as bait for mink traps, as mink are attracted to the scent.

Modern Uses

Today Mountain mint is used in the bath to relieve the discomfort of irritated skin, including chigger bites, as a meat seasoning, applied directly to the tooth as a toothache remedy, burned as incense, added to the dryer as a laundry freshener, moth repellent, carpet freshener and natural insect repellent. Have a musty closet? Make a sachet from the dried plant to freshen your closet and kill mold. It can also be used as an antiseptic mouthwash. Lister, the namesake of Listerine, was the first person to use phenol, the germ killing component of Mountain Mint.

Tea made from the leaves is used to treat a variety of illnesses, including cough, cold, and sinus problems. I have personally used this treatment, and it works very well. Steep about 3 leaves in 2 cup of boiled water for about 5 minutes, and relief is almost immediate.

Due to the phenol content such as carvacrol and thymol, an infusion made from mountain mint can also be used to clean infected wounds. A 2005 study documented the inhibitory and lethal effect of mountain mint against Escherichia coli, Helicobacter pylori, Anthracis and Mycobacterium.

Medicinal Uses

Oil distilled from the plant contains the medically relevant substances pulegone and limonene. Limonene has exceptional tissue healing properties. It is a potent antioxidant with anti-inflammatory effects. Pulegone is an aromatic substance used in perfumes and some flavoring agents, and is a combination of the scents of peppermint, camphor and pennyroyal.

Precautions

Similar to Mountain Mint, Pennyroyal is another member of the mint family that used to be very popular, and was used in flea remedies for pets. It should be avoided, as it has been shown to be toxic, causing deaths in both humans and dogs. Although Mountain mint contains pulegone, the aromatic chemical also found in Pennyroyal, it has not been shown to be hazardous. In a 1996 study on the toxicity of Pennyroyal, menthofuran was found in large amounts in a patient who died, so it is likely pulegone was not the toxic component. Note: Mucomyst is an antidote for Pennyroyal poisoning. Mountain Mint should be avoided in pregnant and nursing mothers and small children.

Economics

For those who are starting a home business gathering and selling herbs, Mountain Mint leaves and seeds are in high demand.

Save the seed heads from your mint plants. They hold microscopic seeds, and can easily be planted by crushing the seed head in your hand over prepared ground.

42

SORRELS

Very popular with children and hikers, sorrels are a popular grazing plant for people and chewing the leaves acts as a thirst quencher. There are 5 types of sorrel common to Missouri, where it is often found in moist meadows, along roadsides and in acid soils.

There are many sub-species of sorrel, but the most popular is sheep sorrel, *Rumex acetosella,* which is also the most studied. It has dark green arrow head shaped leaves at the base, and a 4 – 12 inch high ridged stem that produces light green leaves and maroon flowers arising from a single stalk.

Another commonly found sorrel is *Oxalis stricta,* also called lemon clover or sour grass. The alternate leaves have three heart-shaped clusters that look like clover leaves, and except for the yellow flowers it produces, it can easily be mistaken for giant clover. For those who love to make natural dyes from native plants, boiling the whole plant will produce an orange dye.

Farmers consider sorrels a noxious weed. Sheep sorrel is especially problematic in blue berry crops, as they flourish tin the same environment. It is hard to eradicate as it has a rhizome or stolon, and hand removal is most effective.

Nutritional Uses

The entire plant is edible, although usually only the fresh leaves and shoots are eaten. Sheep sorrel has several uses in food preparation, including a as a garnish, a flavoring agent, in salads, and can be used to curdle cheese or milk. The leaves have a tart lemon flavor, and contain

79 mg of Vitamin C per 100 gm (1 cup) of plant. The daily recommended allowance for Vitamin C is 75 mg for women and 90 mg for men. It also contains 1 gram of protein and 8 percent of the body's daily iron requirement. The plant also contains calcium, with about 60 mg per cup, and more than 500 mg of potassium, plus small amounts of magnesium, phosphorus zinc. The leaves have a tangy lemon flavor, and are considered to be a thirst quencher. A non-lemon lemonade drink can be made by infusing the leaves in hot water for about 10 minutes, adding sweetener and chilling. The French blend dried wood sorrel with sugar for a pre-made lemonade powder. When camping, it makes a great seasoning for fish, and is readily found in the wild. Dried leaves can also be used as a thickening agent.

Sorrels produce green seed pods that are tasty when raw, similar to sugar snap peas with a taste like rhubarb. Juice extracted from the plant can be used as a vinegar substitute.

Medicinal Uses

The sorrels can be used to treat scurvy (vitamin C deficiency) as a diuretic, laxative, fever reducer, astringent and to treat intestinal worms. Traditionally, a tea made from leaves the sorrel plant was used for fever, inflammation and to treat scurvy, while a root extract has been used for diarrhea. The leaves can be used as a poultice for skin disorders. Sheep Sorrel is rich in cancer preventive and antioxidant compounds. Sorrel is an ingredient in the anti-cancer Essiac formula.

Essiac has been widely used in Canada for over 70 years, and is reputed to be a Native American recipe that initially consisted of 4 plants: burdock root, Indian rhubarb, sheep sorrel and the inner bark of the slippery elm.

Treating Infection

A study published in the March, 2015 issue of International Journal of Analytical Chemistry looked at the effect of Yellow Wood Sorrel on bacteria, fungus and some insects. They found significant anti-bacterial effects against E.coli, typhus and dysentery, but not staph aureus. It was also effective against several types of fungi and insects. They concluded that sorrel "plant extracts could be a new source for antibiotics and pesticides with minimum noxious effects on the environment."

Other reported uses

An archaic use for the extract of sorrel leaves is as a stain remover on linen cloth. An ancient Chinese belief was that sorrel juice could remove freckles. It has been successfully used to treat some forms of dysentery by destroying the amoeba that can cause the disease.

Precautions

Due to high oxalic acid content of sorrels, they should only be eaten raw in small amounts, and avoided by those with gout or history of kidney stones. Cooking may remove some of the oxalates.

Oxalis stricta, also called Lemon clover, resembles clover with yellow flowers.

Sheep sorrel has maroon flowers and arrow-head shaped leaves at its base.

43

CARDINAL PLANT – GO CARDS!

It seems very fitting that one of the most striking of all native plants in Missouri is the Cardinal plant, *Lobelia cardinalis*. So named because the color is similar to the robes of the Roman Catholic Cardinals, this marvelous plant is usually found near streams and rivers. As the Cardinal plant flowers between July and October, now is a great time to scout out this unmistakable beauty.

The Cardinal Plant is in the same family as Indian tobacco, *Lobelia inflata*. Not as dramatic in appearance as the Cardinal Plant, Indian tobacco has pale violet-blue flowers, slightly yellow tinged. When you chew the leaves of the plant, it tastes like tobacco, hence the name. Lobelia inflata contains no tobacco or nicotine, but rather a chemical called lobeline that has a stimulating effect on breathing, and has been used in traditional medicine as an asthma treatment. Although all the published studies have been performed on *Lobelia inflata*, the Cardinal Plant also contains the active component lobeline.

Medicinal Uses

Lobeline has been used successfully to treat nicotine addiction because it stimulates nicotine receptors in the body, easing withdrawal symptoms and cravings, similar to Zyban or Chantix. Lobeline is also reported to be mildly sedating. There has been a flurry of studies in the past two years regarding the use of lobeline to treat methamphetamine addiction. This extract from the Lobelia family inhibits the neurochemical and behavioral effects of methamphetamine, without causing tolerance, similar to the way Antabuse works in alcoholics.

When given orally to laboratory rats, lobeline decreased self-administration of methamphetamine by up to 85%. Users become addicted to both cigarettes and methamphetamine due to the huge surge of dopamine, the "feel-good" chemical when they use the drug. Lobeline works by blocking this surge. In 1993, the FDA prohibited the sale of smoking cessation products containing lobeline; about the same time studies on Zyban were started. Prescription Zyban was approved in 1997.

Both the Cardinal Plant and Indian Tobacco have a history of use by the Iroquois, Delaware, Cherokee and Meskwaki tribes who used the plants to treat asthma, bronchitis and cough. Interesting enough, they smoked it for this purpose. It is still used in natural medicine to clear mucus from the respiratory tract, and is considered the best herb for bronchial spasms and as part of a comprehensive treatment program for asthma. Today it is taken by mouth, not smoked. It is sold online for about $9 per ounce, and customers give it rave reviews for both relief of mucus and its calming effects. Although it cannot be marketed to help with nicotine withdrawal, online reviews attest to its effectiveness for this purpose.

Like nicotine, lobelia will also induce vomiting if taken in large amounts, and during the 19th century when it was promoted by herbalist Samuel Thompson, it was prescribed by physicians for this purpose. Like the nicotine it replaces, Lobelia is a potentially toxic herb that has a history of safe use in small doses. The aerial parts of the plant (leaves and seeds) are used for medicinal purposes. Pregnant and breastfeeding women should avoid ingesting this plant.

Now is the time to look for the brilliant Cardinal Flower along rivers and streams. (Photo taken at Sherrill Creek.)

44

SUNFLOWERS – TRUE AMERICAN PLANT

Did you know that Sunflowers are the only seed crop in the world domesticated here in the United States? Sunflowers are mainly grown for the premium oil produced from the seeds, but there are many more uses for this hardy native that you've likely seen growing along the highway, hard to miss with the bright yellow flowers that change position as they track the sun. This quality, heliotropism, is why when planting sunflowers it is best to have your rows run north and south so the plant has more room to rotate in its quest to follow the sun. When fully mature, the sunflower heads face downward, likely protecting them from bird activity and disease. Domestic sunflowers have only one head per plant, while our native varieties can have multiple flower heads.

Sunflowers date back over a thousand years in Missouri, initially cultivated by Native Americans. There are currently 16 species of sunflower in Missouri, and we will discuss two of the most common – the Ashy Sunflower and Jerusalem Artichoke. All sunflowers have a very short production period, - about 100 days from seed to harvest, making them wonderful for impatient gardeners, and those wishing to have double crops on the same piece of land.

Sunflowers actually have 2 types of flowers, ray and disk. The ray flowers are those that look like petals, while the tiny disk flowers are at the center of the sunflower head. Mathematicians are fascinated with the sunflower, as the pattern of the spirals in the flower head follows the famous Fibonacci Sequence, more evidence of intelligent design.

Nutritional Value

In addition to making cooking oil from the seeds, the seeds themselves are loved by both people and wildlife. Very high in energy, 1 cup of seeds has almost 600 calories, packed with essential fatty acids like linoleic and oleic, that help optimize cholesterol levels. That same cup of sunflower seeds contains 37% of the RDA of protein, almost 100% of the RDA for the B vitamins including large amounts of folic acid, 240% of our Vitamin E requirement, and large amounts of needed trace minerals like copper, iron, manganese, phosphorus and Selenium.

Traditional Uses

Sunflower leaves can be used in a strong tea to treat fevers. The Dakota and Pawnee Indians made a drink from the flower heads to treat bronchitis and other lung infections. The seeds are also helpful for colds and cough due to their diuretic and expectorant properties.

Myocardial Infarction

Although most of the studies on sunflowers show their efficacy against lung problems, a 2015 study showed protection against myocardial infarction following doses of 20 mg/kg of sunflower oil for 2 weeks in the laboratory setting.

Ashy Sunflower

Ashy Sunflower is a common sight along sunny roadways in southern Missouri, the only part of the state where it grows. Growing no taller than 4 feet, the Ashy Sunflower, *Helianthus mollis*, is shorter than most sunflowers, with flower heads about 3 and a half inches wide. Considered threatened in the states of Michigan and Ohio, in Missouri the plant is mostly threatened by the birds and wildlife that love to snack on it.

Other Uses

Stems, leaves and flower heads can be can be cut and used as silage for livestock. Domestic birds such as parrots will eat an entire flower head when offered. The interior pith of the stalk is the lightest substance known, and has great commercial value in the packaging industry and is also used in making paper. A yellow dye can be made from the flowers. The leaves are used in herb tobaccos. All parts of the plant contain large amounts of potash, making it valuable in composting.

See next week's column to learn about Jerusalem Artichoke – another native Missouri Sunflower!

The Ashy Sunflower is common along Missouri Highways, and has multiple flower heads on one stalk.

45

SUNFLOWERS – PART 2

Last week we discussed the nutritive and medicinal properties of the native Ashy Sunflower, properties found mainly in the leaves and seeds. Another fascinating and beneficial native sunflower is the Jerusalem Artichoke, ready for harvest NOW!

Jerusalem Artichokes

Not an artichoke at all, the Jerusalem Artichoke, *Helianthus tuberosus*, blooms from July through October. Similar in appearance to the Ashy Sunflower, with multiple flower heads per stem, Jerusalem Artichokes are taller, growing almost 10 feet tall, and the flower heads have a chocolate scent. Despite the name, it is a native Missouri plant. The plant produces edible tubers that are similar in appearance to ginger root, but taste like a nutty artichoke. Jerusalem artichokes were very popular in Europe in the 1600's, and have long been cultivated by Native Americans. Like potatoes, when replanted the tubers last for many years, ensuring an ongoing crop.

Very low in starch, the "artichoke" is about 10% protein, and very rich in carbohydrates, especially inulin, a component of the sugar fructose, which gives the artichoke a sweet taste. (Fructose is almost twice as sweet as table sugar.) Inulin is not absorbed in the digestive tract, so it is used in many foods targeted for diabetics as it will not raise the blood sugar. 1 cup of tubers from the Jerusalem Artichoke contain 650 mg of potassium and significant amounts of iron, niacin, thiamin, phosphorus and copper. Very popular in France, the Jerusalem Artichoke earned the title of "Best Soup Vegetable" in the 2002 Nice Festival for the Heritage of the French Cuisine. For diabetics, there is specialty honey made from pollen of the Jerusalem Artichoke flower.

Medical Evidence

A 2014 report in the British Journal of Nutrition looked at the effect of Jerusalem Artichoke in the prevention of type 2 diabetes and non-alcoholic fatty liver. They found that adding Jerusalem Artichoke to the diet may be beneficial in prevention of these diseases.

Sunflower Oil

A discussion of sunflowers would not be complete without a discussion of its most valuable attribute – the oil. As people turn away from genetically modified oils such as soybean, sunflower oil is becoming ever more popular for cooking and cosmetic uses. The oil is high in beneficial oleic acid and lecithin, with large amount of vitamins A, D and E. Oil extraction from seeds can be performed at home, using an oil press. As sunflower seeds are about 35% oil, a surprising amount of product can be extracted. The material left after oil extraction, called meal, contains up to 42 percent protein and can be used as a food source. Usually seeds are cold processed first for highest purity, and then warm processed to remove remaining oil.

Oil cold pressed from the seed is citron yellow colored with a sweet taste. It is similar to olive oil. The left-over meal can then be warm pressed to produce a lesser grade of oil used in soap and candle making. It is an exceptional burning oil, lasting longer than any other vegetable oil. It can also be substituted for linseed oil in mixing paint, and used as a lubricant.

Precautions

Sunflower seed allergy is very rare, and there are sunflower butter products available as an alternative for those with a peanut allergy.

Jerusalem Artichoke is plentiful along Missouri roadways. At this time of year, the flower heads are mostly gone, but the tall, leafy stalks are unmistakable.

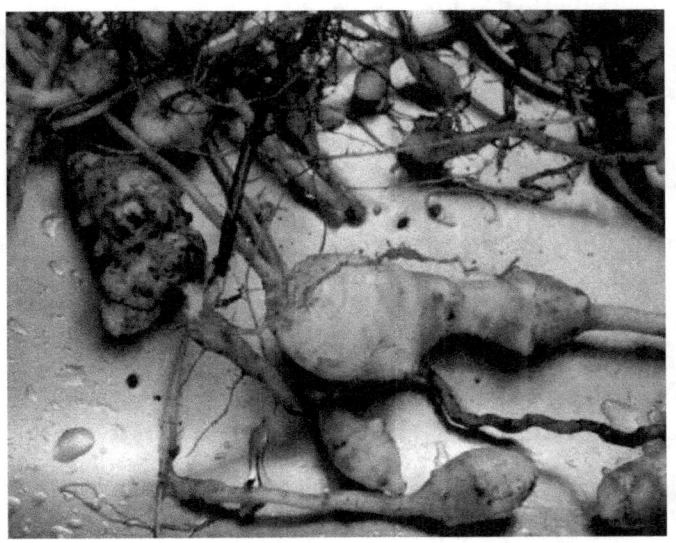

At the root of the plant you will find nutritious tubers, an excellent addition to soup.

46

PINE CONE EXTRACT

I get a lot of emails from folks interested in starting a home-based business using native plants. Pine cone extract is one potential product, receiving 5 star reviews and selling for $11 per ounce online.

In a previous column we discussed the multiple benefits of pine bark; decongestant properties, physical performance and metabolic recovery, wound healing, and as a disinfectant effective against a wide range of bacteria, fungus and virus, including the influenza virus type A, and herpes simplex types 1 and 2.

Not only are the pine needles and bark beneficial, pine cone extract has also has been shown to improve immune response, treat seasonal allergies, inhibit tumors, and even treat acne. Abbreviated as PCE in the literature, pine cone extract has been involved in multiple published studies over the last 10 years, but the medicinal properties have been recognized for almost 2000 years. Over the past century, Japanese residents on the island of Kyushu have successfully used pine cone tea to treat multiple conditions, ranging from colds to cancer, so this population group has been researched extensively.

We have 5 types of pine trees common to Missouri, with the Short Leaf Pine the only native and the most prevalent pine species in Dent and Texas counties. While most of the research studies focus on only one species of Pine, all members of the Pine family share similar properties.

Allergies

A 2009 study found significant evidence that oral administration of PCE from Scotch pines for at least 14 days leads to the reduction of Immune globulin E (IgE) levels in the blood. IgE causes hypersensitivity which triggers various allergic diseases, such as asthma, allergic rhinitis, eczema, chronic itching, atopic dermatitis and food allergies. IgE antibodies are found in the lungs, skin, and mucous membranes, so these are the areas where allergy symptoms are noticeable.

Acne

A 2008 study was able to identify an important diterpene, similar to Benzoyl Peroxide, in a water extract of pine cone from the Japanese Red Pine.   This   component   showed   antibacterial   activity   against Propionibacterium acnes, the bacteria found in acne that lives deep in the follicles and pores. The extract also had antifungal activity.

HIV

Extracts from pine cones have been found to have anti HIV-1 properties. The anti-HIV mechanisms include blocking of HIV entry into the cell and inhibition of virus replication in the body. The potent anti-HIV activities and low toxicity to the cell in the laboratory setting indicate that the pine cone extract from Pinus yunnanensis (Chinese pine) has the potential to become an alternative medicine for HIV infection.

Herpes Virus and Cancer

In A study published in 1989, researchers extracted several antitumor substances from cones of various pine trees. They found that pine cone extract inhibited the plaque formation of Herpes Simplex virus types 1 and 2 (HSV-1, HSV-2) strains in laboratory animals and human cancer cells. An experiment using radiolabeled virus particles indicated that the anti-herpes effect was due to interference with virus adsorption to the cells. This is important because the herpes virus has been linked to several forms of cancer.

Influenza

A 1995 study from Tokyo University for that fractions obtained from pine cone extract suppressed the growth of influenza virus. The inhibitory effects of one of the fractions, Fraction VII, on the formation of RNA-viral protein complex and the viral RNA synthesis were investigated. Pine cone extract worked by stopping the flu virus from replicating.

Making Pine Cone Extract

There has been a flurry of interest in pine cone extracts. On Nov. 23, 2010, patent US7838052 B2 was published by Tampa Bay Research Institute entitled "Pine cone extracts and uses thereof." The extract can easily be made at home, and unlike many plants that require an alcohol-based extraction agent, water works well to extract active ingredients from pine cones.

Bring 2 cups of water to a slow simmer, and add 1 cup of washed, broken up fresh pine cones. Simmer for about 5 minutes, then cover pan and let cool. Strain extract into a clean glass jar, and store in refrigerator. Most people take 1 tablespoon of PCE daily to ward off influenza, treat allergies, and improve acne. It can also be used as a facial cleanser. (Never gather pine cones near a roadway, because they can pick up toxic hydrocarbons from vehicles.)

47

OSAGE ORANGE

Those of us living in the Ozarks have a deep respect for the Osage Orange tree, *Maclura pomifera*. Not just because of its fairly spectacular thorns, but because of the exceptional quality of its wood. From early times, the Osage Indians used the wood for bows and clubs, and early French explorers named the tree *Bois d' arc*, or "wood of the bow." In fact, there is arguably no finer wood used in bow making, and local historian and craftsman Dean Wilson of Licking was featured in the Feb. 2, 1996 edition of Missouri Conservationist describing in detail the intricacies of making the perfect bow with a carefully selected stave from the tree. Osage Orange trees served as the original barbed wire fencing and after four years of growth were said to be "horse-high, bull-strong and hog-tight." Lasting 50 years, a living fence row made of Osage Orange trees outlives most modern fencing materials. Today, the wood of the Osage Orange is finding exceptional utility in making stringed instruments.

A member of the mulberry family, the fruit of the Osage Orange, commonly called a hedge apple, looks like just that, a sort of ungainly orange. It smells slightly of like its namesake, but not all of the fruit is edible, only the seeds. It is a complicated fruit composed of multiple single seeded drupes. Squirrels enjoy the hedge apples, and there have been erroneous reports of toxicity to livestock, most likely due to animals choking on the large fruit. Not all trees will have fruit, because there are both male and female trees, so if planting, it is wise to plant several. The tree generally starts to bear fruit at 10 years. The fruits usually ripen in September and October and are ready to harvest after the first hard frost.

In order to separate seed from the fruit, it must first be soaked in water until soft, then the seeds can be manually removed, and eaten raw or roasted. Studies conducted on the seed found the following nutritional benefits: on a dry weight basis, the seeds are 32.75% protein and 20.76% carbohydrate. Major nutrients include potassium, calcium and magnesium. The main fatty acids are linoleic, oleic, stearic and palmitic, all essential fatty acids. The seed is also rich is tocopherols, a form of Vitamin E.

Insect repellent

Iowa State University conducted studies on hedge apples and discovered they contain tetrahydroxystilbene, an anti-fungal, which repels cockroaches. To date, there have been no published studies on the use of the whole fruit to "repel or control insects in homes," but many people swear by their potency, particularly in controlling spiders. In fact, hedge apples are currently selling locally for approximately $2.00 apiece as we seem to have an inordinate amount of spiders this year.

Skin Treatments

Pomiferin is a unique molecule that can be isolated and purified from Osage Orange fruit. It is a skin protein stimulant, comparable or superior to equivalent concentrations of retinol. It is currently added to some skin and scalp preparations. This component of Osage Orange is effective in stimulating the production of collagen and elastin and improving the appearance and condition of the skin. Pomiferin has also been shown to be effective as an antioxidant, cardio protectant, antimicrobial, antidiabetic, and anti-tumor agent effective against several cancer cell lines.

Cancer fighting

In a study published in 2013, Pomiferin obtained from Osage Orange was found effective against Glioma, the most common primary brain tumor. Recently, growing evidence showed that glioma possesses stem-like cells, which are thought to be resistant to both chemo and radiation and believed to contribute to the poor clinical outcomes of these tumors. Study results suggested that Pomiferin could "kill the cancer stem-like cells in glioma and may serve as a potential therapeutic agent in the future."

In another study from 2007, both pomiferin and asajin isoflavones from Osage Orange were found to inhibit the growth of five human tumor cell lines with highest inhibitory activity on the HCT-15 colon tumor cell line.

Heart Protection

In laboratory studies, Osage Orange extracts were also found to the protective effects on the heart after heart attack. The protection is thought to result from the suppression of oxidative stress with resulting improved ventricular function.

Anti-inflammatory and Pain relief

A 2008 study looked at the effects of Osage Orange extract on edema (swelling) and pain. Two isoflavones were isolated and found to possess anti nociceptive (decrease in pain perception) activity and anti-inflammatory activity at a 100 mg/kg dose. The isoflavones are easily separated from the fruit. In the research study, the fresh whole fruit was cut into smaller pieces and homogenized into a puree using a hand blender. The puree was oven or air dried, and made into a dried powder.

Precautions

Hedge apples have a milky, sticky juice that can cause dermatitis and skin irritation in susceptible people.

48

JUNIPER BERRIES

Missouri has several native trees that produce Juniper berries, one of which is the Eastern Red Cedar (Juniperus Virginiana). Juniper berries are actually edible seed cones that unlike pine cones resemble a soft, fleshy fruit. The berries are green when young, but ripen in 2 – 3 years into a purple/black color. Juniper berries improve with age. Each tree has its own flavor – sort of like the way wines from different regions have their own flavor despite being made from the same variety of grape. Both the berries and needles are rich in essential oils that have antibacterial activity. The ripe berries are sweet, composed of 30-40 percent sugar, mainly glucose and fructose, good to know in case of a diabetic emergency on a hike with no food available. Juniper berries are also an excellent source of Vitamin C.

Long before the modern uses of Juniper berries were discovered, Native Americans used them for spices. If you locate a huge tree, it may well have served the Osage Indians, as the oldest tree reported, 795 years old when it was harvested, was from Missouri. While sometimes the tree gets no larger than a bush, Oregon County boasts the largest living Eastern Red Cedar in Missouri, with a circumference of 176 inches and a height of 70 feet.

The red cedar is sometimes called the pencil tree because its aromatic red wood is used to make pencils. Other uses of the wood include closet and cabinet linings due to the insect-repelling properties. Many farmers use small red cedar trunks as fence posts. Tomato stakes cut from the saplings will last many years. Juniper berries are popular in making alcoholic beverages as their large amounts of sugar enable fermentation and they have antiseptic properties that lengthen product shelf life. In Germany and Poland, Juniper berry juice is a common ingredient in beer. Unlike most beers, the Juniper variety doesn't contain malt, and is a low alcohol beverage. German cooks also use juniper berries as seasoning in traditional sauerkraut and delicious sauerbraten.

Medicinal Uses

Juniper is considered the third most used medicinal plant in parts of northern Europe where it is used for edema, gastrointestinal problems, asthma, coughs, tuberculosis and to regulate menstruation. In Native American medicine, juniper berries were used mainly for breathing problems, but also for gastrointestinal and kidney problems. Essential oil obtained from Juniper berries contains at least 49 different components.

Lithontriptic

Lithontripic is a fancy name for a chemical that breaks up or dissolves kidney stones. Juniper berries possess this property. They also serve as a diuretic, flushing out the kidneys.

Disinfectant

Juniper berry extract has been found effective against both Gram-positive and Gram negative bacteria. Not just effective taken internally, using smoke from burning juniper branches to cleanse an area of infection has been documented throughout the years. In a study published in August, 2014, this application was partially validated when burning juniper branches were found to have insecticidal activity against 2 types of beetles, thought to be due to highly volatile oils including limonene, sabinene and pinene that can be disseminated when burning the plant.

Role as an Antioxidant

Juniper berries have significant anti-oxidant activity, much like grapes. Antioxidants are effective in fighting cancer and diminishing the effects of aging.

Diabetes

In a 1994 research study from Spain, the hypoglycemic activity of a decoction from juniper berries was examined. Juniper berries fed to laboratory animals for 24 days resulted in a significant reduction both in blood glucose levels and in the mortality index, as well as the prevention of the loss of body weight. Other studies have shown the effect of Juniper berry extract on increasing the appetite, likely due to the increase in digestive enzymes and stomach acid secretion, effects that also aid in digestion.

Precautions

At the 41st European conference on Clinical Pharmacy, a paper was presented about an 81 year old man who was taking five to seven juniper berries every morning to prevent getting the flu. He was on Coumadin for atrial fibrillation, and was found to have sub therapeutic levels. His Coumadin dose was increased by 28% while he was taking juniper berries to maintain adequate blood thinning effect, as blood clots are very dangerous in a patient with atrial fibrillation. He did NOT contract the flu.

When used in excess, juniper berries can cause kidney irritation and damage due to the terpene component in the volatile oil. Pregnant and nursing mothers should avoid the use of Juniper.

Juniper berries take up to 3 years to ripen, and are purple/black when mature.

49

YAUPON – WHAT'S IN A NAME?

For those who have found the Kentucky Coffee Tree disappointing (no caffeine!), there is one native plant that does contain caffeine, similar to black or green tea. That plant is Yaupon Holly. Although distribution maps for the plant show it stops at the north border of Arkansas, I can attest to the fact it is present in Texas County, as I recently found a plant growing along Sherrill Creek.

Despite the Latin name *Ilex vomitoria*, the plant does NOT make you vomit. The name apparently evolved from a Native American ceremony involving elite young men in the Timucua and Creek tribes who consumed what they called "the black drink," and vomited afterward as part of the ritual that also included fasting, sleep deprivation, dancing, and binge drinking before important occasions such as getting married or going off to war. Yaupon tea does NOT cause vomiting, although eating the berries may cause nausea. The size of a small bush, this perennial evergreen plant has alternate green leaves and small, red shiny fruits that look like holly berries. Each berry contains 4 seeds. Many birds and forest animals eat the berries which are only produced by the female trees, while deer love the leaves and twigs, which is where the caffeine is found. Like holly, the red berries of Yaupon are plentiful in the winter.

Although most people have never heard of Yaupon, it used to be extremely popular. Spanish settlers in Florida drank Yaupon tea every day in the 1600's, and in the 18th century, European settlers in the Carolinas began drinking the tea introduced to them by the Cherokee, who called Yaupon "the beloved tree." The settlers must have found Yaupon tea very agreeable, as they exported it back to markets in both England and France. While its South American counterpart Yerba Mate has grown in popularity, some researchers think Yaupon fell by the wayside due to its Latin name, and there has even been some effort to rename the plant. In 2002, Fuller et al did extensive chemical analysis of Yaupon, and found NO emetic properties.

Respiratory effects

The active ingredients in Yaupon are both theobromine and caffeine. Theobromine is able to suppress cough in both guinea-pigs and humans without the side effects displayed by other antitussive drugs, such as codeine. Epidemiological evidence suggests that theobromine and caffeine, also found in chocolate, improve lung function and help open the airways of asthma patients.

Colon cancer

In a 2011 study, extracts from yaupon leave were investigated for their cancer prevention and anti-inflammatory activities on human colon cancer cells. Yaupon was found to protect the colon against onset of cancer, and also prevent inflammation.

What's in a name?

In the past 10 years there have been concerted efforts to restore Yaupon to its former status. It makes little sense to import caffeinated teas when Yaupon is native among an estimated 100 million potential customers. An interesting blind study published in September, 2014 gave 75 participants four unidentified teas to taste in random order. After tasting, the participants were asked if they would purchase the tea if it was commercially available. The panelists preferred Yaupon tea, with and without stems, over any form of popular yerba mate. When told the scientific name, however, 42% of the panelists reversed their decision to purchase the tea in the future. The revival underway in regards to Yaupon tea continues, and you can find it online for $13.00 per ounce.

Making Tea from Yaupon

When brewing tea, both the leaves and stems can be used. Including the stems imparts a somewhat milder taste. The simplest method is to cut off a branch containing several leaves and let it air dry on the kitchen counter. Either crush the leaves and put them in a tea ball, or steep the leaves whole for 5 minutes and strain the mixture into your cup.

If you are in hurry to process tea, you can also quick dry in a dehydrator or oven at low heat. This method retains less caffeine. For tea purists, roasting the leave in a 400 degree oven is thought to produce the richest flavor. Place in a single lay on a cookie sheet, and let them roast to a deep brown color, taking care not to scorch.

Yaupon berries resemble the bright berries of the holly bush. The leaves and stems of the plant are thought to be the only native source of caffeine in North America.

50

ERGOT – FRIEND AND FOE

Missouri farmers know Ergot as a toxic fungus that flourishes in humid weather on the heads of pasture grasses, including rye, wheat and fescue. Ergot contains chemicals that constrict blood vessels, and in high amounts can raise body temperature, constrict blood supply to the extremities that can lead to gangrene, and even cause hallucinations. Consumption of ergot has been found to result in miscarriage, although as far back as Hippocrates, it was recommended to treat excessive post-partum bleeding, and is still used today in the form of a drug called Methergine. Over the centuries, eating cereal grains contaminated with ergot has resulted in mass poisonings, such as St. Anthony's Fire, from the Middle Ages. Ergot is also thought to be the cause of seizures leading to accusations of witchcraft at the time of the Salem witch trials. Ergot fungus is fairly easy to identify, and has been compared to the appearance of rodent droppings in the seeds heads of cereal grains. In infected plants, hard, black or dark purple ergot bodies replace the kernels._There is some evidence that grains infected with the ergot fungus are those referred to as "tares" in the Bible.

Despite the hazards of Ergot, it has been produced commercially since it was patented in 1918, and first marketed by Sandoz Pharmaceuticals in 1921. Since the 1950's, several other major pharmaceutical companies including Novartis and Boeringer have offered ergot-based products.

The drug Parlodel is an ergot alkaloid used in Parkinson's disease and the treatment of pituitary tumors, Prior to 2014, Parlodel was used to suppress breast milk production after child birth, but was found to have serious cardiac, neurological and psychiatric side effects.

Migraine

In spite of the many hazards of ergot, a medication prepared from the fungus stands as one of the most effective treatments of intractable migraine headache. Although not considered a first-line treatment, ergotamine tartrate is FDA approved to treat or prevent several forms of vascular headaches, such as migraine and cluster headaches. It works by constricting blood vessels in the brain and stops the development of inflammation. In my own experience in the neurology office, I have never seen DHE (ergotamine) fail to stop a headache, even in patients who have had a chronic headache for *months*. In the emergency room or physician's office, ergotamine in the form of DHE is administered in very small doses IV every 15 minutes until the migraine is gone, usually requiring 3 doses total. How long the patient remains headache-free is variable, but often up to several months. Ergotamine now comes in a nasal spray called Migranal, and there is also a variety combined with caffeine in both oral and suppository form called Cafergot.

Precautions

There has been resurgence in the practice of growing and milling cereal grains, and some folks are doing it quite successfully. The benefits include a product that still contains the bran, and is not bleached. It is estimated that planting 6 pounds of wheat in a 20 x 50 foot area could provide a harvest of 50 pounds of grain. Potential millers should be on the lookout for ergot contamination. If growing your own grain, call the local USDA extension for guidance.

Ergot has severe interactions with some of the anti-retroviral drugs, causing extreme decrease in the circulation of the extremities that can lead to amputation. This is being increasing seen in patients with HIV who are self-treating with ergot, available online. It also interacts with common antibiotics, including erythromycin and clarithromycin and some anti-fungal medications.

If you suffer from migraines, have a talk with your medical provider about ergot-based medications, available by prescription. They should never be taken by pregnant or lactating women, and your prescriber should know all the medications you are taking, both prescribed and over the counter.

In infected plants, hard, black or dark purple ergot bodies replace the kernels.

51

FRANKINCENSE AND MYRRH

When the Magi presented gold, frankincense and myrrh to Jesus, their gift was considered suitable for a King. Today, the healing properties of frankincense and myrrh are becoming increasingly appreciated, and any discussion of the healing properties of plants would be incomplete without including these earliest medicinals.

Frankincense (*boswellia)* is extracted from the resin of a tree that grows mainly in Somalia, but also in the southern region of the Arabian Peninsula. For home gardeners, Frankincense is very difficult to grow in the United States, but patient and meticulous gardeners in Arizona are having some success.

Myrrh (*commiphora-myrrha*) is much easier to grow. Native to Somalia, Yemen, Ethiopia and Eritrea, growing on the coastline along the Red Sea, it can be grown in pots here in Missouri.

Both Frankincense and myrrh are harvested much like maple syrup. A cut is made through the bark into the sap wood, and the resin is tapped. It is then smoked, taken orally, or made into an oil.

Frankincense

Frankincense has traditionally been used as an essential oil and an inhalation agent. A few drops of the oil in a steam inhaler are reported to improve mood, decrease pain, and help with bronchial congestion. There are hundreds of clinical studies ongoing regarding Frankincense, and the following represent only a sampling.

Anti-Cancer

Hepatocellular carcinoma and colorectal cancer are 2 of the major causes of illness and death due to cancer. In a study published earlier this year, researchers investigated the effect of frankincense resin extract on two prevalent cancer cell lines. They found that the cytotoxic activity of the extract was comparable to chemotherapy drugs doxorubicin and 5-fluorouracil.

In addition to liver and colon cancer, frankincense extract is showing promise against breast cancer. Initial studies are finding effectiveness against some cancer cell lines, with less damage to normal tissue.

In 2013, researchers at Leicester University in England identified a chemical compound in frankincense resin that has cancer-killing properties effective against ovarian cancer cells. Cancer cells resistant to conventional therapy were killed with the frankincense preparation.

Prevention of skin damage

Redness, swelling, pain and other skin reactions are common effects experienced by breast cancer patients receiving radiotherapy treatment. Frankincense has strong anti-inflammatory properties, and a cream formulated from the resin was used in a 2015 study looking at methods to reduce skin damage after radiation. The researchers found that "the use of a frankincense-based cream is effective in reducing the use of topical corticosteroids and is able to reduce the grade of erythema and the skin superficial symptoms, being well tolerated by the patients.'

Headache and Pain

Cluster headache is an extremely severe type of headache. A 2012 study involving 4 subjects with chronic cluster headache were given Frankincense resin extract by mouth. The researchers found that frankincense extract by mouth "reduces the intensity and frequency of headaches in patients with chronic cluster headache."

In a 2014 study, 12 healthy volunteers were given a single dose of frankincense (125 mg, 2 capsules). Their pain tolerance and pain threshold were significantly increased over placebo at 1, 2 and 3 hours after administration.

Myrrh

Since ancient times myrrh has been used to treat inflammatory diseases, gynecological problems, pain and infection. In Biblical times, myrrh was a common analgesic and was also used to clean wounds. Pharmacological studies also have showed that myrrh possesses multiple activities, including anti-inflammatory, cytotoxic, anesthetic, and antimicrobial.

Memory loss

A new application of myrrh is the treatment of memory loss. In a study published just last month that looked at the effect of myrrh on memory in laboratory animals, myrrh resin extract taken by mouth for seven days significantly decreased induced memory loss and had a protective effect on the hippocampus of the brain. **The hippocampus is crucial to memory, and is involved in the formation, organization and storing of memories.**

Fungal infections

For centuries, Myrrh has been used for the treatment of skin fungal infections. In a study published in October, 2015, **Myrrh oil was used to treat skin infections due** to 5 different forms of fungus. The authors of the study concluded "The results of our investigation confirmed the traditional uses of myrrh oil as a poultice for the treatment of cutaneous fungal infections."

Inflammation

Both frankincense and myrrh are highly effective in the treatment of inflammation, but the exact mechanism has not been identified. In October, researchers investigated the process by which frankincense and myrrh given in combination helped rheumatoid arthritis sufferers. They found that inflammatory markers were significantly decreased after oral treatment for 17 days.

52

HORSEMINT

Horsemint, also known as Wild Bergamot (*monarda fistulosa*), is a close relative of Beebalm, and indeed, they are often mistaken for each other. Native to the Ozarks, both are in the mint family, and the *Monarda* genus. The medicinal uses are essentially interchangeable, and documented history by several different tribes of Native Americans includes use as an antiseptic, stimulant, carminative (think Gas-X), and for treatment of headache and fever.

Both horsemint and beebalm are perennials, with rose-purple flowers in clusters, blooming from May through August with alternating gray-green leaves. In comparison with horsemint, the leaves on beebalm do not have stems. Both varieties grow to about 3 feet. Like all mint plants, horsemint and beebalm have a square stem and minty fragrance, similar to peppermint. They grow throughout Missouri in fields, and borders of woods and glades, and I have found them in the barb-wire fence row on my property.

The name Wild Bergamot comes from the similarity of the scent of the plant to the Bergamot Orange, grown commercially in Italy, and used in Earl Grey tea, considered a premium blend.

In 2002, researchers in Lithuania noted the use of horsemint as a domestic medicine, being particularly useful in the treatment of digestive disorders. They found both the leaves and flowering stems have anti-helminthic (killing worms in the digestive tract), carminative (stopping gas formation), diuretic, expectorant, febrifuge (fever reducing), rubefacient (bringing blood to the surface of the skin) and stimulant properties. There are at least twenty-six compounds in the essential oil, with higher quantities in the flowers than the leaves.

Dandruff

Seborrheic dermatitis, also known as dandruff, is a common but embarrassing skin condition mainly affecting the scalp. It presents as red skin, and dry, flaky patches of skin.

Oil from the horsemint plant has been investigated as a treatment for this stubborn problem, and in 2009 researchers found that essential oil made from the leaves of horsemint had pronounced therapeutic effects on the treatment of seborrhea, stating "studies of its antibacterial, anti-fungal, and anti-inflammatory activities showed that it inhibits microorganism growth and is superior to hydrocortisone in combination with vitamin B6 by its anti-inflammatory activity."

Insect Repellant

As part of an ongoing research program at the University of Mississippi to identify active mosquito repellents, horsemint oil showed good repellent activity compared to DEET. The isolated compounds carvacrol, thymol, eugenol, and carvacrol methyl ether were found to be the repellent ingredients. Horsemint was also found to kill the larvae of the yellow fever mosquito, without toxicity to humans.

The University of Mississippi has also investigated growing horsemint as a commercial crop for the essential oil and found it has good commerce potential in the southeastern US,

Food storage and preservation

A 2015 study in the journal of Food Science and nutrition evaluated the use of horsemint added as a preservative to frozen fish, in this case bighead carp, and found it reduced the spoilage of fillets and extended shelf life.

A previous study in 2011 showed that horsemint inhibits the growth of organisms that can cause food poisoning, such as E.coli and several other organisms, giving scientific validity to traditional Native American use of the plant for stomach ailments and excessive gas. Old-timers put a little horsemint in a pot of beans to prevent gas. Animals seem to know the benefits of horsemint, and will eat it to calm their stomach.

Stimulant

There are some reports of stimulant effects from horsemint, and a popular drink called Oswego Tea is made from a variety of horsemint with dark crimson flowers.

Horsemint has a square stem with rose-purple flowers in a cluster. It has a pleasant peppermint scent.

53

SELF HEAL – CHECK YOUR LAWN!

Believe it or not, there is actually a native plant in Missouri called self-heal, or all heal; also known by the less glamorous name *prunella vulgaris*. Another member of the mint family, it has a square stem, and is considered a common lawn weed.

Unlike many plants with estrogenic properties, self-heal is an anti-estrogen, used in some body building supplements. In China, an herbal drink is made from the dried aerial parts of the plant and used for treatment of muscle and bone pain. Native Americans used it as a skin poultice for cuts and inflammations.

A perennial, self-heal has easily identified purple or blue or violet flowers in cylindrical spikes, and blooms from May through September. If not in a mowed area, it can grow up to 1 foot in height. The plant is fully edible, and can be eaten raw or boiled. The tender young leaves are best in salads. As an added bonus, it contains the compound rosmarinic acid, also found in rosemary. As the name indicates, self-heal has multiple medicinal uses.

Antimicrobial

Medicinal benefits of self-heal include use as an antibiotic, anti-viral (including herpes simplex) and an anti-oxidant. A 2011 study showed that a water-extract of self-heal inhibits the HIV virus. The anti-viral effects of self-heal are thought to be due to an interruption in viral replication. A salve made from self-heal is helpful for cold sores.

Anti-allergic

In a 2001 study, a water extract of self-heal was shown effective in allergic reactions, even anaphylactic shock, when given as a pre-treatment in a dose of 0.005 to 1 gm/kg. It works against allergic response by inhibiting histamine release from mast cells. (Anaphylaxis is a serious allergic reaction that occurs rapidly, and can cause death. It is usually treated with epinephrine.)

Cancer

In 2014, researchers found that self-heal had a positive effect on human neuroblastoma cells, and decreased cancer cells in a dose-dependent manner. Another study showed significant effect against T-lymphoma cells, by causing apoptosis (programmed cell death) in those cancer cells.

Stroke Prevention

A 2012 study recognized the effectiveness of self-heal as a medical resource in cancer therapy, also as a treatment for high blood pressure and inflammation, and also use as a diuretic. The researchers looked at the effect of the plant on blood clotting, platelet adhesion, and breaking up of clots. They found that self-heal had effective anticoagulant activity and is very soluble. They concluded that "prunella vulgaris (self-heal) can be a potential candidate for anticoagulants and antiplatelets, as well as fibrolytic agents." This is important because medications to dissolve clots, if given within about 3 hours of a stroke, can dissolve the clot and restore function. Current medication used to dissolve clots after stroke is made with recombinant DNA technology, so the possibility of a natural herbal product is of interest to researchers.

Cognitive Performance

A study in the September 2015 issue of Phytotherapy Research found that self-heal is helpful in treating cognitive function and some neurological diseases associated with Alzheimer's disease or schizophrenia. When self-heal was administered to laboratory animals for 14 days, there was significant improvement in brain function, and also increased brain cell proliferation and number of new neurons (neuro genesis) in the hippocampus. This falls in line with the theory of neuronal plasticity, the brain's ability to reorganize itself by forming new neural connections throughout life.

Inflammatory Bowel Disease

In a study published just last month, self-heal was tested for its effect on colitis in laboratory animals. Sufferers from inflammatory bowel disease have reported that self-heal is helping in treating their disease. Researchers reported "Treatment with the *P. vulgaris* extract was able to delay onset of severe colitis and reduce intestinal inflammation." Intestinal tissue of the subjects was markedly improved and more closely resembled the tissue appearance of healthy subjects with no side effects as seen with traditional treatments like Flagyl.

These are just a few of the promising uses of self-heal, and like the name indicates, it has been used for almost every illness for centuries on almost every continent. It has no known side effects, and the aerial parts (above the ground) can be also be used in cooking.

Self-heal is very likely to pop up in your yard this spring – easy to spot with its cylindrical spikes and purple flowers.

54

THE CHESTNUT CATASTROPHE

As the end of the year approaches and a new year begins, we reflect on all the blessings we have received and think of giving back. Over the years this column has been written, only a fraction of God's gifts to be found in our native Ozark plants have been covered. There is one Ozark treasure that is missing – that is the Ozark Chinquapin, our native chestnut tree. (*Note: Don't confuse Chinquapin with the chinkapin oak, so named because of the similiarity of its leaves to the chestnut tree.*)

Described best in 2007 by an unnamed 85 year old Ozarkian, "The Ozark Chinquapin nuts were delicious and we waited for them to fall like you would wait on a crop of corn to ripen,..... they were that important. Up on the hilltop the nuts were so plentiful that we scooped them up with flat blade shovels and loaded them into the wagons to be used as livestock feed, to eat for ourselves, and to sell. Deer, bears, turkeys, squirrels, and a variety of other wildlife fattened up on the sweet crop of nuts that fell every year. But, starting in the 1950's and 60' all of the trees started dying off. Now they are all gone and no one has heard of them."

The Chestnut catastrophe was first widely evident in the Ozarks around 1957, involving the American Chestnut (Castanea dentate), and including the closely related Ozark Chinquapin (Castanea pumila van ozarkensis). The fungus was accidentally, or negligently, introduced from Asia in the late 1800's when property owners were ordering them via catalog. The disease became evident in 1904 when native chestnut trees at the Bronx Zoo began dying after a Chinese Chestnut was planted. Existing healthy Chestnut trees in Missouri today have been tracked to catalog orders of the Chinese chestnut as early as 1912. During WWII, the USDA vigorously campaigned for anyone to plant

Chinese chestnuts. Although Chinese chestnuts carry the deadly fungus, they do not seem to be affected by it.

Ozark Chestnut trees were very productive, with sweet nuts right off the tree. Unlike Chinese chestnuts with 3 nuts in the burr, Ozark Chestnuts have a single nut inside the prickly bur, and are hand-crackable for easy eating. The Ozark Chinquapin has 5 -9' long sharp, coarsely toothed leaves compared with the Chinese Chestnut that has oval-shaped waxy leaves with smaller teeth. The nut of the Ozark Chinquapin is higher than white oak or the American Chestnut in protein, fat, carbohydrates and trace minerals. A mature Chinquapin could produce 6,000 nuts per year.

Not only the nuts were valuable. The tree itself was also used in home remedies, with one recorded account advising 'Tea of year old trees for heart trouble, leaves from young sprouts to cure old sores, cold bark tea with buckeye to stop bleeding after birth; apply warmed galls to make infant's navel recede; boil eaves with mullein and brown sugar for cough syrup; dip leaves and put on sores." (Freinkel, S. 2007. *American Chestnut).* Chestnut trees were so plentiful that farmers turned their livestock loose in the forest, notching their ears to mark ownership. Cattle and hogs both grew fat on chestnuts, acorns and hickory nuts. Many an Ozarkian made a living from the wood of the Chestnut tree, using the wood in construction, and even selling railroad ties made of Chestnut.

The blight affecting our beloved Ozark Chestnut, a tree that formerly comprised up to 30 or 40% of the forest canopy, is the Cryphonectria parasitica fungus. Interesting, the chestnut blight has a blight of its own, a virus that saps the strength of the fungus. Possibly due to the effect of the virus, there are still struggling Chinquapin trees, growing only a few feet in height from the root base, unable to achieve their former stature of up to 60 feet high, and unable to produce seeds and reproduce.

In what can only be described as prophecy, the famous poet Robert Frost wrote the following verse in 1936:

Evil Tendencies Cancel

Will the blight end the chestnut?

The farmers rather guess not

It keeps smouldering at the roots

And sending up new shoots

Til another parasite shall come

To end the blight.

We are still waiting for the blight to end. In the meantime, consider joining the Ozark Chinquapin Foundation by visiting www.ozarkchinquapin.com. Any discussion of restoring the Ozark Chinquapin would be incomplete with mentioning the efforts of Montauk State Park naturalist Steve Bost who has been very active in restoration efforts, and is the founder of the Ozark Chinquapin Foundation.

The nuts of the Chinquapin are found within the prickly burs; note the coarsely toothed leaves that help distinguish the Ozark Chestnut from the Chinese variety.

55

HEALING TOUCH

Sometimes in life the most basic things are the most powerful. Touch is one of those things. Likely each and every one of us can recall the comfort of our mother's hand on our feverish forehead when we were home from school with an illness. How comforting, when we need encouragement, to simply have someone place their hand on our shoulder, with no words spoken? When we are going through a painful procedure, our natural tendency is to reach out and hold someone's hand, anyone's hand.

Hippocrates, the father of medicine, was likely the first to document the power of healing touch. He wrote: "it is believed by experienced doctors that the heat which oozed out of the hand, on being applied to the sick, is highly salutary. It has often appeared, while I have been soothing my patients, as if there was a singular property in my hand to pull and draw away from the affected parts aches and diverse impurities, by laying my hand upon the place, and extending my fingers toward it."

The need for touch is so strong that even in animals it can be the difference between life and death. In some distressing animal studies in the 1930's, baby monkeys were taken away from their mothers, and became obsessively attached to their cloth diapers, seeking any kind of physical contact. The monkeys turned out very emotionally disturbed. The same thing has happened to children raised in Russian orphanages, where there is minimal cuddling and eye contact. Largely due to information gleaned from this sad situation, "Kangaroo Care," skin to skin contact between the front of the baby and the mother's chest for as much time as possible, is now recognized as being very important in the care of a preemie baby, who may have to remain hospitalized for a prolonged period.

Several studies have shown that infants of caregivers who were visited and held more often in the NICU had differences in early neuro behavior, weight gain and immune response, which supports the need for and importance of close touch.

Not only beneficial for children, touch therapy for pain relief and enhanced healing in adults is being validated with research. In a 2008 Cochrane Review of 24 studies involving 1153 subjects, it was found that "Participants exposed to touch had on average of 0.83 units (on a 0 to ten scale) lower pain intensity than unexposed participants." The placebo effect was also explored, with no significant placebo effect identified. Massaging the hands of elderly persons with dementia is an effective tool in helping them to feel more relaxed.

A 2009 study looking at the impact of healing touch on pediatric cancer patients, average age 9 years, found that healing touch "is associated with lowered stress and changes in heart rate variability." At the cellular level, there is a mechanism in the body called the oxyhemoglobin dissociation curve. Simply put, when we are under stress, our cells release oxygen to deal with the stress. In illness, this leaves little oxygen left for healing, so reducing stress is paramount.

Another study published in September 2015 examined the effect of handholding and on anxiety in patients having a vertebroplasty, a painful procedure done while the patient is awake, but under local anesthesia. Psychological anxiety was lower, and blood pressure was also lower in patients who had their hand held by the nurse during the procedure. In addition, being spoken to during the procedure further lessened anxiety and blood pressure.

Massage Therapy

Massage therapy is thought to release serotonin (the body's own feel-good chemical) by stimulating pressure receptors under the skin. Touch may also help to relieve pain via the 'spinal gating theory' whereby if certain sensory stimuli are being sent to the brain, the 'gate" is locked to other painful stimuli, or in more technical terms, activation of nerves which do not transmit pain signals can interfere with signals from pain fibers. I actually tried this once at the dentist with a simple filling. I requested no Novocain, and pinched the web between my thumb and forefinger throughout the procedure, which went smoothly and no pain that I recall.

Massage therapy has been utilized in many hospital settings, especially in the care of hospitalized infants who are in pain. Giving traditional pain medications to infants and children is not without risk, such as affecting breathing, but they obviously experience pain. In one study of 186 infants, the use of massage and healing touch was found to have a beneficial effect on the infants' heart rate, oxygen saturation, and therapist reported pain.

A large study was conducted in 2009 that included 519 children and adolescents hospitalized at Cincinnati Children's Hospital Medical Center. The children involved in the study received massage therapy primarily because of anxiety or pain. Over half of the children (97 of 183), achieved a more than a 30% reduction in pain, whereas more than three quarters (61 of 73) met the 30% pain reduction threshold. Pain reduction was greater than 50% for 72 children (39%).

Remember the healing power of touch. We all have it, and we all need it.

56

MILK THISTLE

Milk Thistle (Silybum marianum) is originally a native of Southern Europe to Asia, but is now found throughout the world. In many places, including Missouri, it is considered an invasive weed. Despite this designation, extract of the plant is becoming increasingly popular, especially in the treatment of liver disease and certain forms of cancer.

The first use of milk thistle for medicinal purposes was described 2000 years ago by the Roman scholar Pliny the Elder, who wrote extensively about natural cures until he died of toxic fumes following the eruption of Mt. Vesuvius. Although the benefit of milk thistle for liver disorders was first noted at the time of Christ, soaring rates of chronic liver disease have caused a tremendous rise in treatments with milk thistle in modern times. Not only good for the liver, milk thistle protects other organs from the effects of radiation and chemotherapy, and also promotes healthy kidneys. Because of its protective effects against UV rays, milk thistle also has a place in the cosmetic industry.

The active ingredient in milk thistle is contained in the seeds, a substance called silymarin. Its protective effects on the cells is thought to be due to its antioxidant and free-radical scavenging properties.

Liver protection

The protective effect of milk thistle on the liver in patients undergoing treatment for cancer has been extensively studied, and shows promise. A 2012 study conducted at Barnes-Jewish Hospital in St. Louis examined the use milk thistle by a 46 year old woman undergoing chemotherapy for acute myeloid leukemia. After 8 days on chemo, she had marked elevation of her liver enzymes, indicating potential liver damage. She underwent numerous tests and treatments, but her liver enzymes continued to rise, and failed to normalize even when chemo was stopped. Finally, on day 47 she was started on milk thistle "based on the recommendation of a homeopathic physician who provided evidence for the recommendation based on a study showing its benefit in preventing liver disease." It is likely her physicians were amazed when one week after starting milk thistle her liver enzymes showed a dramatic decrease. She continued milk thistle when chemotherapy was restarted, and her liver enzymes remained decreased, allowing her to continue treatment.

Mushroom poisoning

In another case, a family of 4 was poisoned when they mistakenly ate Amanita phalloides (death cap) mushrooms. Consumption of these mushrooms has up to a 40% mortality rate in adults, even higher in children. All 4 persons had severe liver damage, and despite conventional treatment, their condition worsened greatly over the next several days. They were then treated with milk thistle, and improved dramatically. All were discharged from the hospital a week later. A study conducted in both North America and Europe found that the quicker milk thistle is taken following Amanita mushroom poisoning, the less severe the liver injury.

Diabetes

Milk thistle has both hypoglycemic and cholesterol lowering properties. It boosts insulin sensitizers in Type-2 diabetics, helping to lower blood sugar. Because of the protective effects on the organs, it can help prevent kidney damage in diabetic patients.

Osteoporosis

Osteoporosis is loss of bone mass leading to fragility of the bones and fractures, most often occurring in post-menopausal women. In a 2013 study, milk thistle was found to hasten healing of fractures in osteoporotic bone, and also helped prevent bone loss in this patient population.

Veterinary use

While milk thistle can't be fed to ruminants, i.e. sheep and cows, due to its potassium nitrate content, there is evidence to show it prevents laminitis in horses. When eaten by ruminants, bacteria in an animal's stomach breaks the chemical down, eventually producing methemoglobin, a chemical that blocks oxygen transport, causing oxygen deprivation in the animal.

Toxicity and Dosing

Milk thistle is thought to have very little toxicity or herb-drug interactions. A study of 2637 people showed minimal side effects, mainly gastrointestinal symptoms at high doses. It is safe for use in pregnancy, and there is evidence it protects the fetus against the effects of alcohol. It also stimulates prolactin, essential for milk production in the nursing mother.

A paper published by the Agency for Health Care Research and Quality found that silymarin (milk thistle seed extract) is typically administered in amounts ranging from 420–480 mg per day in two to three divided doses. Higher doses, up to 600 mg daily in the treatment of Type II diabetes and chronic hepatitis C, have also been documented with no adverse effects.

Considered a toxic weed, milk thistle is especially useful in treating liver disease.

57

ZINC TOXICITY DUE TO DENTURE ADHESIVE

In the past 8 months I have encountered two patients in my nursing practice who were being poisoned by their denture cream. With their consent, I wrote their stories and submitted them to a medical journal, and the article has been fast-tracked for publication. As very few people actually read medical journals, and this information is so important, I want to share it with you.

Traditionally, zinc has been used in denture creams to enhance adhesion to the oral mucosa. Dentures that are properly aligned and fitted should not require the use of adhesives, which can come in the form of paste, power or adhesive pads. Underlying bone structures in the mouth can shrink over time, causing dentures to loosen. Zinc is a leachable mineral that is absorbed by the oral mucosa. Remember that the membranes in the mouth have a lot of blood vessels, and chemicals and drugs can be rapidly absorbed. (For fast headache relief, stick an aspirin in your cheek and let it dissolve.) Many patients use denture adhesives in excess of the recommended amount, which can lead to elevated zinc levels and associated copper depletion resulting in bone marrow suppression and polyneuropathy manifested by numbness, tingling and burning of the extremities, loss of balance and walking problems.

Zinc toxicity

Over the past 10 years the link between the high zinc content in some denture creams has been named as a contributing dietary source in hyperzincemia cases. The estimated zinc intake from denture adhesives can be up to 23 times the FDA approved amount for the treatment of Wilson's disease (an excess of copper in the body). The original formula of Polygrip contained 34 milligrams of zinc in each gram, while Fixodent contained 17 mg/gm. The US recommended daily allowance is 15 mg/day. On Feb. 23, 2011, the FDA identified the problem and sent a letter out to denture adhesive manufacturers in a quest for a solution. Polygrip is now advertising a zinc-free product, but even after removing the source of zinc, copper depletion secondary to zinc toxicity is increasingly diagnosed.

Copper Depletion

Typically, copper deficiency is only seen in malabsorption syndromes and after gastric surgery. With high levels of zinc, there is an increase in methallothineins, proteins that bind zinc to prevent its absorption. Unfortunately, these proteins have a higher affinity for copper than zinc, resulting in copper depletion. With Wilson's disease, characterized by progressive copper accumulation, zinc is used very effectively to deplete excessive copper stores. Deficiencies in copper levels can result in impaired nerve function with many of the following:

- Numbness and weakness initially affecting lower extremities
- Urinary incontinence
- Cognitive decline
- Balance problems
- Hyper reflexes
- Decreased perspiration
- Constipation

Deficiencies in copper can also result in posterior column dysfunction with bone marrow suppression and degeneration of the spinal cord, resulting in the so-called "human swayback disease," normally only seen in cows and sheep with copper deficiency.

Diagnosis

Diagnosis is made after a confirmation of frequent use of a dental adhesive containing zinc. New FDA recommendations suggest that a 2.4-ounce tube of denture adhesive used by a consumer with upper and lower dentures should last seven to eight weeks. Blood tests will confirm the presence of zinc levels exceeding normal levels of 0.66 – 1.10 μg/ml, and serum copper well below the normal range of 0.75-1.45 μg/ml. Nerve conduction studies can show nerve damage.

Treatment

Treatment includes rapid replacement of copper stores, by either oral or IV means. Generally oral replacement is preceded by intravenous administration. Products containing zinc should be avoided.

Prevention

Read labels and avoid denture adhesives that contain zinc! Don't over use dental adhesive. In general, a 2.4 ounce container of dental adhesive should last approximately 7-8 weeks. If you have symptoms of numbness and weakness, seek treatment. If your doctor does heavy metal screening, be sure to ask that zinc and copper levels be included, as they generally are not. Only lead, mercury and arsenic are included in the routine test. This is a devastating but fully preventable disease with a severe residual functional deficit, even after treatment.

Denture Cream Recipe

Karaya gum powder
Tragacanth powder
Clove oil

Blend a 3:1 mixture of tragacanth (in the cake decorating section) and karaya powders. Add clove or peppermint oil to taste. Mix thoroughly. Sprinkle mixture on denture lining and press firmly into place.

58

SNOWY DAYS AND COMFORT FOOD

Being stuck inside on these cold, snowy days affords the perfect opportunity to do some real home style cooking. One project that is a little time-consuming, but delicious, is making pasta.

Once you taste fresh, home-made pasta, you will quickly realize the store-bought variety is just one step up from cardboard. And once you make your own pasta, I promise you will be hooked.

The basic pasta recipe requires only 3 ingredients: flour, eggs and water. Of course, fresh farm eggs work best. There are a lot of recipes out there, but this is my favorite:

4 eggs at room temperature (important).

3 cups unbleached all-purpose flour

½ cup warm water (amount varies)

Mix flour and eggs in a bowl with a fork, or with the dough hook on an electric mixer. Slowly work the flour into the eggs. Add just enough water to make the mixture come together in a ball, moist enough it holds together, but doesn't stick to the bowl.

Let the dough rest in a bowl covered with a towel for 30 minutes. Cut off a piece at a time, and press it flat with your hand. You can roll it out with a rolling pin, or roll it through a pasta machine (see picture). Roll dough to desired thickness. I make it a little thinner than I want, because it expands when you boil it. Now cut your pasta into strings with a sharp knife or your pasta machine. If you are hand cutting, you will most likely have a wider fettucine noodle. Dust the dough with a little flour if it seems moist to keep it from sticking together. After you cut the pasta into strings, hang it over wire coat hangers to dry until you are ready to drop it into a pot of boiling salted water. Fresh pasta takes a little longer to cook than store-bought, approximately 15 minutes. Homemade pasta is best fresh, remember it has no preservatives, but can be stored in the refrigerator for at least a week. You can also freeze your pasta for up to a year.

Once you have the recipe down pat, you will likely want to try variations. Fresh, boiled spinach can be added to your dough, but usually requires a food processor for thorough mixing. Dried or freshly chopped herbs can also be added to your pasta, with basil, garlic and fennel a few of my favorites. Be sure that herbs are thoroughly ground before adding to the dough mixture, this can be easily accomplished by running them through a coffee grinder.

You can also use this recipe for ravioli. Roll the dough into a thin sheet, and cut into 2 ½ inch squares. Place a dab of cheese, meat, or a mixture into the center of a square, and top with a second square after brushing the edges with a little egg white. Crimp the corners with fork. Your home-made ravioli can be boiled and served in tomato or Alfredo sauce. For St. Louis style toasted ravioli, freeze your raviolis, and when ready to cook, dip them in a milk and egg mixture and coat in breadcrumbs. Fry the ravioli in 2 inches of hot oil, 1 minute on each side. Drain on paper towels.

If you don't have a wooden rack, wire coat hangers work great to dry your pasta. Pasta can be hand cut, but a pasta machine (hand crank) has several settings to make a variety of noodles.

59

TOOTHACHE TREE

Don't you just love it when the name of a plant describes its function? If you've ever had a toothache, and been unable to get to the dentist, the Native American remedy may have been nearby. The Common Prickly Ash, whose Latin name *Zanthoxylum americanum* literally means American yellow wood, grows in wooded areas, clearings and along river banks here in Missouri, but generally outside of the Ozarks. The tree is often found in thickets, because in addition to seeds, it can also grow from underground roots, and in Arkansas it has the descriptive nicknames "tearblanket" and "wait-a-bit". The tree is easy to identify by its paired thorns on the branches that also have 5-11 dark green alternating leaflets. Able to grow about 10 – 12 feet tall, the tree usually presents as a small shrub. The toothache tree produces large amounts of berries in late summer that turn reddish-brown as they mature. If you are looking for this tree in the winter, look for the paired thorns and gray to brown bark. You can scrape the bark, and if it smells like lemon zest, you have likely identified your toothpaste tree.

Toothache and other uses

Early settlers were taught by Native Americans that chewing live bark and berries from the tree numbed tooth pain. They used the chewed, pounded or powdered inner bark as a local anesthetic by putting bark in the mouth cavity or around the tooth. There is also record of the bark being smoked. The famous tracker Tom Brown, Jr. tells of substituting prickly-ash berries for Novocain when he needed dental work. (Personal experience shows the numbing lasts about 10 minutes.) The bark infusion was also used as a wash for sore joints, and the bark and berries were used to make an expectorant or cough syrup. The berry infusion was sprayed on the chest for lung problems. The bark has been used traditionally to treat rheumatism by applying an inner-bark poultice to the affected area. An inner bark infusion was also used sparingly by mouth for heart trouble and circulation problems. In Edgar Cayce's writings, he described making a strong solution of prickly ash bark, adding enough salt to make a thin paste and applying it to the gums to strengthen the tissue around the teeth.

The toothache tree has also been shown to have antifungal and antibiotic properties and effectiveness in treating high blood pressure. There is some early research showing success against some cancers such as leukemia and lymphoma.

Antifungal

A 2005 study on the antifungal properties of the leaf, fruit, stem and bark of prickly ash found a wide range of effects on 11 different strains of fungi, including the common yeast Candida albicans and dangerous Aspergillus fumigatus. The fruit and leaf extracts were the most active against fungus. The researchers concluded "The results provide a phytochemical basis for the very widespread use of *Z. americanum* in indigenous North American ethnomedical tradition for conditions that may be related to fungal infections."

Antibiotic

A 2015 study looking at the antibacterial activity of prickly ash seed proteins revealed that the peptides showed inhibitory effects on Escherichia coli, Salmonella, Bacillus subtilis, and Staphylococcus aureus. The antimicrobial activity of these peptides increased in a dose-dependent dependent manner.

Hypertension

A study published in January, 2016 looked at how the seeds of Prickly Ash affect angiotensin-I converting enzyme. They found significant inhibitory effect against this enzyme that can contribute to high blood pressure, much in the way as the ACE inhibitors Captopril and Lisinopril. They concluded that extracts from prickly ash seeds could "be a potential resource for exploring functional food or pharmaceuticals against hypertension."

Cooking

Prickly ash berries are used to make Szechuan pepper, one of the ingredients in 5 spice powder. The seed husks only are roasted and ground before use. The seeds themselves are not used as they don't grind well, and have a poor flavor. (Don't throw the seeds away, as they sell for up to one dollar apiece on line.) While traditionally the closely related Chinese prickly ash has been used to make Szechuan pepper, a ban in the US from 1968 to 2005 prompted the use of the less flavorful American Prickly Ash to manufacture the product. (The ban was enacted due to authorities suspecting Chinese Szechuan peppercorns carried a canker that was harmful to the citrus tree. This was found not to be true, and the ban was lifted.)

Precautions

A high furanocoumarin content was detected in fruit and leaf and low furanocoumarin levels were found in bark and wood. Furanocoumarins may be toxic, so should be used with caution. As they metabolize to coumarin, they may increase bleeding time and cause hemorrhage. In humans these compounds can cause the "grapefruit juice effect" and prevent the absorption and metabolism of certain drugs.

The toothache tree is identified by its paired thorns and alternating leaflets. Scrape off some bark to test for the distinctive lemon scent.

60

RHUBARB

My grandmother loved rhubarb. Year after year, it was the first thing to appear in her tiny garden, with its green and pink shoots arriving just after the ground thawed. Grandma's rhubarb excitement in the spring was matched only by seeing the first Canadian Geese in the fall.

While grandma focused on rhubarb as a pie ingredient, its use as a food has actually been very brief, coinciding with increased availability of sugar, as the tart stalks are not very palatable without it. In comparison, the medicinal uses of rhubarb go back at least 5000 years, and the name comes from *Rha*, the ancient name for the river Volga, and *Barb* for the Barbarian territories outside of ancient Greece. Rhubarb was once so highly valued that 300 years ago it sold in London for 14 shillings a pound, the equivalent of $285 per pound in today's currency.

Historical uses of rhubarb include use as a laxative, treatment for jaundice, intestinal bleeding, menstrual problems, conjunctivitis, traumatic injuries, ulcers, burns and to lower cholesterol and raise calcium levels. Somewhere along the line, rhubarb took a wrong turn, and is just now making a comeback, both as food and medicine.

Nutrition

One cup of diced rhubarb has 9.8 mg of Vitamin C, 35.7 mcg of Vitamin K, 105 mg of Calcium, 1.1 mg of protein and 121 mg of omega 6 fatty acids.

Medicinal Uses

Memory

An interesting study in 2015 looked at the effect of rhubarb on memory in laboratory rats given rhubarb extract for 20 days. Memory was measured by using maze tasks, with ability to find the way out of a maze again after previously navigating it successfully. The rats receiving rhubarb extract spent much less time completing the maze, suggesting a possible treatment for Alzheimer's.

Chronic kidney Disease

Chronic kidney disease (CKD) is a major public health problem worldwide, and sufferers can face a lifetime of dialysis treatments. Rhubarb has been shown to have protective activity on the kidneys in patients with CKD, especially in preventing fibrosis of the renal tubule, a hugely important structure in the kidney that filters the blood and removes wastes to be excreted from the body as urine. Hundreds of studies have shown that treatment with Rhubarb has shown favorable effects in humans and animal with CKD. A 2015 study looking at how this works found that rhubarb helped a damaged kidney remove toxins by improving the function of the renal tubule.

Pancreatitis

Rhubarb seems particularly helpful in treating severe pancreatitis, a very painful disorder. In a 2014 study involving 126 patients with pancreatitis, those treated with tube feedings containing rhubarb extract had the shortest period of abdominal pain and the fastest recovery, including shorter ICU and hospital stays.

Another study from 2014 added rhubarb extract to the standard treatment of pancreatitis with somatostatin. Researchers found that compared with the sole use of somatostatin, adding rhubarb extract shortened the duration of abdominal pain, hastened the return of serum amylase to normal, and reduced the incidence of complications.

Menopause

Rhubarb root contains lindleyin, an estrogen-like substance. In a 12 week study of 109 women with menopause related symptoms, rhubarb extract showed significant improvement in number and severity of hot flashes.

Other uses

A rich brown dye can be made from rhubarb root.

Precautions

Rhubarb is one of only eight foods--spinach, rhubarb, beets, nuts, chocolate, tea, wheat bran, and strawberries—that can cause a significant increase in urinary oxalate excretion, a concern in people with a history of calcium oxalate kidney stones, but thought to be safe if eaten in moderation. Rhubarb damaged by cold should not be eaten, as the oxalates can migrate from the leaves to the stalk increasing the risk of stone formation.

Dosage

When used for medicinal purposes, a typical dosage is ½ to 1 teaspoons of root boiled in one cup of water 3 times daily.

61

TICKSEED

Tickseed, *coreopsis tinctoria*, is a beautiful native plant that got the nickname because its seeds look like ticks. Growing up to 40 inches tall, tickseed is often mistaken for Black-eyed Susan at a distance with its bright yellow flowers with brown centers. Many Native American tribes have used tickseed for medicinal purposes. The Zuni tribe of Indians used the flowers to make a mahogany dye, and women tribe members drank an infusion of the plant if they wanted their baby to be female. The Cherokees used an infusion of the root for diarrhea, and the Navaho used a cold infusion of the dried plant as a treatment for "lightning" infection and used the root as "life medicine." Tickseed is found throughout the Ozarks, and is a food plant for many birds and small mammals.

Nutrition

Before coffee became plentiful, petals from the plants were used to make a hot beverage. While the plant does not contain caffeine, it does contain caffeic acid, a key ingredient in coffee. A popular tea made from the flower heads is marketed on Amazon at $4.85 per ounce. Recommendations for brewing are as follows: Use about 1 teaspoon for every cup of water. Infuse in hot water for 2 to 4 minutes for the first and second brewing. Gradually increase steeping time and temperature for subsequent brewing.

Breast Cancer

A study published last year in Clinical Cancer Research found that caffeic acid found in tickseed blocked estrogen receptors in breast cancer cells, impairing the progression of the cancer cell, and ultimately leading to cell death. Caffeine was also found to help in this process. In addition, both caffeic acid and caffeine boosted the effect of the drug Tamoxifen, commonly used to treat breast cancer.

Beta-sitosterol

Another beneficial chemical found in tickseed is beta-sitosterol. Although this chemical is thought to be effective against many disease conditions including tuberculosis and gallstones, there is clear evidence of its benefit in treating high cholesterol and enlarged prostate. It is thought to reduce cholesterol levels by limiting absorption into the body. The chemical can bind to the prostate, reducing swelling, and aiding the urinary stream.

Insulin sensitivity

An infusion of Coreopsis tinctoria flowering tops is traditionally used in Portugal to control high blood sugar. In a 2015 study using laboratory animals, tea made from the flower heads of tickseed fed for 8 weeks was found to decrease insulin resistance along 10 metabolic pathways, resulting in normal blood sugar levels.

In another study published in 2010, glucose intolerant laboratory animals fed tickseed flower head tea for 3 weeks showed recovery of glucose tolerance, thought to be due to a recovery of the beta cells in the pancreas. (Beta cells are where insulin is made in our body.) Chronic exposure to elevated blood glucose levels due to decreased insulin secretion or insulin resistance is a defining feature of Type 2 diabetes, and in a vicious cycle contributes to ongoing toxicity and harm to the Beta Cells in the pancreas. Tickseed extracts and pure compounds have been shown to have a protective effect on these important cells.

High Blood Pressure

Extract from the flower heads of Tickseed has been shown to lower blood pressure in multiple studies, dramatically lowering the systolic pressure (the top number). It appears to work by several mechanisms. Tickseed lowers levels of the toxic stress hormone malondialdehyde and angiotensin II in the blood, and increases the level of nitric oxide (a chemical that dilates blood vessels). A study published in 2013 also showed the relaxation effect that tickseed extracts has on the blood vessels that researchers attributed to the effect on calcium movement through the cell membrane. This effect on blood pressure can be compared with calcium channel blockers available commercially, such as Norvasc, Cardizem, Procardia, Verapamil and several others. Persons taking these medications should avoid ingesting tickseed due to a possible additive effect.

Tickseed grows throughout the Ozarks and is plentiful along roadways where it can be mistaken for Black-eyed Susan with its bright yellow flowers and dark center.

62

FLEABANE FOR VISION

A member of the daisy family, Philadelphia Fleabane, *erigeron philadephicus,* is a perennial plant that is scattered throughout Missouri, but hard to find in western parts of the Ozarks. There are four other species of Fleabane in Missouri, located throughout the state. The plant has arrow shaped lower leaves and daisy-like flower heads that are initially white, turning to light pink/lavender.

An excellent food plant for butterflies and moths, fleabane flowers provide nectar for other insects. Native Americans used the plant as a cold remedy, to treat diarrhea and difficulty urinating, and to control excessive bleeding after child birth. The leaves are edible and used in folk medicine to treat low blood sugar, stomach ache, indigestion, and diarrhea caused by pathogenic organisms. The name likely comes from the use of the plant to clear intestinal parasites.

Vision Loss

Likely Fleabane's most important role is the prevention of vision loss. A study published in 2009 gives some insights as to why fleabane can help vision, especially in patients with glaucoma. As pressure in the eye increases, retinal ganglion cells are damaged. Fleabane extract has a protective effect on these cells, even when eye pressures are artificially elevated in the laboratory setting, preserving vision.

A study published in 2012 looked at combining an injection of fleabane extract with laser therapy to improve vision with diabetic retinopathy.

After treatment, microcirculation in the eye was markedly improved in 90% of the cases.

A study in the 2015 International Journal of Ophthalmology looked at the vision protection process and found that fleabane extract suppresses outward potassium channel currents in the retina, an effect that prevents vision loss and retinal damage caused by glaucoma.

Hypoglycemia

Fleabane flowers are effective in treating low blood sugar, possibly due to the number of yeast isolates (up to 79 strains) found on the flowers. Compare to eating a slice of bread! Livestock will consume fleabane with no ill effects, and in one study dealing with lambs, there was significant improvement in weight gain and similar or improved nutritional markers compared with usual feed.

Anti-inflammatory

Fleabane has significant anti-inflammatory effects, and has been the subject of much research. One mechanism of action is the suppression of inflammatory substances in the body. The Navaho used fleabane in lotions for body aches and headache.

Astringent

Fleabane has astringent properties, and has been used as a topical application for hemorrhoids, to stop bleeding from a minor wound, and as a medicinal bath. There are records of fleabane taken internally for bleeding from the urinary tract and non-menstrual bleeding. Fleabane is also included in several homeopathic preparations for the relief of chronic nose bleeds. The astringent property likely helps to relieve diarrhea.

Cough Suppressant

A study from November 2015 found that an extract from fleabane flowers has anti-tussive (cough suppressing) properties. Another recent study from September 2015 found that fleabane decreased the incidence and length of convulsive seizures. These are new studies which have not yet been replicated, so the jury is still out if these are valid uses.

Dosage

The PDR for Natural Medicines recommends the following dosage: using the dried flower tops, make into a tea and drink up to 3 cups daily.

A member of the daisy family has arrow shaped lower leaves and daisy-like flower heads.

63

GET THE LEAD OUT

There is a lead crisis looming in our country, and it is being fueled by the increase in water fluoridation. I was born in Flint, Michigan and lived there until age 6. My father was from the Appalachian Mountains of east Tennessee, and was kind of dropped off there when he got out of the Navy. He met my mom in the boarding house grandma ran after grandfather's death. The problem with being born in Flint is the fact that in 1945 Grand Rapids was the first US city to add fluoride, followed by Flint, just in time to fully fluoridate a young kid like me, and I have the tooth fractures to prove it.

Fluoride is not naturally found in the body, and whenever you introduce an unknown quantity to any living system, there are going to be problems. Fluoride, like lead, is a calcium imitator, therein lays the problem. Both substances replace healthy calcium, and in the case of teeth, fluoride causes a frequently occurring problem caused dental fluorosis. Simply put, dental fluorosis is the replacement of calcium in your teeth by fluoride, causing cosmetic mottling, but more importantly fluoride fracture lines. When fluoride replaces calcium, it can cause teeth to break off, often at the gum line, and almost always on the inner aspect of the tooth that comes in contact with fluoridated beverages.

But fluoride is much more hazardous than broken teeth. The relation of fluoride and lead is coming to the forefront. Both **fluoride** and **lead** can cross the blood-brain barrier and produce toxic effects on the central neural system, resulting in low learning and memory abilities, especially in children because of their rapidly developing nervous systems. In 2012, the Harvard School of Public Health issued a statement on "The

impact of fluoridation on neurological development in children."
Researchers found an average loss of 7 IQ points in children exposed to
fluoride from drinking water.

Water fluoridation has always been unpopular. From the very start
water fluoridation has been an unwanted intervention, and the
overwhelming majority of the communities actually able to vote against
fluoridation have rejected it. Fluoridation was not established through
public referenda, but rather through executive actions by government
bodies, including city councils. And city councils have the ability to stop
fluoridating your water overnight, but that is about to change.

Fluoride is classifed as a pharmaceutical because it is has no nutritive
qualities, and is added to the water to treat a disease (cavities). Over
97% of Western Europe has rejected fluoride as it is considered
unethical to mass medicate an entire population without the required
informed consent. While topical applications of fluoride to the teeth
through toothpaste and mouthwash have been shown to prevent tooth
decay, keep in mind that these products contain pharmaceutical grade
fluoride, as opposed to industrial grade fluoride, *fluorosilicic acid*, that is
added to our water. Fluorosilic acid has been proven to be
contaminated with arsenic, lead, and other toxins.

There is no need to ever swallow fluoride in any form, and even your
tube of toothpaste cautions you to immediately contact Poison Control
if you do so. An analysis of phone calls regarding fluoride exposure
made to New Jersey Poison Control Center from 2010 to 2012
documented 2,476 reports of excessive fluoride exposure, with the
majority of phone calls made by mothers whose children had swallowed
a fluoridated dental product. Initial toxicity was treated by the
administration of calcium as an antidote, but the long-term effects are
still not known.

*Continued next week – how fluoride increases lead levels in drinking
water, and what you can do to help.*

64

GET THE LEAD OUT – PART 2

Last week we talked about the lead crisis and the effect of fluoridated drinking water. This article will look at the problem in more depth, and discuss actions you can take as a citizen to ensure pure drinking water for generations to come.

The relationship between fluoride and lead has been recognized for decades. A study published in *Neurotoxicology* in Dec. 2000 found that for every age and race group there was a consistently significant elevation of fluoride-treated community water and elevated blood lead.

As far back as 1964, a pediatrics textbook noted that the incidence of lead poisoning was rising in certain fluoridated metropolitan areas in the eastern United States. Blame was placed on children eating lead paint, but children had been eating paint chips long before the crisis arose in 1964. In the interim, a new source of lead was provided to children – lead contaminated fluoridated water, also capable of leaching lead from pipes. There is also lead in brass fittings on water supply lines, which is added to increase flexibility. Data collected by the Centers for Disease Control (CDC) show that children drinking water treated with FSA and other fluorosilicate chemicals are *20 percent more likely* to have dangerous levels of lead in their blood. The CDC has yet to warn the public about the fluoridation/lead risk, but continues to promote water fluoridation.

 Several recent studies are examining the relation of fluoridated water and lead levels. A 2010 study in the journal *Toxicology* examined the fact that higher blood levels of lead have been reported in children living in communities with fluoride-treated water. Researchers found that fluoride consistently increases lead levels in both blood and calcified tissues, showing an association between increased blood levels in children living in water-fluoridated areas.

In a manuscript entitles "How does fluorosilicic acid leach lead?" by Dr. Sauerhaber, he describes the process as follows; 'When diluted in water, fluorosilicic acid breaks down in drinking water into fluoride ion, hydrogen fluoride, and orthosilicic acid, H_4SiO_4. Orthosilicic acid is classed as a weak acid and is often dismissed as relatively harmless. Unfortunately for our health, it is able to dissolve – slowly but surely – lead salts out of lead based pipes and fittings, especially brass."

Call to Action

There is a very important bill currently in Senate Committee, HB1717, that requires the public water system to notify the Department of Natural Resources and the Department of Health and Senior Services 90 days prior to any vote to cease fluoridation. You can consider this a fluoride protection bill, as there is no requirement to notify these entities prior to ADDING fluoride to the drinking water, which on the face of it would be of greater concern to the DNR as fluorosilicic acid is considered a pollutant, and companies are fined if they dump it in rivers or streams. Somehow it is okay to add it to our drinking water, which eventually ends up in the rivers and streams. This bill will make it almost impossible for your city council to remove fluoride from your drinking water. I have experienced firsthand the huge resources put forth by the government to keep fluoride in place. In order to kill this bill in the Senate Committee, contact your State Senator, or send them a copy of this article.

65

SPIDERWORTS – NATURE'S RADIATION DETECTOR

Ever since the disaster at Japan's Fukushima nuclear plant five years ago, folks have been understandably concerned about radiation levels. While just now irradiated flotsam and jetsam are hitting the west coast, air currents are carrying radiating particles eastward. Unfortunately there have been large increases in thyroid cancers in the affected areas due to exposure to radioiodine. One of my scientific friends monitors the radiation count daily in our area. Most days it is a normal low level, but there is a brief spike following heavy rainfall. This spike is not enough to be of concern, and I would let you know if it was. Very few of us own a radiation meter, but did you know that Missouri's native spiderwort is nature's own radiation detector?

Plant Identification

Missouri has 8 species of Spiderworts, *Tradescantia sp*, a perennial plant. It has 3 blue/purple petals, not to be confused with the native common violet with 5 petals, with the lower 3 usually larger. Spiderwort blooms between May and July with each flower open for only one day. The plant has 12 inch long bluish-green leaves that are long and narrow with a middle seam, folded lengthwise. Spiderwort is pollinated by bumblebees and fully edible, and enjoyed by small mammals and livestock .

Radiation monitor

Spiderworts are unique in their ability to monitor radiation in the area in which they grow. Once exposed to radiation, the sensitive hairs in the stamen mutate and change color. This remarkable ability of this largely overlooked plant has been investigated world-wide with stunning results to the extent scientists have declared spiderwort better than a mechanical monitor, and able to detect radiation in very small amounts.

Monitoring factory emissions with a plant

In a 2016 study from Brazil, researchers used the spiderwort plant to assess the toxicity of emissions from a ceramics plant. For comparison purposes the spiderwort plant was also monitored in a suburban residential area. Toxicity assessments were determined monthly, while heavy metal bioaccumulation was measured at the end of the total exposure period. Markers of genetic toxicity were significantly higher in spiderwort plants exposed in the ceramic plant emission monitored area compared to the residential site. With respect to heavy metal bioaccumulation in spiderwort leaves, cadmium and chromium concentrations were significantly higher in plants at the ceramic industry emission monitoring site. Researchers concluded that Spiderwort was found to be sensitive to air contamination by heavy metals from emissions generated by the ceramic industry, confirming that this plant species may be employed as a reference organism in biomonitoring studies.

Outdoor smoking areas

Since smoking has been banned inside most public buildings, outdoor smoking areas have been in use. In a 2015 study published in the journal of Environmental Science, researchers conducted a 10 day study assessing the accumulation of particulate matter from tobacco products in the leaves of the spiderwort plant. The median concentration of particulate matter in the smoking area in all days of monitoring was double that of the control area. In addition, the elements aluminum, cadmium, copper, nickel, lead, antimony and selenium found in spiderwort were in higher concentration in the smoking area when compared to control area. Under the study conditions, vegetal biomonitoring proved to be an effective tool for assessing environmental tobacco smoke exposure in outdoor areas.

Other Uses

Although also renowned for its ability to effectively remove volatile organic pollutants from the air, Spiderwort has also been traditionally used as an anti-inflammatory and anti-toxic supplement, and to improve blood circulation. Research has shown Spiderwort to be active against Gram-negative bacteria, which may explain its traditional use in wound healing.

Radiation monitoring at home

The fuzzy yellow hairs at the center of spiderwort flower will turn blue when exposed to even low levels of radiation. This is a mutation provoked by radiation above the normal background level. The level of radiation to which the plant was exposed can be estimated by counting the number of blue hairs in relation to yellow hairs. The hairs grow in sequence, so if you monitor the plant daily, you can tell when the radiation exposure occurred, and even the wind direction carrying the radiation.

When exposed to even low doses of radiation, the stamen hairs of the Spiderwort change from yellow to blue.

66

GALLS, WHAT ARE THEY GOOD FOR?

They are brown and dried now, but anyone walking in woods this summer likely spotted the "green apples" on some of the oak trees. Upon close examination, these "apples" have the weight and consistency of ping-pong balls. Commonly called oak-apple galls, these remarkable plant structures have been studied, observed, and utilized since well before the birth of Christ. Pliny the Elder, noteworthy Roman naturalist, documented the medicinal use of gall extracts around 50 A.D.

So what is a gall exactly? It looks edible, could you eat it? Plant galls are caused by an insect or mite which induces the growth of the gall. The insect then resides within the gall which provides protection, nourishment and water. There are over 2000 types of galls in North America, and certain insects use certain trees and plants. Of the oak apple galls, there are more than 20 different types, but only one wasp species produces the 1 – 1 ½ galls that look like green apples on our local oak trees. Arguably, the oak apple gall is the most beneficial gall of all, not just to the wasp inhabiting it, but also for humans. Oak apple galls are intricately linked in our history, and many important documents were written with gall ink, including the Dead Sea Scrolls, the Magna Carta, the Declaration of Independence, the US Constitution and the Bill of Rights. Van Gogh drew with gall ink, Bach composed with it, and Da Vinci used it in his writings. Galls are so important that a whole area of study is based on them, called Cecidology.

Galls have a wide variety of size, color and shape, but every gall can be matched to the insect that stimulates its growth. One type of gall wasp (Amphibolips inanis) is responsible for the empty, green oak apple galls that we see. This wasp is not harmful to humans, or even the tree that it inhabits.

The major beneficial ingredient found in oak apple galls is tannic acid, making them excellent for tanning and dyeing material. Inks made from oak apple galls are high quality and permanent, explaining its use in important historic documents. Iron gall ink has only four ingredients, water, oak galls, ferrous sulfate, and gum Arabic, a process that creates gallic acid. The method for making ink is simple, as this 1770 recipe shows: Take 2 ounces of crushed oak galls soaked overnight in a pint of water. Strain into 1 ounce of ferrous sulfate, add ½ ounce gum arabic and stir until fully dissolved.

In addition to a time-revered source of permanent ink, oak galls have very unique and potent properties that are the focus of current research studies, mainly focusing on their antibacterial properties. Native Americans ground galls into a sort of antibacterial powder, used for eyewash and skin poultices. Galls have also been reported to have antihistamine and anti-inflammatory properties. Oak gall extract is highly astringent, making it beneficial for hemorrhage or diarrhea.

Antibacterial Properties

A study from 2014 found that oak apple gall extract is particularly effective against streptococcus mutans, the bacteria that is associated with dental plaque and cavities.

Another 2014 study found that gall extract works well to control drug resistant bacteria found in burn wounds. It makes sense that there would be no resistance against the highly unique chemicals found in an oak apple gall.

Gall extract has also been proven active against staphylococcus aureus and E. coli, where it works by destroying the offending cell membrane.

Can you eat them?

A lot of animals like eating galls, not just the insect inside, but the gall itself which contains edible nutritious starch. Galls are also considered a survival food, and I have some friends who enjoy eating them.

Galling as a hobby

Once you go galling, you will be hooked! In addition to oak apple galls, there are thousands of relatives, all specific to the insect and its plant host. Don't be afraid to break open the gall in look inside to see inside the little house built by an insect.

Oak apple galls look like little green apples, but have the weight of a ping-pong ball.

67

PASSION FLOWER

Without a doubt, Passion Flower (*passiflora incarnata*), is the most exotic of all Missouri native plants. A perennial vine, the plant blooms from June-September with elaborate purple and pink flowers that rival that of an orchid in their sophistication. Unlike orchids, the Passion Flower produces a nutritious and edible fruit, great for making jelly. The fruits are commonly called "maypops," due to the fact they first ripen in May, and pop when crushed. Native in Missouri south of the Missouri River, Passion Flower can be found in fence rows, along road sides, and in sandy fields. Unlike its tropical relatives, the Missouri native can withstand winters down to -4°F.

Nutrition

While leaves and flowers from passion flower can be used to make tea, the main nutritive qualities are found in its sweet, yellow fruit that is the size of a small egg. 3.5 ounces of passion flower contains 97 calories, 30 mg of Vitamin C, and significant amounts of Vitamin A, beta carotene, Vitamins B2, B3 and B9, iron, phosphorus and potassium.

Medicinal Uses

The use of passion flower in medicine was first described in Germany in 1787, where it was used to treat seizures in the elderly. Even older reports detail its effects on insomnia and so-called spasmodic disorders. It is used in Europe today to treat insomnia and anxiety, heart palpitations and as a sedative. Passion Flower is sold on Amazon in a liquid drop form for anxiety with a 5 star rating. Some interesting product reviews claim that it aids in stopping drinking, lowers blood pressure, decreases anxiety, aids sleep and acts as a blood thinner.

Anxiety

The most prevalent medical application for passion Fruit is treatment of anxiety. Unfortunately, anxiety medications are over prescribed to the elderly, and many seniors have become dependent. The EMPOWER trial looked at natural, non-addicting alternatives in treating anxiety in older adults. Passion Flower is one natural alternative that has been proven safe and effective in multiple clinical studies.

A 2013 study found pre-treatment with Passion Flower was significantly effective in reducing anxiety in dental patients. In this randomized- one sided blind clinical trial, 63 patients, with moderate, high and severe anxiety in need of periodontal treatment were randomly divided into 3 groups of 21.The first group was given Passion flower drops and the second group were given placebo drops and to the third group neither drug nor placebo were given. These results demonstrated a significant difference in the anxiety levels before and after the Passion flower administration in the Passion Flower group and also between the Passion Flower group and the other two groups.

A 2001 study compared Passion Flower with oxazepam in the treatment of generalized anxiety disorder. The study was performed on 36 out-patients diagnosed with generalized anxiety. Patients were allocated in a random fashion: 18 to the Passiflora extract 45 drops/day plus placebo tablet group, and 18 to oxazepam 30 mg/day plus placebo drop for a 4 week trial. No significant difference was observed between the two protocols at the end of trial. Oxazepam showed a rapid onset of action. On the other hand, significantly more problems relating to impairment of job performance were encountered with subjects on oxazepam. Researchers concluded that passion flower extract is an effective drug for the management of generalized anxiety disorder, and the low incidence of impairment of job performance compared to oxazepam is an advantage.

Many surgical patients have preoperative anxiety; therefore, the development of a strong anxiety agent with minimal side effects is desirable. In a 2008 study, Passion Flower was evaluated as a pre medication prior to surgery. Patients who received Passion Flower extract before surgery had significantly lower anxiety, and prompt recovery of psychomotor function (ability to think and move) post operatively.

Absence seizures

The tops (aerial parts) of the passion flower are being manufactured commercially as a drug called Pasipay used to treat seizures. A 2007 study found a dose of 0.4 mg/kg of passion flower was effective in delaying the onset of a seizure and decreasing seizure length in patients with absence seizures (also known as petit mal).

Other Uses

Additional medical uses include the treatment of neuropathic pain, sleep disorders, spatial memory (memory needed to navigate), and high blood pressure, although there is much more research to be done in these areas. Possibly the most important use of Passion Flower is as a magical addition to your garden, and as a food plant the butterflies and bees will thank you.

Found only south of the Missouri River, the Passion Flower is a perennial vine that blooms from June - September with heart-stopping beauty.

68

PINEAPPLE WEED

I've always loved chamomile tea, and included it in my aromatherapy class when I worked with troubled teens,. The teens were delighted with the scent of the plant, and several began a habit of drinking a cup of calming chamomile tea at bedtime. Generally "store bought" chamomile tea is from Germany, but a type of wild chamomile, *matricaria discoidea,* grows wild throughout Missouri to the extent it is considered a weed. In the Ozarks, wild chamomile is referred to as "pineapple weed," as its leaves give off a pineapple smell when crushed. The flower head of the pineapple weed is cone shaped, comprised of densely packed yellow petals that appear from March through September. The leaves are arranged alternately along the stem and smell sweet when crushed. Pineapple weed grows from 2-16 inches tall. The flowers are used in salads, but tend to become bitter at the end of season, so are best when picked early. The plant usually grows in disturbed areas, in compacted soil, along roadsides, and even in the cracks of sidewalks.

Pineapple weed has a long history of medicinal uses, and the aerial parts of the plant, leaves and flowers have been used to treat menstrual cramps, stomach pain, diarrhea and constipation, infected sores, fevers, and some heart ailments. Several American Indian tribes considered pineapple weed a cure-all, and it has been used in sweat lodges for both its calming effect and pleasant aroma.

Essential oil obtained from pineapple weed includes several compounds, including the following listed according to strength: *myrcene* , which has a pain-killing and anti-inflammatory effect that can be counteracted with narcan, indicating it may stimulate release of internal opiods; *farnesene* – a natural insect repellent, and *germacrene*

– an antimicrobial.

Medicinal Uses

Stomach Ulcers

The bacterium *h. pylori*, not stress, is the cause of stomach ulcers. Pineapple weed has been shown to decrease cell aggregation of this organism, leading the authors of a 1998 study to conclude that pineapple weed may support traditional antibiotics in the treatment of ulcers. In a similar fashion, pineapple weed has been shown to block the aggregation of e.coli, another disease causing organism.

Aphthous Stomatitis

Aphthous stomatitis is a common condition producing painful ulcerations in the mouth. To date, there has been no optimal treatment. Topical and systemic steroids commonly prescribed for the condition have local and systemic side-effects. A 2014 study assessed the efficacy of a chamomile mouth rinse on reducing the signs and symptoms of aphthous lesions in comparison with a placebo mouth rinse. In a study with 36 patients, the ability of a chamomile mouth rinse to control the pain and burning sensation and the number and size of the ulcers was evaluated. Chamomile mouth rinse was effective in the treatment of stomatitis, controlling the pain and burning sensation and decreasing the number of ulcers without producing any adverse side effects.

Sleep

Chamomile is the most commonly used herbal for sleep disorders. One possible mechanism in its role as a sleep aid is it the effect it has on anxiety as documented in a 2011 study. Considered a 'mild sedative' chamomile has no reported side effects or safety considerations.

Pain

Pineapple weed has pain relieving properties, and the crushed flowers can be placed in a tea bag for a teething baby. A tea can also be made from the aerial parts, and will provide a mild anti-inflammatory and pain relieving effect.

A 2016 study looks at using chamomile for pain in conjunction with a COX-inhibitor (like Celebrex). They found that chamomile enhances the pain relief of the Cox-inhibitor, and also protects the sotmach lining (Celebrex and other non-steroidal anti-inflammatory drugs can cause stomach bleeding). One mechanism by which chamomile works is by blocking prostaglandins, substances that cause pain.

Knee Osteoarthritis

In a 2015 study, patients were randomized and treated with topical chamomile oil, diclofenac or placebo, 3 times daily for 3 weeks. They were allowed to use Tylenol as an analgesic. The chamomile oil significantly reduced the patients' need for Tylenol, and there were beneficial effects on physical function, and stiffness of the joint.

Precautions

The plant contains coumarin, a blood thinner that is helpful in preventing strokes, but can cause dangerous bleeding if taken in large quantities or combined with prescription blood thinners.

Rachael West makes a flavorful and healthy tea with native violets and wild chamomile. (photo courtesy of Once Upon A Weed)

69

WILD VIOLETS

One of the most edible of Missouri native plants are wild violets. With almost 20 varieties in Missouri, a forager can readily gather a large bowl of the blue, purple, white and gray petals for use in a variety of foods, including violet jelly, violet syrup, infused vinegar, and as a salad garnish. Violets always have 5 petals, and the leaves have a heart shape.

The entire plant is edible, and the leaves and stem contain vitamins A and C. In 1979, Erichson-Brown reported that the basal leaves of the violet when collected in the early spring have twice the vitamin C of oranges, and more than twice the Vitamin A of spinach. The flowers themselves are rich in vitamin C. Violets also contain 30 amino acids, the building blocks of protein, and are particularly rich in lysine, an amino acid well known for its antiviral properties. Lysine is particularly helpful in preventing outbreaks of cold sores, and as an essential amino acid, it cannot be manufactured in the body but must be gleaned from food sources.

Medicinal Uses

Violets have a long history of use as a cough remedy, especially for bronchitis. Preparations made from violets quell cough by both anti-inflammatory and expectorant properties.

A 2015 study looked at the effect of violet syrup on relief of cough in children with intermittent asthma. In a well-designed double-blind study including 182 children ages 2 to 12; violet syrup was compared with placebo and common standard treatments for cough. This study showed that the adjuvant use of violet syrup with traditional treatments for cough can enhance the cough suppression in children with intermittent asthma.

A study published in 2015 may detail the most complete chemical analysis of the violet, and violets were found to be closely related to the plant family Salicaceae, plants from which aspirin is derived. (Aspirin is actually acetylsalicylic acid). The Cherokee Indians knew what they were doing when they used violet leaves in a poultice to relieve headaches, a remedy that was passed on to early settlers. A violet poultice can also be applied to boils.

The book Native American Ethnobotany by Merman describes the use of an infusion of the violet plant to treat dysentery, coughs and colds.

Other Uses

In order to repel insects on corn, first soak the corn seeds in water in which violet roots have been soaked prior to planting.

For a beautiful and unique garnish, dip violet flowers into gently whisked egg whites, melted sugar and lemon juice, then quickly drop into ice water to set the sugar coating. Use on cakes, salads, and other desserts for a gourmet touch.

Precautions

There are no known side effects reported with the use of violets as either food or medicine.

Violet Syrup

1 cup of violet flowers

1 cup boiling water

1 cup sugar

1 Tbs. lemon juice

Put the washed flowers in a glass measuring cup and cover with the boiling water overnight. Pour off the liquid into a saucepan, add sugar and bring to a boil until slightly thickened. When heated, the syrup will turn from purple to a greenish tint – add 1 Tbs. of lemon juice and watch the beautiful violet color develop! By adding pectin, this recipe can be modified to make jelly.

Now is the time to pick wild violets. A syrup made from the plant is a time-honored remedy for cough.

70

SOLOMON'S SEAL

Solomon's Seal (polygonatum sp) earned its name due to root scars on the rhizome that are thought to resemble King Solomon's seal – an emblem similar to the Star of David.

The plant has some nutritional properties, but is mainly a pharmaceutical. A member of the lily family, Solomon's Seal presents in a cluster of single stalks with alternate leaves that can grow up to several feet. Around the month of May, it forms drooping clusters of small white flowers that later produce blue berries.

Considered a forage food, the root has been used in place of potato due to its rich starch content, and the shoots prepared like asparagus.

In medicine, Solomon's Seal is used mostly for skeletal, joint and muscle problems.
It also works well as a demulcent and treatment for chronic, nagging cough according to purchaser reviews at Amazon.com. The rhizome itself has been used to make a tonic to treat gout and arthritis. In addition to traditional uses, scientists are discovering some novel uses for Solomon's Seal, most involving the rhizome, or root.

Alzheimer's Disease

An exciting study from 2007 talks about the role of Solomon's seal in protecting the brain from beta amyloid, with important implications for prevention of Alzheimer's Disease (AD). Amyloid is a sticky protein that clumps together forming plaques and problems wherever it occurs. When amyloid accumulates in the brain, it causes the tangles and interruption in synapses that trigger the recognizable symptoms of AD. Scientists have identified rare genes that virtually guarantee an individual will develop Alzheimer's. All of these genes increase production or accumulation of beta-amyloid, so a widely available native plant that can protect the brain from amyloid is of huge significance.

Cancer prevention

A 2015 study investigates the role of Solomon's Seal as an anti-cancer drug. Solomon's seal contains a unique lectin. Lectins are a type of protein found in plants. They play a role in immune function, cell growth, cell death and body fat regulation. Lectins are resistant to human digestion, and enter the blood unchanged. The lectins found in Solomon's Seal have anti-cancer properties, causing lung cancer and some forms of breast cancer cells to die without affecting healthy cells.

An earlier study in 2014 had similar results, with Solomon's Seal causing cell death in non-small cell lung cancer with no significant effect on healthy, normal cells. The study lead the authors to conclude, "Due to the anti-tumor activities, lectin from Solomon's Seal might become a potent as effective drugs in cancer treatment."

Chronic cough

Solomon's Seal is most popular for its role in treating chronic cough, which seems to be a very common complaint. In addition to user testimonies, scientific research supports its effectiveness. A 2013 study looked into the trachea relaxant and anti-inflammatory effects of Solomon's Seal which supports its medicinal use in hyperactive airway complaints and inflammatory disorders. Researchers found that Solomon's Seal decreased swelling, sensitivity and spasms in the trachea that can contribute to chronic cough.

Diabetes

Multiple studies have shown a blood sugar lowering effect in diabetics who include an extract from the rhizome (root) of Solomon's Seal in their diet.

Solomon's Seal presents in a cluster of single stalks with alternate leaves that can grow up to several feet. Around the month of May, it forms drooping clusters of small white flowers.

71

PURPLE DEAD NETTLE

A fuzzy plant with a square stem that doesn't look edible, purple dead nettle, *lamium purpureum*, isn't dead at all. In this case, dead refers to the fact the plant won't sting you, unlike stinging nettle.

A member of the mint family with a distinctive square stem, purple dead nettle has fuzzy green leaves has sweet nectar-filled flowers if you catch it at the right time. Although widely considered an invasive weed, it is a pollen plant enjoyed by bees. It often grows next to henbit dead nettle, which looks similar, but has unstalked leaves unlike the stalked leaves of purple dead nettle.

Nutrition

As a source of nutrition, purple dead nettle is a major source of carbohydrates, especially in the form of manninotriose, found in high concentrations in the early spring stems and roots of the plant. Manninotriose is a soluble sugar, good for quick energy, which also has a role as an antioxidant. It is also a natural source of Vitamin C.

Pain relief

Purple dead nettle has been used to treat arthritic pain for centuries. A 2008 study investigated this property. Researchers concluded that the plant extract at a dosage of 200 mg per kg of body weight "displayed remarkable anti-inflammatory and pain reduction properties." It was also found to markedly reduce edema (swelling). The leaves can be used as a poultice on external wounds or swollen areas. Extract from the root and leaves can also be made into a pain relieving salve.

Antioxidant and free-radical scavenging

Exposure to radiation, chemicals and other environmental agents can cause our cells to oxidize and create toxic chemicals called free radicals that are responsible for aging and tissue damage. Purple dead nettle has strong antioxidant activity of up to 78%.

Seasonal allergies

Purple dead nettle can also be brewed as a tea, and is reportedly good for the kidneys and helping to control seasonal allergies, partially due to its ability to reduce the release of histamine, the chemical that causes allergy symptoms, such as sneezing and runny nose. Don't drink too much, because when used in large amounts, it has a laxative effect.

Antimicrobial

In 2007, researchers documented a wide range of antimicrobial and antifungal properties found in dead purple nettle. The plant contains an antibacterial essential oil called germacrene D, effective against staphylococcus, enterococcus, e.coli, pseudomonas and candida.

Purple Dead Nettle Pesto

2 cups purple dead nettle leaves and flowers

5 small garlic bulbs (can substitute wild garlic)

1/4 cup toasted walnuts

Salt and pepper to taste

1/3 cup olive oil

Combine all ingredients in food processor until blended. Slowly add olive oil until pesto reaches the desired consistency.

Great served with crackers as a unique dip.

Purple Dead Nettle is considered by some to be an annoying weed,

but it is nutritional with several medicinal uses.

72

SERVICEBERRY

Our beautiful native Serviceberry, Amelanchier arborea, greets us as one of the first trees to bloom in the spring. Due to its white blossoms, it is sometimes mistaken for dogwood, which blooms about two weeks later. Upon closer inspection, it is very easy to discriminate the serviceberry from the dogwood as the latter have 4 paired white leaves while serviceberries have clusters of flowers at the ends of the branches, with white, fragile, downy petals in drooping clusters. Dogwood trees bloom after the serviceberry flowers have gone. An extremely hardy deciduous shrub, Serviceberry ranges in height from 6 to 10 ft. and can be found on rocky, dry slopes. The shrub lives about 60 years. It is non-invasive and easy to grow.

There is quite a bit of history in relation to the name "serviceberry." In Early American literature, the tree was referred to as a "sarvis" tree. Similar to the way Rolla got its name, the Sarvis tree was named because Ozarkians pronounced Service as Sarvis. It was so named because the tree bloomed shortly after the snow melted and the circuit rider preacher was able to ride to town to hold services, both wedding and funeral. More reliable than the calendar, when the Sarvis tree was blooming it was a good indicator that the ground had thawed and was soft enough to dig a grave.

Back in those days, it was not uncommon for a widower to have a funeral service for his first wife who died and was held in what was essentially cold storage in the barn over the winter, and on the same day marry his new wife, who immediately took on the role of mother to his children.

The purple berries make excellent jam and jelly, but good luck beating the birds to them! Forlong term use, the berries can be dehydrated like raisins. As the tree is also native to Canada, there are many medicinal uses documented by native Canadians. The bark was used as a tea for stomach upset and used to hasten uterine recovery after childbirth. The wood has been prized by both Native Americans and Canadians in making arrows, spear shafts and tool handles where its close grain results in a superior product.

Nutrition

Little is written regarding the medicinal uses of serviceberry, but the nutritional content of the leaves and bark have been extensively studied. The bark contains potassium, magnesium, and 1.15% of its dry weight is calcium. The leaves also contain the above nutrients, plus nitrogen, a protein building block.

The berries themselves contain large amounts of benzaldehyde, used to flavor many products, and imparting an almond/cherry flavor. In Canada, service berries are called "Saskatoon berries." The Ocean Spray juice company is looking to expand into the service berry market, as a 3 year Canadian study found them a potent antioxidant, comparable to blueberries, blackberries and grape seed extract.

Serviceberry Relish

2 cups ripe serviceberries
1/4 cup cold water
2 cups sugar
1 tsp cinnamon
¼ cup minced orange or lemon peel
2 oz. liquid pectin

Wash berries and crush with a slotted spoon. Bring to a boil in a deep saucepan with cinnamon and water while stirring constantly. Reduce to low heat and simmer for 10 minutes, with pan covered. Remove from heat and add sugar and pectin. Mix well. Bring to a boil for 1 full minute.

To remove any foam, stir in ¼ tablespoon of butter. Stir in minced citrus peel. Spoon or pour into hot, sterile jelly jars and seal.

Serviceberry fruits closely resemble blueberries.

73

INDIAN PAINTBRUSH

Indian Paintbrush (Castillega) is blooming now, and is popular with the ruby-throated hummingbird as a pollination plant. The plant grows on an upright stalk, 4 to 20 inches tall with hairy leaves and stems. It is sometimes called prairie fire, due to its clusters of spiky blooms resembling paintbrushes dipped in red paint. In the Ozarks it typically grows in forest clearings and grassy fields. A biennial plant, named after the 18th century Spanish botanist, Don Domingo Castillejo. It develops rosettes the first year and stalks of blooms in the second year and usually dies after setting seed, reseeding itself every autumn.

Labeled a hemi-parasite, Indian Paintbrush can grow on its own, but its roots have been known to take over the roots of other plants for nutrients, as is usually the case when the plants reaches taller heights.

Nutrition

Indian Paintbrush flowers are edible and sweet, and have been included in the diets of several Native American tribes. The plant has many health benefits, but the plant can absorb selenium, especially if grown in sandy soils. Selenium is a mineral that's essential to the body in trace amounts, but can be toxic in large amounts. Despite potential toxicity, Selenium has attracted attention because of its antioxidant properties. As you recall, antioxidants protect cells from damage and aging. There is also significant evidence that selenium reduces the odds of prostate cancer.

Dietary deficiencies of selenium may have negative impacts on human health, such as increasing the risk of infertility in men, prostate cancer, kidney disease, or the risk of the occurrence of neurological diseases such as multiple sclerosis and epilepsy. Low selenium levels have been associated with rheumatoid arthritis. Approximately 10 years have elapsed since recommended dietary intakes of selenium were introduced.

Medical Uses

Selenium has also been studied for the treatment of dozens of conditions, including asthma, arthritis and infertility. Researchers have long thought the effectiveness of Indian Paintbrush is due to its selenium content. By taking the root of this plant and making it into tea, it becomes similar to selenium tea. While the flowers also contain traces of selenium, the concentration is much smaller than found in the root. Taken in proper amounts, selenium may be useful for the treatment of arthritis, Hashimoto's thyroiditis, elevated cholesterol, prostate cancer, heart disease and diabetes. A poultice of the plant can be used to soothe burns and stings from insect bites.

Thyroid Function

Selenium is an important element that exerts its effects through enzymes called selenoproteins. The thyroid gland has the highest selenium concentration in the body, and selenium is crucial in thyroid hormone metabolism.

Arthritis

A 2004 study of Selenium supplementation in patients with rheumatoid arthritis at a dose of 600 µg/day showed significant reduction of joint pain and a lack of side effects.

Cancer prevention

Numerous studies have demonstrated the benefits of selenium supplementation in the treatment of neoplasms and autoimmune thyroid disorders. The protective effects of selenium in the etiology of cancer diseases result from its effect on cell membranes protecting against oxidative stress, and also from the enhancement of cellular immune response. It has also been found that selenium inhibits tumor cell proliferation. In addition, selenium alleviates the side effects of chemotherapy.

Other Uses

A 2016 study just published in Neurotoxicology shows that selenium may decrease the risk of ALS (Lou Gehrig's Disease) following a case-control study of 163 patients from the National Registry of Veterans with ALS and 229 matched control patients.

A hair rinse can be made from Indian Paintbrush, useful as a conditioner and to treat dandruff, and there are records of its use for this purpose by the Chippewa Indians. The most popular dandruff shampoos today contain selenium.

About toxicity

An excess of selenium in the diet causes chronic food poisoning symptoms such as vomiting, nausea, and diarrhea at a dose exceeding 850 µg/day. In most cases, humans and animals have low selenium levels as they don't receive enough from their diet.

Currently, many research centers in the world have been working on obtaining new food products that constitute sources of selenium. Indian Paintbrush is an excellent native source of this essential mineral.

Our native Indian Paintbrush is an excellent source of Selenium.

74

LEADPLANT

Prized by Native Americans, and Nothing to do with Lead

Another very nice plant with a misleading name, the leadplant *(amorpha canescens)* does not contain lead. There is an unfounded old myth that the plant grows in lead-laden grounds, causing the grayish tint to the leaves, which is not the case. The term canescens is a Latin term meaning "becoming grey."

A member of the pea family (fabaceae), the leadplant is native to North America. It is has tiny purple flowers with yellow stamens that bloom from May through August and alternate leaves that look like feathers. It is considered a hairy plant, because it is covered with protective fine, hair-like structures. It produces small pods which each contain one seed. Look for it in open woodlands and in fields and prairies.

Traditional Uses

Leadplant has been used by various Indian tribes to treat a variety of conditions. It has also been used as a smoking mixture when combined with buffalo fat.

Meskwaki Tribe

The Meskwaki used an infusion of leaves to kill pinworms and any intestinal worms. They also used an infusion of leaves to treat eczema.

Ojibwa Tribe

The Ojibwa valued the leadplant for its analgesic properties, and used a decoction of the root for stomach pain.

Omaha Tribe

The Omaha also used leadplant for pain, and applied a moxa of twigs for pain associated with neuralgia and rheumatism. For those not familiar with the term moxa, dried leaves of certain plants are added to a cone placed against the skin, which is then lighted to produce counter-irritation.

The Omaha also used dried, powdered leaves in cuts and open wounds.

Sickle Cell Disorder

Despite the extensive history of documented uses of leadplant by Indian Tribes, pharmaceutical research has been limited. One study published in June of 2016 investigated the use of leadplant in treating sickle cell disorder. It was observed that leaves were the most common plant part used, followed by root and stem bark in the preparation for sickle cell management.

Essential Oils

The leadplant yields an astounding 109 essential oils from the fruit and leaves, including pinene, myrcene, limonene and 3-Carene in the highest percentages. Most of the medicinal properties arise from the active ingredients in the essential oils.

Pinene

Pinene is the same aromatic compound found in conifers (think pine trees), and has several useful effects, including anti-microbial and anti-inflammatory.

Myrcene

Myrcene has a both analgesic and anti-inflammatory effects. It works by blocking pain-causing prostaglandin P2, and since its pain relieving effects can be blocked by naloxone, it likely stimulates release of our body's own opiates.

Limonene

Limonene has been used to promote weight loss, treat cancer, and is added to medicinal ointments to help them penetrate the skin to treat underlying tissues.

3-Carene

3-Carene has been found to be an effective anti-inflammatory. It has also been used to dry up runny noses and persistent menstrual flows.

Other Uses

An infusion of the dried leaves makes a pleasant tasting tea. There are no known side-effects.

Leadplant has tiny purple flowers with yellow stamens that bloom from May through August and alternate hairy leaves that look like feathers. Courtesy of Missouri Dept. of Conservation

75

BUTTERFLY MILKWEED: A FRIEND TO EVERYONE

It's pretty evident the Monarch Butterflies are in trouble. For many of us, it has been years since we've seen a Monarch, a common sight in our childhood. What has happened to the Monarchs? Scientists blame loss of the milkweed plant; host plant of the Monarch, on farming practices with genetically modified plants that render even the native plants infertile and herbicides that kill the plant itself.

Monarchs will soon be extinct without milkweed, as it is the only plant on which monarch butterflies lay their eggs, and the only food source for the larvae. Milkweed gets its name from the milky sap, which consists of a form of latex that contains several active compounds. The sap has a high dextrose content, and has been used as a sweetener.

Not only is milkweed critical for Monarch butterflies, it has unique healing properties for respiratory conditions, and has been used to treat many lung diseases since the 1800's, earning it the nickname Pleurisy root. The Latin name, *Asclepias tuberosa*, is taken from the Greek god of medicine and healing.

Medicinal Uses

Heart Disease

Milkweeds secrete latex containing cardiac glycosides that are medicinally valuable in the treatment of heart disease, and are similar to the cardiac drug digoxin, that strengthens and slows the heart, but can be toxic in high doses.

Skin regeneration

A 2011 study using an extract from the root of the milkweed plant caused normal human skin fibroblasts to proliferate. A fibroblast is a type of cell that builds the structural framework for skin and connective tissue, and these important cells play a critical role in wound healing.

Other Uses

A poultice of the roots can be used in treating swelling and skin ulcers. A poultice can also be applied to remove warts.

While the root is used for medicinal purposes, the aerial, or above ground parts of the plant have been used for both food and clothing. Milkweed pods are usually ready for picking in the fall. The soft seed fluff is warmer than goose down and has been used in bedding and pillows. The hollow, wax-covered milkweed filaments possess good insulation properties and have been used to make candlewicks, twine and fabric. In WWII, 5000 tons of milkweed floss was collected in the United States to substitute for kapok, a traditional insulation material. Milkweed is grown today for use in hypoallergenic pillows. Milkweed fibers have also been used to clean up oil spills due to their absorptive properties.

Precautions

Milkweed has been found to contain estrogen-like substances that can cause uterine contraction, so ingestion should be avoided in pregnant women. Large doses should always be avoided, as they can cause vomiting, diarrhea and heart problems.

How to Help the Monarch Butterfly

The best way to help the Monarch Butterfly is to plant milkweed in your yard or garden, and avoid spraying pesticides. Let's all help bring the

Monarch back for our children and grandchildren to enjoy!

To bring back the Monarch Butterfly, plant Butterfly Milkweed everywhere!

76

DOGBANE

Around the turn of the last Century, Dogbane *(apocynum cannabinum)* was an extremely popular apothecary offering. Credited with being the "most powerful diuretic known." dogbane was used to treat critical conditions such as congestive heart failure and pleural effusion, or fluid around the lungs.

Dogbane contains a chemical called cymarin in its roots. Cymarin is a cardiac stimulant with strong activity on the heart, similar to the plant digitalis that is used to make the drug Digoxin. Both dogbane and digitalis strengthen and slow the heart rate, but can be toxic in large doses. Dogbane was listed up until 1952 in the United States Pharmacopeia, but in the 1950s scientists at Merck and Searle introduced new pharmaceuticals, and the natural product disappeared from the literature.

Also known by the descriptive names, rheumatism root, wild cotton and Indian hemp, dogbane is a native perennial throughout the United States. The Latin name Apocynum means "stay away dogs," hence the common name dogbane.

The plant contains cannabinoids, but its properties are related to its use as a hemp-like fiber, rather than a psychoactive drug containing THC. Fiber obtained from the dogbane stem is a very high quality flax substitute that retains its shape and strength, even when wet. Native Americans used dogbane for twine, baskets, mats, clothing nets, fishing line and hunting bows by stripping the inner bark from the fresh plant, yielding fibers that can be twisted into 2-ply string. Dogbane fibers have been found at archeological digs in sites over 2000 years old. Dogbane stalks are so valuable for many uses that you can purchase them online for $1 apiece. Stalks are generally harvested in the fall when the aerial parts of the plant are less toxic. At this time, the stalk becomes stiff and can be cut close to the ground. The sap remains in the root.

Dogbane has several medicinal uses, primarily using the seeds, root and bark. The most active part of the plant medicinally is the fresh root, but due to potential toxicity must be used with great care, and only in small amounts. Major uses by Native Americans included rheumatism, coughs, asthma, and internal parasites. To treat cardiac problems, like a fast heart rate with low blood pressure, a weak tea made from the dried root has been used. The milky latex sap has also been applied to warts, and a poultice of leaves can be applied for rheumatism and to treat wounds.

Anticancer activity

A 2016 study reviewed the use of dogbane as a natural treatment for congestive heart failure. It works by binding to sodium and potassium in a way that makes the heart beat more efficiently. This same action affects tumor cells by causing the cell to die. The leaves, flesh, seeds and juices of dogbane contain the active substance cardenolide that has the capability of regulating cancer cell survival and death through multiple signaling pathways.

Other Uses

A form of latex can be squeezed from the plant, and if allowed to stand overnight can harden, making a form of chewing gum after being mixed with clean clay.

Dogbane can be planted in lead-contaminated areas to remove lead from soil and water, and accumulate it within the plant itself.

Dogbane plant growing along Sparrow Drive. The plant has a straight reddish color stalk and broad green leaves with smooth edges.

77

CHICORY – A PROBIOTIC WORTH EXPLORING

Chicory belongs to the dandelion family, and usually has bright blue flowers. It is common in much of North America, including Missouri, where over time it has become a native. A good forage plant for livestock, chicory is also good forage for us humans. Food uses include salad leaves or as a coffee substitute,

Wild Chicory can have a bitter taste, but cooking and discarding the water reduces the bitterness. Leaves can then be braised with garlic, onion, and bacon for a gourmet side dish, or used as a replacement for spinach in many dishes.

Nutrition

1 cup of chicory has 96 calories, 1.2 gm. of dietary fiber, 0.5 gm of protein, 33% of the RDA of Vit. A and 11% of the RDA for Vit. C.

Chicory Root

Not just the leaves of the chicory plant are valuable. The roots can be roasted and ground into a coffee substitute, or added to different coffee blends, especially popular with natives of New Orleans. During hard economic times, chicory was widely used as a coffee extender. In 1970, researchers discovered that chicory root contains up to 23% inulin. Inulin is a very valuable starch that has attained the GRAS (generally recognized as safe) status in USA and is found in about 36,000 species of plants, with chicory being the richest source.

Inulin

Inulin is used in the food industry as a natural sweetener with one tenth the sweetening power of table sugar. Inulin has the added advantage of being a probiotic, and also a good source of dietary fiber. When chicory root is roasted, the inulin caramelizes and converts to fruit sugar that counteracts the bitterness of the raw root, and also provides a rich, brown color. Chicory does not contain caffeine, but when brewed with coffee still results in a satisfying dark brown beverage.

Blood Sugar and Liver Function

Chicory has been found to have beneficial effects on blood sugar levels in diabetics, and also liver function. In a 2016 study looking at the effect of chicory on liver enzymes, calcium concentrations and blood pressure in patients with Type 2 diabetes, 46 diabetic female patients were randomly assigned into intervention (n=27) and control (n=22) groups. Subjects in the intervention group received a daily dose of 10 grams of chicory and subjects in the control group received a placebo for two months. At the end of the study, there were significant reductions in fasting serum glucose, Hb A_1C, and liver enzymes AST and ALP in the chicory-treated group. Systolic and diastolic blood pressures were also reduced in chicory-treated group. Serum calcium significantly increased after chicory supplementation but no change in placebo treated group occurred.

Eye Health

Chicory leaves are loaded with lutein and zeaxanthin, carotenoids that support eye health.
The Nurses' Health Study that followed over 100,000 nurses since 1989 found that the need for cataract surgery declined by almost 25% in women over the age of 45 who had adequate amounts of lutein and zeaxanthin in their diet.
Prevention of Skin Damage

A 2016 study looked at the effect of chicory as a cosmetic ingredient to prevent skin damage. They concluded that chicory root extract showed protective and restructuring effects on the skin and stands out as an innovative ingredient to improve skin barrier function.

Internal Parasites

Chicory root is well known for effect on internal parasites, and use as a livestock forage can decrease the need for wormer. Chicory can actually be substituted for oats in horse feed due to the protein and fat content.

Other Uses

Extracts of chicory flower are popular in Europe, and it is used as a tonic. The Cherokee Indians used the root extract as a nerve tonic.

Chicory is added to Alpo dog food, and there is a patent on is use as "a method for improving activity in a pet; especially elderly cats and dogs." The positive effect is attributed mainly to the probiotic activity of inulin contained in the plant.

In summer and fall, the blue flowers of chicory are easy to spot along the roadsides

78

HOPTREE

A Native Plant With Some of the Benefits of Ginseng

While walking along Sherrill Creek in north east Texas County, I spotted a unique tree, the ptelea trifoliatea, or common hoptree. Sometimes called wafer ash because of its wafer-like seed coverings, it is a deciduous tree that grows up to 26 feet and bears flowers and winged fruit. The plant got the name hoptree after 19th century German immigrants used its seed instead of hops to make beer.

Winged fruits, also called *samaras*, are of interest to children everywhere, and are either helicopters (double-winged) or flutterers (single-winged). Is there any child on earth who has not played with a "helicopter" from a maple tree, watching it make its fluttering way in the wind? The seed can be either in the center of the wing, as in the case of the hoptree; or on one side, making the seed rotate as it falls, as is the case with the maple tree. Having seeds packed in an aerodynamic covering helps the plant with seed dispersal, and ensures survival of its species. The amazing design of the samara with their proven aerodynamic capabilities has been the inspiration for many aviation patents.

The hoptree is a native here in Missouri, although not very plentiful. Unfortunately, the hoptree is endangered in New Jersey, New York, and Pennsylvania, and is considered a rare species in Canada. It likes to grow in sandy soil, on the more open side of creeks and streams, exactly where I found it.

Medicinal uses

The medicinal uses of hoptree come from the many chemical components of the plant. Native American tribes used hoptree extracts as a general health cure-all or tonic. Like ginseng, the hoptree is one of only a few plants that are considered to improve the functioning of all the body systems. Hoptrees have also been found to have properties that make other medicines more effective, and have not been shown to have any adverse effects.

Listed in King's American Dispensatory in 1898, hoptree extract was recommended for use after prolonged fever and cases debility where tonics are indicated. It was also listed in the American Pharmacopoeia from 1878 to 1941. Hoptree was often recommended for the treatment of asthma. It was also touted as a permanent cure for erysipelatous inflammation, an acute, febrile infectious disease caused by a form of streptococcus, resulting in diffusely spreading deep-red inflammation of the skin or mucous membranes. It is also used in chronic rheumatism.

The most frequently reported medicinal properties include the appetite stimulating and fever reducing properties of root bark, used in Louisiana before the introduction of quinine for these same indications. The root bark has also been shown to have some anti-malarial and anti-tuberculosis properties.

Hoptree is currently used in the treatment of gastric disorders like irritable bowel syndrome due to its ability to reduce spasms. It can be found online in homeopathic preparations from France, where it is widely used. It is a popular natural remedy throughout Eastern Europe and India.

Essential Oils

The leaf essential oils of the hoptree plant can be isolated by water distillation. The most abundant essential oil components obtained from the leaf are myrcene (an anti-inflammatory) and phellandrene (used in fragrances). The bark contains at least three active constituents, a powerful volatile oil, a salt, acrid resin, and an alkaloid: Berberine (a compound that benefits diabetes and metabolic syndrome). The alkaloid Arginine that reduces healing time and helps decrease blood pressure is also present in the root.

Dosage

The dose of the powdered bark is 10 to 30 grains. The infusion of the bark is taken by tablespoon three or four times daily.

If you are fortunate enough to have a hoptree on your place, treasure and take care of it. The hoptree is also host plant of the giant swallowtail butterfly, Papilio cresphontes.

Hoptree, also called wafer ash, grows on sandy banks along streams. It produces winged fruits in a paper-like samara.

79

ALOE VERA

While not a native Missouri plant, Aloe Vera is so important in the medical world it is a definite must in your herbal pharmacy. It is unclear where Aloe Vera originated, as it has been cultivated throughout the world. In the United States, it is naturalized in Florida, Arizona and Texas. The first authentic record of *Aloe* as a plant with healing properties was found on a Mesopotamian clay tablet dated at 2100 BC. Aloe was officially listed as a purgative and skin protectant by the U.S. pharmacopoeia in 1820 and was clinically used in the 1930s for the treatment of radiotherapy burns to the skin and mucous membranes. Aloe Vera remains an important traditional medicine in many countries.

There are 420 species of Aloe, with Aloe Vera considered to be the most biologically active of the varieties. More than 75 potentially active constituents have been identified in the plant. The familiar gel is produced by the inner part of the plant leaves. The gel itself provides nutrients such as vitamins A, C and E, minerals and amino acids. A 2005 study showed that Aloe Vera gel also enhances vitamin C and E's bioavailability in the body. It is thought that Aloe taken along with these vitamins acts by protecting against their degradation in the intestinal tract. There is also evidence that if co-administered, Aloe may also enhance the absorption of other poorly absorbed drugs.

Antibacterial

The antibacterial efficacy of Aloe is attributed to its property of inhibiting protein synthesis in bacterial cells. It also has moisturizing actions, wound healing, and anti-inflammatory effects. The bacteria *S. pyogenes* and *S. faecalis* are inhibited by Aloe Vera gel and it is bactericidal against *Pseudomonas aeruginosa*, actually killing the bacteria.

Dental applications

Aloe has several dental uses, and has been used to apply to the sites of periodontal surgery or when gum tissues have been traumatized, scratched, or burned. Lesions in the mouth, such as ulcers, canker sores or herpes lesions are improved by the direct application of Aloe. Denture wearers with a sore mouth due to ill-fitting dentures can benefit from Aloe due to its soothing, anti-inflammatory properties and protection against bacterial growth.

Reducing blood glucose and lipids

A 1985 study involving 5000 patients ages 35-65 with heart disease, 3167 of which were Type-2 diabetics, found preliminary evidence to suggest that oral administration of Aloe Vera might be effective in reducing blood glucose in diabetic patients and in lowering blood lipid levels. Marked reductions were noted in serum cholesterol, triglycerides, and total lipid levels, along with an increase in HDL (good) cholesterol. All but 177 of the diabetic patients demonstrated a normalization of fasting and postprandial blood glucose levels that enabled them to go off medication by the end of 2 months of therapy.

In the first of two related clinical trials, 72 diabetic women without drug therapy were administered one tablespoon of Aloe Vera gel or placebo for 6 weeks. Blood glucose and serum triglyceride levels were significantly decreased with Aloe Vera treatment, although cholesterol concentrations were unaffected

Wound Healing

The first case report of the beneficial effects of *Aloe Vera* in the treatment of skin and wound healing was published in 1935, with fresh whole-leaf extract reported to provide rapid relief from the itching and burning associated with severe radiation dermatitis and complete skin regeneration. A 2007 review of Aloe Vera use in burns concluded, "Cumulative evidence tends to support that Aloe Vera might be an effective intervention used in burn wound healing for first to second degree burns."

Topical application of Aloe Vera may also be effective for genital herpes and psoriasis. In a randomized, double-blind, controlled trial of Aloe Vera or placebo cream in 60 patients with chronic psoriasis, the cure rate in the Aloe group was 83% (with no relapses at 12 months of follow-up) compared to only 7% in the placebo group

Using the duration of wound healing as an outcome measure, the meta-analysis of the efficacy of Aloe Vera in burn wound healing concluded that Aloe Vera treatments reduced healing time by approximately 9 days compared to conventional treatment groups

80

GMOS EXPLAINED

At every turn, labeling of GMO (genetically modified) food is being derailed. In an extensive review of the literature, studies on the safety of GM plants and food products are very scarce, with most of the research dedicated to ways to modify public perception of genetically modified foods. Of the few very short-term safety studies conducted, mostly by biotechnology companies promoting GMOs, no safety problems have been identified. The problem remains that no long-term studies have been completed.

Definition

The term GMO is commonly used to refer to crop plants; especially soybeans, corn, rice and wheat, created for human consumption after being genetically modified in the laboratory. Genetic modification is achieved by inserting genes from other plants and non-plant organisms into the target plant.

In 2012, California could have been the first state in the U.S. to require labeling of genetically modified foods, but after Monsanto spent 44 million to defeat the measure at the polls, it failed. One might wonder, if GMOs are so great, wouldn't companies want to declare that on the label? In another failed promise, while campaigning in 2007, Barak Obama promised to require labeling of GMOs if elected. Since then, labeling initiatives have also failed in Oregon and Colorado. In an effort to head off further GMO labeling initiatives, in March of this year a bill to outlaw state GMO labeling passed the senate committee to which it was assigned.

Human health risks

GMOs also huge risk of fatal food allergies. When introducing a new gene into a food, there is always the danger of causing unexpected allergic reactions, another reason why labeling is important – to protect those with severe food allergies.

Cancer

Animal toxicity studies with certain GM foods, especially Bt corn, have shown that they may toxically affect several organs and systems. The results of most studies with GM foods in animals indicate that they may cause some common toxic effects such as hepatic, pancreatic, renal, or reproductive effects and may alter the hematological, biochemical, and immunologic parameters.

Harm to other organisms

A laboratory study published in the journal Nature showed that pollen from Bt corn caused high mortality rates in monarch butterfly caterpillars, an at-risk species. While Bt corn is insect resistant, it kills many species of larvae indiscriminately.

Gene Transfer

Genetically modified plants have been known to cross breed, carrying pesticide resistance into the weeds. Genetically modified genes can also travel over into normal crops planted nearby. Cross pollination readily occurs, as demonstrated by the fact Monsanto has filed hundred of patent infringements lawsuits, demanding royalties from farmers who now have the unwanted genetically modified genes in their crops due to cross-pollination.

The Terminator Gene

Although there is plenty of evidence that "suicide" seeds exist, there is no documentation that the technology is currently in use. The sterile or "suicide" seeds are produced by means of genetic use restriction technology, which makes crops die off after one harvest without producing offspring. As a result, farmers have to buy new seeds for each planting, which reduces their self-sufficiency and makes them dependent on major seed and chemical companies.

Bt Corn

Bt Corn has been genetically altered to contain the Bt endotoxin, highly effective at killing insects that can damage corn. Virtually all corn, with the exception of popcorn, has been genetically modified.

A study in the Journal of American Science showed that Bt corn proved fatal to rats that were fed the corn for only 91 days. In other studies, a GMO corn diet caused changes in organ weight and blood chemistry. Researchers found clear signs of damage to liver, kidneys and small intestines of rats fed GMO corn. Bt corn also has a negative effect on the foundation of sperm cells and male fertility.

A study published in the International Journal of Biological Science found the Bt corn mainly affects kidney and liver function of rats, but could also result in changes in the heart, adrenals, spleen and blood cells. The researchers raised concern that since GMOs have never before been part of the human or animal diets, the health consequences for those that consume them over long periods are unknown.

Another study published in Reproductive Toxicology found that 93% of pregnant women and 80% of their unborn fetuses had Bt toxin in their blood samples.

Action

Choose organic (look for the USDA Organic label), eat fresh, and check the ingredients. Also, since GMO labeling has been subverted, many organic producers are labeling their products non-GMO.

81

ROSE GENTIAN

Those lovely pink bouquets that are popping up around the county this month are rose gentian, *sabata angularis*, also called rose pink or bitter bloom. A biennial native, they flower and produce seed in their second year, then die, meaning the flowers you see today won't be in the same place next year. The plant grows sporadically, and is sometimes hard to locate.

The name Gentian is a tribute to Gentius, an Illyrian king who is thought to have discovered tonic properties in plants from the Gentianaceae family. The term *Sabata* in the name may come from a legend that Pilgrims arriving in Massachusetts first saw the flower on the Sabbath, and thereafter used it to decorate their church. More likely however, the plant genus was named in honor of Liberato Sabbati, an Italian botanist from the 18th century.

Rose Gentian in an upright plant, growing from 2 to 3 feet tall, with opposite oval green leaves. It grows in clumps, with several plants together, resembling a bouquet. The flowers have 5 petals with a distinct yellow-green pentagonal center, with five protruding yellow stamens. It grows in open woods, fields and prairies, and along roadsides. Flowers are usually pink, but there is also a white variety.

The USDA website lists *Sabatia angularis* as threatened in Michigan and endangered in New York. It is also rare in eastern Kansas, and virtually unknown in the western United States.

Medicinal uses

The root of the plant can be used for medical purposes, and is most often made into a herbal tea used as a tonic with mild stimulating properties. Traditional applications include use as a digestive to treat dyspepsia and aid in digestion. It has also been used to treat fevers, high blood pressure, muscle spasms, sinusitis, rheumatism, gout, malaria and intestinal worms. A warm infusion is said to promote menstrual flow.

Rose Gentian, like most herbs in the Gentianaceae family, is considered a bitter, a class of natural preparations used to increase appetite. It is reported to mainly affect the stomach, gallbladder and spleen, and helps to maintain the portal circulation (the blood supply from the liver to the intestines).

Other Uses

Several beverages are made with gentian root, including some distilled alcoholic beverages, and it is a common flavor used in after-dinner liqueurs in Germany, valued for its digestive properties.

You made have heard the term gentian violet, which is a manufactured chemical dye that doesn't come from plants but does have antibacterial, antifungal and anthelmintic uses.

Dosage and Preparation

The plant is best when harvested in full bloom. When used as a bitter, a liquid extract is made by infusing one ounce of the root in a pint of hot water with a fluid ounce taken every 2 – 3 hours.

The unmistakable pink flowers of rose gentian with a pentagonal green center.

82

THE POWER OF POSITIONING

When discussing natural cures, sometimes the simplest things are overlooked. One of these is body position.

I've been interested in body position since the early 1990's, when I did my master's thesis on the effect of position on oxygen saturation in the body. By simply changing position, you can boost your oxygen level by up to 30%, an intervention that can be critical in a person with lung disease. Even healthy people have higher oxygen levels when laying on their right side, due to the fact you have one extra lung lobe on the right with more oxygen carrying capability. For folks with a bad lung on one side, the rule is "good lung down," so laying on the side with the healthier lung, or even on your stomach will raise the oxygen level in your blood.

Another time when body position can be used to your benefit is with certain types of pain. Last week a friend contacted me with severe pain under her left rib cage. She had been to 2 urgent care centers which were closed, and asked me if I could make a suggestion. Before going to the Emergency Room, I suggested she try the knee chest position, which consists of lying on your stomach, with knees tucked under your chest and bottom in the air for 10 minutes. She did this, and her pain was relieved. Why did this work? Often pain in the left abdominal area is due to a gas pocket. The knee chest position helps the gas to move along, taking pressure off sensitive nerves.

Gas pains can also be felt in the collarbone region. This is called Kehr's sign, caused by irritation of the diaphragm that travels along the phrenic nerve to the shoulder region. The phenomenon is due to referred pain, and is actually fairly common. When using the knee chest position, pain is usually relieved in less than 10 minutes.

Sometimes abdominal pain is due to a prior surgery or a pulled muscle, or the person is unable to get into the knee chest position. Simply placing a pillow under the knees will take pressure off the abdominal muscles and give relief.

Splinting can be used along with position. With a shoulder injury, placing a small folded pad of blanket in about a two-foot square below the affected scapula while lying on your back will give instant pain relief. There are a lot of moving parts in a shoulder joint, and this helps to keep them stable.

Lower back pain is a fairly common problem. At its worst, it is accompanied by spasms. An acupressure technique to relieve spasms in the lower back consists of lying on your back, with knees in the air and bent, and using the fingertips of both hands to apply pressure behind both knees for 1 – 2 minutes. This is especially effective for pain due to spasms.

Another common condition that responds to simple positioning is a crick in the neck. Anyone who has ever awakened with a stiff neck knows just how uncomfortable it is. This problem is often caused by sleeping on too many pillows, or with your neck in an awkward position, and usually responds on its own in a few days. You can hasten the healing process by sleeping on your back with only one flat pillow, with the bottom of the pillow at the level of your shoulders, preventing your neck from being flexed.

These are simple things you can try at home if you encounter any of these problems. Of course, for ongoing issues that don't resolve quickly, you should see your health care provider.

83

EASTERN RED CEDAR

It has been estimated that at least 25 percent of pharmaceuticals are made from plants (I think the percentage is much higher), but less than 2 percent of all plants have been evaluated for their medicinal properties. There is a great deal of basic research consisting of scientific inquiry into the active components of plants, but actually very little utilization of plants to treat specific diseases. With that being said, every plant is precious, and potentially a lifesaver. Although some plants are admittedly noxious, like spotted knapweed, if a species becomes extinct, we could be losing one of God's gifts to mankind. On the World Health Organization list of Essential Medicines, podophyllotoxin, one of the components in Eastern Red Cedar, is listed as one of the most important medications needed in a basic health system.

In a previous article, we discussed Juniper berries; an entity unto themselves. Eastern Red Cedar is one of the trees that produce the berries, but the tree itself has so much more to offer. Eastern Red Cedar (Juniperus virginiana) is a valuable source of extracts and oils that provide decay resistance against termites and wood decay fungi, one of the reasons that cedar is utilized to make long lasting tomato stakes and fence posts. Cedar trees are also tolerant of cold temperatures, diseases and pollution.

Extracts

Extracts from Red Cedar have important commercial value and have been used extensively to make alcoholic and nonalcoholic beverages, frozen desserts, baked goods, and to process meat products. The main essential oils in cedar wood oil are pinene, phellandrene, caryophyllene, safrole and cubebene. Red Cedar also yields significant amounts of podophyllotoxin (PPT). The other major source of PPT is found in May Apples, harvested commercially by pharmaceutical companies, placing them on the verge of extinction. Podophyllotoxin is so valuable that the USDA is developing resources to protect and increase May Apple crops and alternatively develop better extraction methods for the chemical from Red Cedar. Red Cedar has lower concentrations of the valuable chemical, but is much more readily available.

Podophyllotoxin

Podophyllotoxin can be extracted from the roots and leaves (needles) of the Red Cedar. Under the trade names Condylox, a gel; Podofilox, a solution; and Wartec, a solution or cream, it is used on the skin to treat genital warts caused by human papillomavirus, and also other warts. PPT has many other medical applications including use as purgative, vesicant, antirheumatic, antiviral, and antitumor agent. Etoposide and teniposide are PPT derivatives with significant anticancer activity used in various chemotherapies, including lung cancer, lymphomas, and genital tumors. Etoposide has proven effective in the treatment of several types of cancers that don't respond to other agents. New patents were filed in 2015 in an attempt to isolate more medically active substances from PPT, that will likely result in increased demand for the product.

Other Uses

Anti-inflammatory

In Turkey, essential oils from Red Cedar are used to treat rheumatism, bronchitis, cough, fungal infections and hemorrhoids. The traditional use of Red Cedar extract in the treatment of rheumatism was validated in a 2013 study that found it to have significant anti-inflammatory activity.

Biomonitor

Eastern Red Cedar has been used a biomonitor in polluted areas due to its ability to uptake heavy metals, including Cadmium, Chromium, mercury and lead from the soil.

Insect Repellent

Cedar wood oil made from the heartwood, center of the plant, is an agent that can be used to protect wood from insects and microbes, as a mosquito and cockroach repellent. To extract the essential oil, sapwood is removed using a band saw, and then the trimmed heartwood is turned into sawdust and held in a sealed jar prior to steam extraction.

Cautions

Podophyllotoxin lotions or gels should be used during pregnancy because these medications can be harmful to the fetus.

84

SKULLCAP – POSITIVE EFFECTS ON SLEEP AND MOOD

Skullcap (*scutellaria* species) has been extensively used in traditional medicine in Asia, Europe and North America. A perennial plant, the above ground parts are used to make medicine, and are collected during the summer while plant is in full bloom, dried and then stored for later processing.

The nickname skullcap comes from the calyx at the base of the flowers that resembles a helmet, while the generic name comes from the Latin scutella, (little dish). The leaves are opposite with scalloped or saw-toothed edges, heart shaped at the base of the plant. The blue to lavender flowers typically bloom from May to August, and have a distinctive hooded tube shape with upper and lower lips. In the early 19th Century, the plant was referred to a mad dog skullcap, as it once was considered a cure for rabies.

Skullcap has proven to be a powerful medicinal herb. The chemicals in skullcap are thought to work by preventing inflammation and spasm. It has been used to reduce fever. It is used to treat several disorders of the nervous system, including seizures, insomnia, anxiety, delirium tremors and withdrawal from benzodiazepines and barbiturates.

Demand for skullcap in world markets appears to be growing. Harvesting and sales of the herb increased by 250% from 1997 to 2001 and between 2000 and 2001 the increase was 23%. The increase in demand continues at about 30% per year, and is believed to be due to its preference as a sedative alternative to kava kava, which, due to toxicity fears, is no longer widely used. An online search will return results for buyers of skullcap – making it a good plant for those with home-based herb businesses.

Food Allergies

A 2014 study examined the effect of skullcap on food allergies. Food allergy symptoms can include itching, vomiting, and diarrhea, and can even be lethal in some sensitive individuals. In one study where skullcap was taken by mouth every day for 17 days, food allergy symptoms were significantly decreased.

Rabies

When researching skullcap, references to its use as a cure for rabies surface. In the late 1700's, Dr. Lawrence Van Derveer used skullcap as a treatment for rabies, with Dr. Joseph Bates reporting in an 1855 edition of the Boston Medical Journal that Van Derveer was believed to have cured more that 300 people of canine madness." Following these claims, skullcap was thoroughly tested as a cure for rabies and was found to be completely useless.

Anxiety and Related Disorders

The most prominent use of skullcap is as a "nervine," an agent that acts on the nervous system. This may explain its effectiveness in the treatment of some seizures, especially the non-epileptic type "pseudo-seizures" that are anxiety-based. Skullcap contains small quantities of the substances melatonin and serotonin, explaining both its effect on sleep and mood.

Physical symptoms of anxiety include pallor, sweating, hyperventilation, irritable bowel, trouble swallowing, heart palpitations, nausea, muscle tension and back pain. Anxiety sufferers may also be easily fatigued and/or experience sleep problems. Treatments for anxiety often include the use of benzodiazepines or barbiturates, both of which are very addicting and can have serious side effects.

In 2012, a study with 31 subjects titled, "American skullcap: a study of its effects on mood in healthy volunteers," was conducted to validate the use of skullcap for anxiety.

Participants in the study kept diaries, and one study participant reported after just 5 days of taking skullcap capsules, "I felt more sociable, not anxious - not worried about anything. I had no panic attacks. I felt good even though I was ill with a cold, I had problems at work and my boyfriend was away. My mind was not racing and I was thinking clearer.'

Perhaps the most important finding from the participant diary results was the finding of resolution of chronic symptoms of longstanding conditions such as allergies, IBS, muscle pain and premenstrual symptoms.

Study researchers concluded that skullcap "had significant anxiety reducing and mood enhancing effects on some people. Also significant was the lack of toxicity, adverse reactions or definite side effects that could be attributed to the herb and the fact there were no rebound reactions such as tolerance, dependability or excitability. This lack of harmful or unpleasant effects is central to the clinical efficacy of an anxiolytic."

Precautions

In the 1970s and 1980s there were reports of liver damage from use of skullcap. The cause of hepatotoxicity was subsequently attributed to Teucrium being used in some European commercial preparations in place of skullcap. Any herbal preparation should be used with extreme caution in pregnant women.

Skullcap is a distinctive plant with its hooded lavender flowers and saw toothed leaves.

85

BLACK EYED SUSAN – NOT JUST A PRETTY FACE

In Missouri, black-eyed Susan, Rudbeckia hirta, is a native plant found in all 48 of the contiguous states in the U.S. Several Indian tribes discovered early on the medicinal uses of the plant, including making a tea from the root to treat worms and colds and an external wash or poultice to treat earaches, sores, snakebites and swelling. While typically the aerial parts are used in medications, a juice made from the root was used to treat earaches.

A popular biennial garden plant in the sunflower family, black-eyed Susan grows well along roadsides as well as in gardens. The plant grows 2-3 ft tall, with hirsute (hairy) leaves. In the summer and fall, it displays yellow ray flowers and brownish purple disk flowers. The plant reproduces by seed and grows in many kinds of soil.

Nutrition

Parts of the plant have nutritional value. In a 2008 study of 10 native prairie species, including 5 grasses, 3 legumes and 2 forbs, Black-eyed Susan yielded the most biomass with crude protein levels high enough to maintain non lactating cows, and adequate concentration of eleven different minerals, only lacking in sodium.

Anti-viral effects

A 2011 study looked at the anti-viral effects of black-eyed Susan. The plant contains chlorogenic acids (CGA's), including quinic acid and cinnamic acid, that have a variety of biological activities like antioxidant, anti-inflammatory, anti-HIV, anti-HBV and inhibition of mutagenesis and carcinogenesis, and are considered to be beneficial to human health.

The study found high levels of CGA's present in the leaves of black-eyed Susan, thought to provide a scientific basis for its antiviral properties.

Antibacterial

According to a 2010 study, extracts of black-eyed Susan had significant inhibitory effect on microorganisms including Kelebsiella pneumoniae, Staphylococcus aureus, Pseudomonas aeruginosa, Escherichia coli, Bacillus anthracis and Streptococcus pyogene. Methanol and ethanol extracts produced a stronger antibacterial product in comparison to aqueous extract.

Anti-inflammatory

In 2013, a new substance called redbeckolide was isolated from the flowers of black-eyed Susan, and the result provided partial evidence for the usage of the plant as an effective traditional medicine. Rudbeckolide was found to be a potent 5-LOX inhibitor, similar to the cox-2 inhibitors that block inflammation in tissues. Colds, earaches, sores and snakebites are examples of inflammatory conditions in which the juice, tea and other preparations of black-eyed Susan have been used traditionally to treat.

Dye-making

A popular biennial garden plant, black eyed susan grows well along roadsides as well as in gardens. The flowers, leaves and stems can be used to achieve olive and green and gold colors in wool yarns. Experts recommend keeping the flowers and herbage separate to achieve different ranges of color, using the flowers only or flowers and herbage together.

86

ARNICA – GREAT FOR PETS AND PEOPLE ALIKE

Arnica Montana, commonly called Arnica, is one of the best anti-inflammatory substances available in nature. Prevalent in Canada, Siberia and Europe, Arnica also grows in the northern United States, and can be cultivated in Missouri.

I first became familiar with Arnica as a component of a homeopathic medication I frequently use, called Traumeel©. Made by the Heel Corporation for over 60 years in Germany, Traumeel consists of 12 natural ingredients, including milfoil, monkshood, belladonna, calendula, 2 varieties of echinacea, witch hazel, hepar sulfuris, St. John's Wort, mercurius and comfrey in addition to arnica montana (mountain Arnica) Traumeel comes in pill, ointment and liquid form.

While all these components have healing properties, when they are combined together, they work synergistically, making the preparation so effective that is the only homeopathic medication listed in the PDR (Physician's Desk Reference.)

The problem with Traumeel comes from the fact it can be difficult to obtain, requiring paying custom fees when importing from Germany. With a little patience and ingenuity, you can make your own! The next several columns will deal with the components of this healing medication.

Arnica has been in use for centuries, especially used externally to treat bruises and sprains. The medicinal properties come from the flowers of the plant. When applied as an ointment, Arnica increases blood supply to the area, stimulating the circulation and bringing healing, oxygenated blood to damaged tissue. There is recent evidence that when taken internally, it is beneficial for the heart and immune system, and there is some evidence it slows the heart rate. Applied topically, arnica also decreases bruising and hastens the reabsorption of hematomas.

Given initially for shock, injury and pain, arnica is hard to beat. I have used it successfully in several instances to treat my animals. In one case a snake bit my dog, making two puncture wounds in her nose causing swelling making it difficult for her to breathe. (Of course, these problems always happen on Sunday evening with no vet available.) I was able to get several drops of arnica extract down her throat, and in hours the swelling resolved and she was resting and breathing comfortably. More recently, a colt jumped the fence, cutting a back leg on the barbed wire. I added several drops of arnica extract to his feed, and the next morning the swelling was greatly decreased and he was walking and grazing without difficulty.

Coronary Artery Disease

A study published in February 2016 documented the effect of Arnica on reducing cardiovascular events in patients with stable coronary disease. The study included 44 patients, (31 males and 13 females) with coronary artery disease. 25 patients were treated with aspirin or Plavix plus a statin drug, and for the other 18 subjects, Arnica was added to the standard protocol. The primary outcome was to evaluate the incidence of acute coronary syndrome, out-of-hospital cardiac arrest, or ischemic stroke. Results: Researchers found in the group of patients (18) who received the standard therapeutic protocol plus Arnica, only one cardiovascular event occurred (5.6%), while in the group treated only with standard therapy 4 events were recorded in 25 patients (16%). Researchers concluded that Arnica in combination with standard therapies is effective in reducing the incidence of cardiovascular events in patients with stable coronary artery disease.

Continued next week...

87

ARNICA – PART 2

Last week we discussed the use of Arnica for cardiovascular events. Arnica has several other proven applications, including treatment of pain and inflammation, and has even proven effective against some fairly rare diseases.

Most of Arnica's anti-inflammatory and pain-relieving properties are attributed to its thymol derivatives. Thymol helps to dilate capillaries, helping to bring oxygenated blood to injured tissue. Arnica has also been found to stimulate white blood cells that act as macrophages, cleaning up trapped blood and other fluids from joints and muscles.

Amaurosis

Arnica has been documented in the Materia Medica and Therapeutics as a successful treatment for amaurosis; a temporary loss of vision in one eye caused by decreased blood flow to the retina.

Pain and inflammation

A review article published in Jan. 2016 in the American Journal of Therapeutics looked at the use of Arnica in the treatment of several inflammatory conditions in pain management and postoperative settings. The authors concluded that Arnica montana is more effective than placebo when used for the treatment of several conditions including post-traumatic and postoperative pain, edema, and bruising.

In March 2016, a study was conducted to investigate the effects of topically applied Arnica and treatment on the regression of postoperative edema and ecchymosis in patients who had undergone a rhinoplasty (nose job). One hundred eight patients were included in the study and the study authors' results suggested that a rapid regression of edema and ecchymosis might be achieved by local treatments of arnica and mucopolysaccharide polysulfate cream.

Arnica after knee surgery

In a study conducted in the year 2000, concentrated Arnica 30x was applied after artificial knee joint replacement resulting in a 50% decrease in post-operative swelling.

Growing Arnica in Missouri

Arnica montana is an endangered medicinal plant species in Europe. Studies are underway to find ways to introduce more plants overseas, as Arnica is one of the most important plants used in natural medicine. When starting from seed, it can take 2 years to grow Arnica to the flowering stage, so it is wise to start with seedlings. If you want to grow it in the home garden, you'll need to be in a cool climate zone (USDA cooler zones of 5 to 9), making Missouri ideal.

Safety

In regular doses, up to 30 times concentrated, Arnica is considered safe. The reader may recall when Alexa Ray Joel (daughter of singer Billy Joel) overdosed on medication. She actually overdosed on Traumeel tablets, containing Arnica. She was hospitalized as a precaution, but no ill effects were noted. There are reports in the literature of death being caused by two ounces of tincture of arnica.

How to Make Arnica Oil

The highest content of volatile oils is found in the flower heads of the Arnica plant. Flower heads should be harvested in full bloom, and then dried.

Pure arnica essential oil is made via steam distillation or CO_2 extraction, and is expensive, approximately $7.50 per ounce. The good news is that you can easily make your own. Here's a step-by-step process from Annie's Remedy:

Materials:
• Dried and coarsely ground arnica blossoms
• Olive oil
• Mason jar
• Bottle

Procedure:
1. Fill the mason jar with arnica flowers and olive oil. Make sure there is enough oil to completely cover the herbs, but leave enough room for expansion.
2. Infuse it with a slow and steady heat for two to three weeks. You can put it in a place with sunlight or use an oven with pilot light on.
3. Strain the oil, and pour into a clean bottle for use.

To prolong the infused oil's shelf life, add a teaspoon of rosemary antioxidant or citric acid.

Dosing: 1/4 to 10 drops

88

COMFREY – THE BONE KNITTING PLANT

Comfrey *(Symphytum officinale)* is another popular plant used in natural medicine with an impressive record. A perennial herb, comfrey is native to Europe, but has been naturalized to North America, and can be easily grown in Missouri.

In Europe, comfrey has the nicknames knitbone or boneset. Its Latin name *Symphytum* comes from the word *symphis*, meaning the process of bones growing together. In addition to treating painful muscle and joint complaints, Comfrey has also been used to treat bronchial problems, ulcers, severe burns, acne and other skin conditions.

Two of its main components, namely allantoin and rosmarinic acid, are likely responsible for the healing effects of comfrey. Allantoin stimulates cell growth and repair while depressing inflammation, and can assist in callus formation as a broken bone heals. It also strongly promotes the cell growth in connective tissues such as tendons and ligaments. In addition, comfrey contains 18 amino acids (the building blocks of protein), vitamins A, B, and C, calcium, potassium, iron, sulfur, copper and selenium, steroidal saponins, ellagic acid and inulin.

Due to the allantoin content, comfrey has a moisturizing and keratolytic effect, acting to increase the water content of the skin and improving the removal of upper layers of dead skin cells which increases the smoothness of the skin and promotes wound healing.

Rosmarinic acid possesses antioxidant, antiviral, and anti-inflammatory effects. Extract of comfrey root has shown microbial activity against

Escherichia coli and Salmonella.

Medicinal uses

Comfrey root extract preparations are marketed in more than ten countries. Multiple clinical trials have been conducted to show the efficacy of comfrey root extract in treating bone and joint ailments.

Back Pain

In a double blind, placebo-controlled multi-center hospital study, 120 patients with acute upper or lower back pain were treated with comfrey root extract applied externally vs. a placebo. Patients were treated 4 times a day, with 4 gram per application. The results showed a significant treatment difference in those treated with comfrey. Pain intensity decreased on average approximately 95.2% in the comfrey extract group. For the first time, a fast-acting effect of comfrey ointment was noted. At 1 hour after application, pain had already decreased 33%.

Osteoarthritis

In another study that included 220 patients with painful osteoarthritis of the knee, 2 grams of comfrey ointment was applied three times daily for 21 days. The study showed significant improvement in four measures – Pain at rest and on movement, quality of life, knee mobility and joint circumference.

Ankle Sprain

In another clinical study involving 184 patients with unilateral ankle sprains, a 6 cm long layer of Comfrey ointment was applied to the ankles of half of the patients, with diclofenac gel applied to the other half. After 7 days of treatment, a 95% improvement was found in the comfrey treatment group, with a corresponding improvement of 85% in the diclofenac group.

Precautions

In 2001, the FDA issued a ban of comfrey products marketed for internal use, and a warning label for those intended for external use. In addition to restrictions on oral use, some experts recommend applying comfrey extracts no longer than 10 days in a row, and no more than 4–6 weeks a year. These concerns are due to pyrrolizidine contained in the plant that has been associated with liver toxicity.

*Comfrey root extract cream has been shown to be safe for use in children at the same dosage used for adults.

Home made Comfrey Oil

Ingredients

8 oz. washed, dried and chopped comfrey root
Olive oil to cover

Put chopped comfrey in to a glass container, preferably dark. Cover with olive oil, and shake jar daily for approximately 3 weeks. Strain the mixture into a clean container. (Used WASHED dryer cloths make great straining cloths!)

89

BELLADONNA

Atropa belladonna, also known as deadly nightshade, is not native to United States but can be grown here. In the late 1970's and early 1980's, belladonna was commonly used in hospitals in the form of a suppository – the "B & O" (belladonna and opium) suppository. Today this anti-spasm medicine is considered toxic, but as Paracelsus stated, "the dose makes the poison."

The root, leaves and berries of the plant all contain compounds used in pharmaceuticals, including atropine, hyoscyamine and scopolamine. In natural medicine, the leaf is most commonly used as it is considered safer than the more potent root. The seeds and fruit should be avoided due to the potency. The name belladonna comes from the Italian "pretty woman," because atropine in the plant causes the pupils to dilate.

Atropine

Atropine has many medicinal uses. It is given prior to surgery to dry up oral secretions and used in cardiology to increase the heart rate. Atropine drops are used in ophthalmology to dilate the pupils.

Hyoscyamine

Hyoscyamine is used to treat spasms and tremors. The once popular B&O suppository mentioned above worked wonderfully to treat bladder spasms in patients with urinary catheters, or those undergoing surgeries in the urinary tract, including prostate surgery. Hyoscyamine is effective in the treatment of irritable bowel syndrome and colitis. It is also used to treat anticholinesterase poisoing from organophosphates found in many common insecticides and herbicides.

Scopolamine

Scopolamine is used to treat motion sickness and nausea. It also dries up oral secretions, and has been used extensively in pre and post surgical cases in the past. Scopolamine has been known to cause delirium, so it has fallen out of favor in hospitals, other than use as a skin patch to dry up secretions.

Medicinal Uses
Irritable Bowel

Belladonna is an inexpensive and effective treatment for gastrointestinal disorders and smooth muscle spasm. It is an ingredient in over the counter medications for colicky babies. There is one case documented in the literature where a painful intestinal obstruction was relieved after taking just 4 pills (6 grains) of belladonna extract.

Peptic Ulcer and GERD

Belladonna blocks receptors in smooth muscles in the intestines, acting to decrease spasm and moderately decrease pancreatic and gastric secretions. The decrease in secretions helps the ulcer heal, without causing the side effects caused by proton pump inhibitors. It also relieves pain.

Migraine

Belladonna is proving successful in treating migraine headache, especially throbbing headaches that come on suddenly and worsen with movement and light. There are dozens of user comments on Amazon attesting to the efficiency of Belladonna in treating headache.

A 2013 study looked at the use of belladonna to prevent and treat migraines in children. The study was conducted in 12 countries worldwide and included 168 children. The frequency, severity, and duration of migraine attacks decreased significantly during the 3-month follow-up period and belladonna, mainly at a dilution of 9C (1 drop in of belladonna in 99 ml of diluent, repeated 6 times.) A significant decrease in the frequency, severity, and duration of migraine attacks was observed and, consequently, reduced absenteeism from school.

Dose and Safety

The berries produced by the Belladonna plant look identical to blueberries, and there are cases of children having toxic symptoms including delirium, rapid heart rate, blurred vision and urinary retention after eating the berries. When used as a 1:3-1:5 tincture from fresh or dried leaf, doses range from 8-10 drops twice to three times daily for an average-size adult. Belladonna drops advertised on Amazon range from 3x to 30x on the homeopathic dilution scale, with the higher number being more dilute, as the number reflects serial dilution of the product.

Adverse effects with high doses include flushed skin, dry mouth and nervousness. Higher doses can cause confusion and fast heart rate progressing to lethargy and coma. Death is very rare, and an overdose can be treated with a drug called physostigmine. Belladonna is contraindicated in patients with glaucoma, benign prostatic hyperplasia, arrhythmias and megacolon.

90

ST. JOHN'S WORT

St. John's Wort (Hypericum perforatum) is a native of Europe, but has been introduced to the U. S. where it is considered a noxious weed in 7 states. In some areas, it is referred to as goatweed.

St. John's Wort is a perennial plant with extensive rhizomes. It has a taproot and the vertical roots can extend up to 5 feet. It has erect stems, reddish at the base, that branch off in the upper sections, and can grow as high as 3 feet. Leaves are a yellow-green in an opposite pattern. If you hold the leaf up to sun, you will see scattered perforations that let light through, hence the use of perforatum in the Latin name. The yellow flowers are 1 inch in diameter with five petals with black dots around the edges. The plant produces abundant seeds that smell like turpentine. The plant provides a source of pollen for pollinators.

Medicinal Uses

St. John's Wort has been documented to have antidepressant and anti-inflammatory properties. Other medicinal uses include treatment of insomnia, gout and diarrhea.

Depression

Among all natural treatments for depression, St. John's Wort has been most widely scientifically documented. In Germany, prior to the decision in 1996 that St. John's Wort did not meet the criteria for the regulatory guidelines of the European Union, St. John's Wort was prescribed more often than Prozac for mild to moderate depression.

However, St. John's Wort is still prescribed today, especially in children.

The prestigious Cochrane review that evaluates research in regard to health care issues examined 29 clinical trials on St. John's Wort in 2008, and concluded it was superior to placebo in patients with major depression, as effective as standard antidepressants, and had fewer side effects.

Inflammation

Since the time of John the Baptist, St. John's Wort has been used to make what is know as "red oil." The flowers only are gathered and soaked in olive oil for a few weeks, turning bright red in the process. The oil can be applied to the skin for arthritis pain, or to treat cuts and scrapes. It is also effective against vitiligo, (a condition where the skin loses its melanin, creating white patches),

Chronic Fatigue
A 2002 study on chronic fatigue found that St. John's Wort, 10 mg/kg by mouth had greater beneficial effect on symptoms than Prozac, and the authors concluded that St. John's Wort "could be useful in the treatment of Chronic Fatigue syndrome."

Side effects

St John's Wort has been shown to decrease the effectiveness of birth control pills. It has been known to cause photosensitivity, a condition that causes a skin reaction when exposed to sunlight. St. John's Wort may also aggravate psychosis in schizophrenic patients and cause manic episodes in those with bipolar disorder. It should not be combined with pharmaceutical antidepressants. St. John's Wort can speed up the metabolism of several drugs, including immunosuppressants, resulting in sub-therapeutic drug levels.

Other Uses

The hypericin in St. John's Wort is known as one of the most powerful photosensitizers in nature with excellent fluorescent properties. In five patients with a recurrence of a malignant glioma, a formulation of hypericin was given intravenously 6 hours before the surgical procedure. Tumor resection was aided when in all patients tumor tissue was clearly distinguishable from normal brain tissue by showing up with a red fluorescent color which was colored blue under a special fluorescent filter. The coloration of the tumor tissue greatly aided in removal of the cancer.

St. John's Wort grows well in Missouri.

91

YELLOW DOCK (RUMEX CRISPUS)

It's Autumn, making it the perfect time to dig roots from some medicinal plants. One of those plants is Yellow Dock, and while the tender young leaves can be eaten as greens in the spring, fall is the time to harvest the root of the plant. Originally native to Europe, Yellow Dock is now naturalized in the United States.

Yellow dock grows in disturbed soil, along roadsides and forest edges and in fields. The plant has lance shaped leaves with curly edges, hence the nickname Curly Dock. A member of the buckwheat family, in July and August the long green flower stalks are filled with rust-colored seeds.

Nutrition

Yellow Dock can be used as a wild green, but only the young leaves should be used as the plant becomes bitter with maturity. Even the young leaves should be boiled in at least 2 sets of water if consuming large quantities, in order to remove oxalic acid, but are okay to eat raw in smaller amounts. The leaves provide Vitamins A and C, and one cup contains over 100% of the daily requirement of these vitamins. The leaves are also good sources of protein, calcium, iron and potassium.

The seeds can be harvested, dried, and then ground into a flour. The dock seed flour can then be used to make unleavened crackers by adding just salt, water, and "regular" flour in equal amounts to the dock seed flour.

Medicinal Uses

While the seeds and leaves are edible, the root of yellow dock holds the medicinal properties, with most products made from root extract. In

1860, D. Leathe's Yellow Dock Syrup was a popular commodity, sold by the best apothecaries in Boston.

Anemia

Due to its high iron content, herbalists often recommend Yellow Dock root extract for treating anemia. It is often combined with stinging nettle for additional iron supplementation.

Obesity

An intriguing study from 2013 looked at the anti-obesity effect of ethanol extract of Yellow Dock on obesity. Yellow Dock was found to be an effective candidate for treating obesity, working by breaking down fat cells and preventing accumulation of adipose tissue. The researchers stated, "further studies will be needed to identify the active compounds that confer the anti-obesity activity of Rumex crispus (Yellow Dock).

Antioxidant

In a 2006 study, the anti-oxidant effects of 36 different plants when applied to the skin were investigated. In addition, the anti-wrinkle effects were also investigated to determine if the plants had commercial value in cosmetic preparations. The results showed that the Yellow Dock extract had the most significant free radical scavenging activity and cell-protecting effects. (Recall that free-radicals are unstable atoms that contribute to aging). It also had significant activity on elastase, important in maintaining skin elasticity. Extract of yellow dock also has a sunscreen effect when applied to the skin.

Diabetes

In a 2015 study that looked at the effect of a 6% extract of yellow dock root on diabetes in laboratory animals, blood sugar levels were decreased, especially in the third and fourth week of administration.

Respiratory Conditions

Yellow Dock has mainly been used for respiratory conditions, especially a tickling cough in the back of the throat.

Athlete's Foot

There is a record of the Zuni Indians using extract from Yellow Dock to treat athlete's foot.

Precautions

Those with a history of kidney stones should not use yellow dock, since the oxalates and tannins present in yellow dock may aggravate that condition. Yellow dock can also have a laxative effect.

The seeds of Yellow Dock turn rust brown in the fall and can be ground into flour. Note the resemblance to buckwheat.

The leaves of Yellow Dock are lance-like and curled at the edges.

92

CHESTNUTS – NEW TOOL AGAINST MRSA

American chestnuts are hard to find after a deadly fungus that killed most of the trees decades ago. Prior to that time, chestnuts were known as the "Redwoods of the East," due to the immense size of the trees, and made up 25 percent of Northeastern American forests.

What you are likely to find in Missouri today are Chinese chestnuts. Although not native, they grow well here, and are worthwhile to plant due to their medicinal properties. Growers in Missouri are marketing the chestnut as a health food, and the University of Missouri's Center for Agroforestry is taking an interest.

Nutrition

Chestnuts are becoming very popular, as they are low fat and gluten free. Chestnuts are so popular in the U.S. that we import 4,000 metric tons annually. Chestnuts are used to make gluten flour, and they are also used to make craft beers. Bees get the nectar from the flowers to make chestnut honey, more nutrient rich than most honeys, and a particularly good source of potassium, calcium, and manganese.

Medicinal qualities

Chestnut leaves contain remarkable elements that can disarm dangerous staph bacteria without causing drug resistance. Chestnut leaf extract is rich in ursene and oleanene that block Staph aureus, without contributing to the emerging epidemic of methicillin resistant staph aureus. In the words of researcher Cassandra Quave of Emory

University, "We've identified a family of compounds from this plant that have an interesting medicinal mechanism," Quave says. "Rather than killing staph, this botanical extract works by taking away staph's weapons, essentially shutting off the ability of the bacteria to create toxins that cause tissue damage. In other words, it takes the teeth out of the bacteria's bite. We've demonstrated in the lab that our extract disarms even the hyper-virulent MRSA strains capable of causing serious infections in healthy athletes, at the same time, the extract doesn't disturb the normal, healthy bacteria on human skin. It's all about restoring balance."

In traditional medicine, a tea was made from the leaves of the chestnut leave and used to treat skin infections and inflammations. In laboratory studies, a single, fairly dilute source of extract cleared up MRSA lesions in lab mice.

Researchers at Emory University identified possible uses for chestnut leaf extract including a preventative spray for athletic equipment that is often contaminated with staph.

Recently, it has been reported that chestnut inner shell extracts inhibited the development of hepatic steatosis in mice fed a high-fat diet.

Antioxidant Effects

Chestnut flowers have an outstanding antioxidant capacity, also displaying antimicrobial and antitumor effects. Studies on chestnut by-products revealed a good profile of bioactive compounds with antioxidant, anticarcinogenic and cardioprotective properties.

A 2010 study analyzed the antioxidant and anti-melanin properties of pre-bloom and full-bloom chestnut flowers. The extracts had high amounts of phenolics, gallic acid, flavonoids and quercetin. These extracts exhibited strong antioxidant activity. In addition, the extract effectively protected the skin against ultraviolet rays.

Chestnut flour

For those who are glucose intolerant, chestnut flour made from the low fat nuts is an excellent substitute, with some modifications for better consistency. Chestnut flour provides both health and nutritional benefits. Cookie samples prepared by replacement of 40% rice flour with chestnut flour had the softest texture, and elevated levels of chestnut flour increased hardness values.

Cosmetic Uses

The inner shell of the chestnut has been used in cosmetic materials, especially in Korea, where it is mixed with honey and sold as an anti-wrinkle and anti-aging compound. Research has indicated that the inner shell of the chestnut slows the production of the pigment melanin with the effect of decreasing or preventing age spots.

The chestnut inner shell has been used as a cosmetic material for a long time in Korea, and previous research has demonstrated that chestnut fruits and leaves contain phenolic compounds. However, little is known about the potential uses of chestnut shell. Chestnut has been sold as an anti-wrinkle and anti-aging compound when mixed with honey, and previous research on the chestnut inner shell has suggested that this material inhibited the biosynthesis of melanin.

93

JEWELWEED – NATURE'S CURE FOR POISON IVY

Impatiens capensis, commonly known in Missouri as jewelweed, is an annual plant native to North America. It grows in ditches, beside creeks, and in the bottomland of pastures. The plants grow as high as five feet tall, and produce easy to recognize orange flowers. The plant produces seedpods with explosive seeds that pop out of the pod at the lightest touch. When held underwater, the leaves appear silver, possibly the origin of the nickname jewelweed.

There is documentation of use the juice from the leaves and stems by Native Americans in the treatment of skin rashes. The plant is gaining increased popularity as a treatment for poison ivy, and is the subject of several research studies.

Jewelweed and Poison Ivy

Another study published in 2006 in the Journal of the American Pharmaceutical Association concluded that jewelweed juice, or concentrated solutions of jewelweed, were capable of inactivating more dilute poison ivy extracts.

Native Americans of the eastern and midwestern U.S. and Canada used jewelweed to prevent and treat skin reactions to Toxidodendron radicans (poison ivy) and Urtica dioica (stinging nettle).

A 2012 study sought to validate the use of jewelweed in poison ivy dermatitis prevention and to refute other scientific papers denying its efficacy. Additionally, the content of lawsone, the purported effective agent in jewelweed preparations, was measured to see if its concentration correlated with jewelweed preparation efficacy. Poison ivy was brushed onto forearms of volunteers in 6 locations and exposed areas were treated with jewelweed extracts, fresh plant mashes, soaps made of plant extracts, water and Dawn® dish soap. Rash development was scored on a scale of 0-14. Jewelweed mash was effective in reducing poison ivy dermatitis, supporting its use. However, jewelweed extracts were not effective; leading researchers to conclude that saponins, the soapy component of jewelweed are the effective agents.

In a follow up of the 2012 study, a second study published in 2015 looked closely at saponins found in jewelweed. Saponins are natural soapy components found within plants. For the study, jewelweed leaves were extracted with methanol and water to obtain a saponin containing extract. The presence of saponins in the extracts was proven by the observation of foaming in the extract fluid. Efficacy of the saponin containing extracts in rash reduction was tested by brushing poison ivy onto the forearms of 23 volunteers and treating these exposed areas with distilled water (control), saponin containing extracts, fresh plant mashes, and soaps made with and without plant extracts. Both saponin containing extracts and all soaps tested were effective in reducing poison ivy dermatitis and researchers concluded that saponin content correlates with poison ivy rash prevention.

In addition to inactivating poison ivy, the 2012 study found additional biologic activity provided by saponins. The extracts were further tested for biological activity against both gram negative and gram-positive bacteria and against cancer cell lines A-375, HT-29, and MCF-7. No apparent antibiotic effect was observed against any bacteria tested; however, dose response cytotoxicity was documented against MCF-7 breast cancer cells and cytostatic activity was seen against the HT-29 colon cancer cell lines.

Other Uses

Jewelweed has been shown to be an excellent food source for migrating ruby-throated hummingbirds.

Jewelweed Soap

2 cups lard
1/2 cup coconut oil
1/2 cup lye water
jewelweed mash

1. First make jewelweed mash by chopping up stems and leaves of the jewelweed plant. Cook in a small amount of gently simmering water until the plants parts are soft and come apart easily. Using a hand mixer, beat the mixture until there are no large parts.
2. Melt the lard and coconut oil, stirring in the jewelweed mash.
3. In an outdoor area, slowly add the lye water to the mixture, combining thoroughly.
4. Pour into soap molds, and allow to cure for 4 weeks.

Jewelweed soap can also be purchased on Amazon at about $10 per bar.

Jewelweed is easy to recognize by its orange flowers

94

FLOWERING DOGWOOD – MISSOURI'S STATE TREE

We all love the dogwood for its beautiful blooms, but also because their presence announces springtime. Dogwood flowers have four white petals, and the leaves are egg shaped in an alternated pattern. The dogwood we commonly see in Missouri is the Flowering Dogwood, *Cornus florida*. The tree can grow up to 40 feet tall, but according to legend, after Jesus Christ was crucified on a cross made of dogwood, God mandated that dogwoods would again never grow tall enough for that purpose.

Even when not in bloom, dogwood trees are easily identified by their bark. When mature, the gray bark cracks into little squares with the resemblance of alligator hide.

Many may not be aware that the dogwood produces a fruit. The fruit appears between August and November in clusters of 2 to 6, in the form of a bright red drupe that contains one to two seeds. The edible drupe has an orange center that is tart/sweet when ripe. Dogwood fruit has long been used both food and medicine. Due to the high vitamin C content, a traditional use has been to fight colds and the flu. Dogwoods are food plants for several species of moths and butterflies and game birds feed on the seeds.

Other varieties of dogwood have a sweet fruit, especially the Chinese Dogwood, and are sold as fruit trees. The fruit of our native tree, while edible, is often bitter, but is loved by wildlife. In fact, the berries, seeds, flowers, bark and leaves are all food sources for birds, small mammals, foxes, deer, and even bears. The high calcium and fat content of the dogwood make it very nutritious.

Woodworking

Fine-grained dogwood is much in demand for crafting items requiring a hard, strong wood. The wood wears evenly and resists splitting, Dogwood twigs have even been used as primitive toothbrushes.

Medicinal Uses

Dogwood was used by Confederate soldiers during the Civil War in the form of a bark tea used to treat pain and fever, and a poultice made from leaves to treat wounds. Dogwood bark has been also used as a substitute for quinine, a component shown to be effective against malaria.

During World War II, when the quinine supplies of the United States were cut off by enemy forces, the potential of dogwood bark as a quinine replacement was again considered when it was found to be active in treating avian malaria.

Almost all parts of dogwood trees can be used for medicinal purposes: the bark, roots, berries, twigs, leaves and flowers. Native Americans also used the root of dogwood trees to treat malaria. The inner bark of the roots contain components called anthocyanins, pigments with associated flavonoids that have demonstrated the ability to protect against many human diseases. They inhibit COX-1 and 2 enzymes by up to 48%, bringing a strong anti-inflammatory property. This finding may validate the use of dogwood bark tea for pain. Anthocyanins also block the growth of certain types of cancer cells in the breast, lungs, colon, and central nervous system. Other ailments that have been treated with dogwood include insomnia, asthma, fevers, muscular problems, whooping cough, toothache and even mange in dogs.

Other uses

Native Americans used the marker of dogwood blooming as an indication of when to plant their crops, especially corn.

Dogwood roots can also be used to make dyes. The roots of the different species of dogwood provide different colors.

From August through November, the dogwood bears an edible, but not very tasty fruit.

95

POACHING PLANTS

Plants are very valuable resources. We may take them for granted as they appear to be plentiful, but as both the medicinal and nutritional values become more known, some plants are on the brink of endangerment. With approximately 25 percent of pharmaceuticals made from plant extracts or components, large pharmaceutical companies either buy native plants, or grow their own. One example is Abbott Pharmaceuticals who purchases approximately 300,000 pounds of mayapple collected in the wild annually. Mayapple is used in the preparation of a form of chemotherapy that works against drug resistant tumors. Reportedly, Abbott Laboratory is considering cultivating the plant on a commercial scale.

Other popular plants subject to poaching are sassafras, purple coneflower, and ginseng. Unfortunately, some of the most medically effective plants are being over harvested, and even obtained illegally. The Missouri Department of Conservation receives calls every year by homeowners who discover holes are their property, indicating that plants have been illegally poached. Missouri state law prohibits the harvesting of plants from highway rights-of-way. Collecting is also illegal in state parks, national forests and conservation areas. It goes without saying that harvesting plants without landowner permission is also illegal, and you could possibly be charged with trespassing or theft.

Desirable plants often grow in patches or colonies in the wild, making it fairly easy to completely eradicate the plant from a certain area by an over-zealous harvester.

Sassafras

If you want a cup of sassafras tea, it can be tempting to help yourself to a root from a neighbor's land, as it can't be purchased commercially. Fortunately, sassafras can be easily harvested without harming the plant. Sassafras tends to grow in groves with trees that are connected horizontally below ground. By digging in between the trees, you can dig up a small section of connecting root, not harming the tree. Be sure to ask your neighbor first, and bring them some freshly harvested root.

Purple Coneflower

Purple Cornflower is used to make the extract Echinacea. Due to the popularity of echinacea in treating colds and the flu, many species of coneflowers in Missouri have been affected by poaching and over-harvesting of the root, which has a ready market. When harvesting cornflower, take seeds from the plant and sow them back in the area from which the plant was harvested. If harvested in late fall (the best time), save the seeds and store them in a sealed container in the refrigerator (to simulate winter), planting them in the early spring.

Ginseng

In some states, but not Missouri, you are required to have a license to harvest ginseng. Wild ginseng can only be harvested from Sept. 1 – Dec. 31st. because if harvested too early, the plant will not have yet produced viable seeds necessary to ensure a sustainable crop of wild ginseng. Dried ginseng may be purchased, sold or transported from Sept. 15 through March 15; wet or undried ginseng may be purchased, sold or transported from Sept. 1 through March 15, and certified roots may be possessed, purchased, sold, transported or exported throughout the year. The Missouri Dept. of Conservation certifies roots to meet requirements for tracking annual harvests, and roots require certification prior to shipment out of Missouri, or if they will be held between March 15 and Sept. 1.

Harvested ginseng plants or roots must possess at least three true leaves (prongs). The fruiting stalk and stem, except the mature fruits, must be kept with the plant until it is returned to the harvester's home or place of business. The seeds from each harvested plant must be planted within 100 feet of the parent plant.

All of the rules and regulations regarding wild ginseng are designed to protect this valuable plant. Ginseng is a highly poached plant, with roots that can sell for up to $800 per pound overseas.

Hazards of over-harvesting

Like people, plants are genetically diverse, and when a certain plant is overharvested, thoughtless harvesters are shrinking the gene pool – leading to increased disease in the plant population, In addition, overharvesting may cause the loss of specific genes in a plant that could hold the key to a cure for a previously incurable disease. Even worse, the plant can be completely eradicated. Researchers are looking into growing native medicinal plants commercially in hopes of taking the strain off wild plants.

The good news is that native plants are a truly renewable resource. With careful consideration and harvesting practices, we can ensure their benefits will be available to following generations. For every plant you harvest, try to plant a few seeds.

96

STONECROP

There are as many as 600 species of sedum, commonly called stonecrop, as the plant grows well on stones (and roofs, as we shall see). Sedum is a perennial leaf succulent, found mainly in the northern hemisphere. The variety common to Missouri is *Sedum ternatum*, also known as Three-Leafed Stonecrop.

Plant characteristics

Three-leafed stonecrop is favored as a natural ground cover. It has fleshy leaves that occur in circles of three. In the spring, it produces tiny white flowers with 4 petals with purple stamens. It grows well in full and partly sunny sites and along stream banks. Its succulent leaves enable it to retain moisture in shallow soil, such as that found on stony ledges.

Medicinal uses

Sedum is finally attracting the attention of researchers centuries after its clinical use was first described in a variety ancient medical texts, especially those from Italy. The species has been frequently used for various conditions, including the treatment of insect bites, burns, corns, ulcers, warts, abscesses and wounds. The fresh leaves are applied as poultice or ointment for topical application, whereas the juice from crushed leaves is used to heal scars. Stonecrop is used in modern natural medicine to treat open wounds and severe burns, including second and third degree, and traumatic injuries involving bone.

The main active ingredients in stonecrop are flavonoids and

polysaccharides, but coumarins, amino acids and triterpenes are also present. Among the flavonoids contained in the palnt are kaempferol and quercetin, considered anti-cancer substances.

The mechanism by which stonecrop repairs damaged tissue is thought to be due to actions at the cellular level, including regeneration of new tissue, including replacement of collagen, reduction of pathogenic bacteria, and reshaping of the new tissue in its final structure. Sedum is especially active against strains of Strep and Staph bacteria. Preparations obtained from Sedum leaves have also been shown to modulate the inflammatory response, resulting in less pain and swelling.

The best harvest season for Medicinal Sedum is the full-bloom period between the end of April and the beginning of May.

Pain Relief

A study in 2009 sought to identify the compounds in stonecrop responsible for pain relief and anti-inflammatory effects. Kamepferol was shown to account for the "renowned medicinal use of Sedum against pain and inflammatory troubles."

Wound Healing

Stonecrop has been used in clinical practice for many years to treat skin wounds. Multiple products are available online including moisturizers and skin care treatments. Multiple studies have shown that stonecrop increases skin hydration, protecting it from drying out and aging. Application of the extract stimulates collagen and helps in tissue regeneration, improving the appearance of scars.

Other Uses

Vegetated "Green" Roofs

Roofs covered with vegetation are increasingly used around the world to improve building efficiency with both heating and cooling. Stonecrop has been found to cool roofs significantly more than other vegetation, providing constant, near 100% vegetative cover.

Soil Restoration

Stonecrop is useful in saving soil contaminated with copper and cadmium. The plant bio-accumulates these heavy metals, extracting them from the soil

Stonecrop with its whorls of 3 leaves and white petals. (Photo courtesy of Missouri Botanical Garden)

97

ANGELICA

Angelica is a tall, aromatic plant with large white flowers in umbrels, similar to Queen Anne's Lace, that bloom in July. The plant grows up to 6 feet. It is native to Eastern North America. You can find it in bottomlands, along stream banks and shady roadsides. It has a smooth, dark purple hollow stem that has many uses. Leaves are dark green, divided into three parts. The plant is biennial, producing seed in its second year, dying after the seed ripens. The plant got its name from a legend whereby the plant was revealed in an angel's dream as a cure for the plague. The leaves, stems, root and seeds all taste like licorice. The plant has been used for both food and for its medicinal applications.

Nutritional Use

The root of the Angelica plant contains vitamins B1, B2 and B12, zinc, potassium, magnesium, iron, and sugars fructose, sucrose and glucose, in addition to other trace minerals. In cooking, fresh leaves can be added to salads. The shoots have a sweet taste and can be substituted for celery or crystallized with sugar as a snack. The leaves, seeds and roots can all be used to make a tea that tastes like licorice.

Medicinal Uses

Some of the main constituents of Angelica include valeric acid, angelic acid (anti-spasmodic and sedative), angelicin, safrole (a natural pesticide), scopoletin (a blood thinner), and linoleic acid (an essential fatty acid). Angelica is sold as an extract on Amazon, and testimonials are posted as to its effectiveness in aiding digestion. It is commonly used to treat symptoms of upset stomach, acid reflux, cramping, nausea, and vomiting.

Angelica is also helpful as a face wash for cystic acne, and a powder made from the dried root is effective against athlete's food. The extract is used as a medicinal gargle for sore throat, and makes a pain-relieving poultice for aching joints and swollen tissue.

Commercial cutlivation focuses on the root, as that is the source of the plant's medicinal properties. Essential oil extracted from the plant contains over 60 active components. β–phellandrene and α–pinene, both pleasant scents, have the highest concentration in root oil but sabiene (a spice), myrcene (an anti-inflammatory), limonene (relieves acid reflux and heartburn), 3–carene and p–cymene (also found in cumin and thyme) are also present in large amounts.

Diabetes

A 2016 study looked at protective effects of angelica against hyperglycemia and liver injury in type 2 diabetics. The study found that angelica had beneficial effects in preventing hyperglycemia, stimulating insulin secretion, promoting hepatic glycogen synthesis, reducing liver fat accumulation, and attenuating liver injury.

Other Uses

In Lapland the angelica plant is used to make a traditional musical instrument called the fadno, a reed instrument similar to a flute.

The plant was smoked by Missouri tribes for colds and respiratory ailments and Alaska natives applied boiled roots as a poultice, and drank an infusion to heal both internal and external wounds.

Dosing

Typical dosing for stomach upset is 1/5 of a teaspoon three times daily.

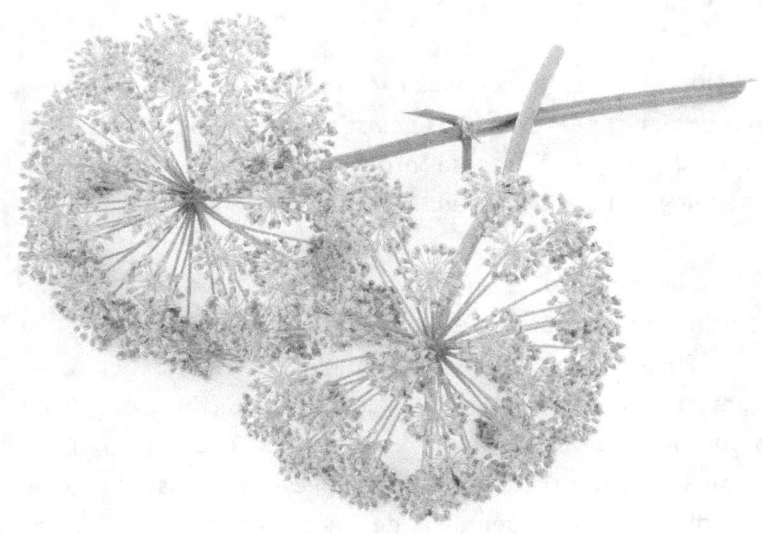

Angelica produces white flowers in umbrels, similar to wild carrot.

Three uses for angelica: crystallized stalk, dried root and extract.

98

REINDEER LICHEN

Reindeer lichen (*Cladonia rangiferina*) is unique, year-round native crop. It grows throughout the state, on open ground, and in shaded woods. I've found hundreds growing in the thin soil on rocks on the bluffs above the highway near my house. As an unusual food source, it would be hard to beat reindeer lichen, as it can be used in soups, jellies and to make flour.

Lichens aren't plants, but a complicated living organism, made up of a fungus and algae. The fungus portion is the most dominant, but has no means of producing food, so the algae portion performs photosynthesis, feeding the fungi so the lichen can grow and spread. Lichen often has 2 forms of algae, green and blue green, also called cyanobacteria, which has some characteristics of bacteria, and responds to antibiotics, not algaecide.

Dozens of active compounds have been isolated from Reindeer moss, some of which have been found to be active against MRSA (methicillin resistant staph aureus) and VRE (vancomycin-resistant Eeterococci, two very tough infections to treat.

Mad Cow Disease

A 2011 study found that Reindeer lichen can degrade the deadly prion that causes mad cow disease, also know as spongiform encephalopathy, through the enzyme serine protease. The study authors suggest that some lichens could have potential to inactivate prion infectivity on the landscape or be a source for agents to degrade prions. This also has implications for treating Chronic Wasting Disease in the deer population, another deadly prion disease.

Prion disease is a disease like no other. Not a virus, nor a bacteria, prions are abnormal protein particles found mostly in central nervous system tissue, and disease is contracted by ingesting the infected tissue. The disease is progressive and 100% fatal, and I have cared for only 3 of these patients in the course of my career. Symptoms begin with mood changes, lack of judgment and increasing anxiety. Speech becomes hard to understand, progressing to being nonverbal. The patient develops increasing rigidity and tremor. Hallucinations are common. Death almost always occurs in under a year. As a nurse, it is very had to care for these patients, as any attempts to comfort them causes increased anxiety and agitation.

 Diagnosis can only be made by brain biopsy, but unfortunately the surgical instruments cannot be adequately sterilized to remove prions as they are resistant to heat or chemicals.. I have encountered one patient in my career thought to have contracted mad cow disease via contaminated instruments. Today, brain biopsies are only performed on deceased individuals on the pathologist's table. If contamination is suspected, surgical instruments used must be incinerated at temperatures of 1000 degrees F. or higher, and obviously not reused.

Kidney Stones

There is record of the use of lichen by tribes in the Himalayas to treat kidney stones. A tea can be made from gathered lichen that is effective against diarrhea.

Nutritional Use

Lichens are generally regarded as low in protein but high in carbohydrate. Reindeer lichen get their name from the fact that they are a preferred source of food for caribou.

Dried lichen can be made into a flour substitute by drying and then crushing it into the consistency you prefer, then using it as a flour substitute in a 75/25 flour to lichen ratio.

Deodorant

There are several deodorants made from lichen extract. For those wishing to avoid aluminum, lichen extract has excellent antiperspirant properties.

Lichen can be found in large patches, it takes only a few minutes to fill a small bag. Note the characteristic reindeer "antlers."

99

CLEANSE ME WITH HYSSOP

Cleanse me with hyssop, and I will be clean; wash me, and I will be whiter than snow. Psalm 51:7

Hyssop is a commonly used medicinal plant, acting as a pain reliever, antiseptic and cough suppressant. Different varieties of hyssop grow throughout the world, and in Missouri, we are most likely to find anise hyssop *(agastache foeniculum),* thought to be the plant described by Lewis Meriweather in the journals documenting the 1804 – 1806 Lewis and Clark expedition. Meriweather wrote "I observed some flax growing *in* the bottoms on this river, but saw no clover or timothy, as I had seen on the *Missouri* and Jefferson river. There is a kind of wild sage or *hyssop*, as high as a man's head, full of branches and leaves, which grows *in* these bottoms. ..."

A herbaceous perennial, anise hyssop is native to North American and displays purple blooms from June to September. The plant spreads by rhizomes and self-seeding; is drought –resistant and likes full sun. Due to rhizomes, it is usually found in clumps. Like other members of the mint family, hyssop has a square stem. It is a good pollen plant for bees, resulting in a rich, aromatic honey. The plant is also attractive to hummingbirds and butterflies.

Nutritional Use

The sweet-smelling minty leaves can be used to make herbal tea or jelly. The dried leaves are also used in potpourri. Seeds from the plant are an interesting addition to cookies or muffins, imparting a unique flavor.

Medicinal Use

Traditionally, a poultice made from the plant was used to treat cuts and wounds. A tea made from the leaves with added honey has been used to treat cough, sore throat and wheezing. A decoction with vinegar and hyssop leaves was used as a toothache remedy. A 2004 study utilizing an inhaled flower infusion found it was both soothing and improved sleep. Other applications include supporting cardiac performance and improving condition of blood vessels.

In Mexico, hyssop is a medicinal plant widely used in traditional medicine for the treatment of anxiety, hypertension, and relief of heart disease, insomnia, and diabetes, as well as to reduce stomach ache.

Dried, cut hyssop is available on Amazon, where the product has 5 star reviews with testimonials ranging from its effect of fighting shingles to treating seasonal allergies. Many folks make a tea for use before bedtime to insure a good night's sleep.

Blood pressure

Hyssop has been found to have a beneficial effect on blood pressure, and a study conducted in 2015 attributes this at least partially to the relaxing effect on cardiac muscle and blood vessels. The relaxation effect of hyssop is due to both calcium channel blockade and opening of potassium channels (an effect caused by common heart medications), lowering both systolic and diastolic blood pressure but not affecting heart rate. The study corroborated the use of hyssop as a medication to lower blood pressure.

Harvesting

For optimal effect, hyssop is harvested twice a year, at the end of spring and onset of autumn, preferably when flowering. The stalks are cut and hung to dry, then kept from sun exposure to prevent oxidation of chemicals. Complete drying usually takes six days, after which the leaves are removed, and chopped finely with flowers added

Other uses

Both coneflower and hyssop have been found effective in dissipating petroleum found in the soil, removing 71.1% and 72.5% of petroleum hydrocarbons, respectively. A paper published in 2014 discussed a community project in which one of Chicago's abandoned service stations was transformed into a lovely community garden in the middle of the city.

A herbaceous perennial, anise hyssop is native to North American and displays purple blooms from June to September.

100

THE HEALTH IMPORTANCE OF NATURAL HONEY

Honey is a naturally sweet substance produced by honeybees from the nectar of blossoms that the bees collect and then combine with specific substances of their own. The bees store honey to ripen and mature in the honeycomb they create. Honey includes carbohydrates, phosphorus, sucrose, potassium, glucose, magnesium, fructose, zinc, sodium fiber, Vitamins B2, B3, B5, B6 and B9, protein fat, water, Vitamin C, calcium and iron. Not many other food sources can boast such a wide array of beneficial nutrients.

Honey and Diabetics

Honey contains sugars in the form of dextrose (31%), fructose (38%) and sucrose (1.3%). On a weight basis, honey is as sweet as granulated sugar, with more sweetening power at a lower dextrose load – beneficial to both Type 1 and Type II diabetics due to a lower glycemic effect with less rise in blood sugar.

Sports Nutrition

Honey can boost athletic performance. When ingested just prior to exercise, it is released into the system at a steady rate throughout the event. When consumed during exercise, honey helps muscles stays nourished and delays fatigue. Ingesting honey post-exercise along with a protein source within 30 minutes after exercise allows the body to refuel and decreases muscle soreness.

Honey in medicine

The medicinal uses of honey have been found on papyrus documents dating back to 1550 BC, with hundreds of applications. The science of the healing properties of honey and other bee products is so extensive, it has its own name – Apitherapy. Different types of honey have different uses, for example, Dandelion honey is used in traditional medicine for liver, kidney, gastric, gall bladder and intestine diseases, while Sunflower honey is used for smooth muscle spasms in asthma. Buckwheat honey improves digestion, and is high in antioxidants, while Chestnut honey enhances blood circulation and protects against anemia. Clover honey is a calmative, and Manuka honey is used for its wound healing and antibacterial properties.

Wound Infections

Honey is an ancient cure for wound infections, but in modern times there is increasing interest in the antimicrobial properties of honey. In most honey types, antimicrobial activity is due to the generation of hydrogen peroxide (H_2O_2), but this can vary greatly among samples. Manuka honey seems to be especially promising against both H. pylori (the organism that causes stomach ulcers), and Staph aureas, a number one cause of wound infections. When used on wounds, honey not only has anti-bacterial properties, it provides a protective layer and a moist wound environment necessary for wound healing. Years ago, wounds were treated with dry heat, and I can remember applying many a heat lamp to a non-healing wound. That practice has been discarded as it has been proven wounds heal best in moist environments; a fact that explains why a wound covered with a Band-Aid heals more quickly than one opened to air.

Diabetic Foot Ulcers

Foot ulcers are a common complication of diabetes, due to both decrease in circulation to the foot, and loss of sensation leading to injury. These ulcers are very serious, and can lead to amputation. In a

2010 case report of a 79-year-old man with type II diabetes with foot ulcers for which he originally received traditional therapy, deep tissue cultures showed the wound was infected with antibiotic resistant VRE and MRSA. Before a trial of topical honey was tried, the patient lost 3 toes, after which a once-daily thick application of local honey was tried. Saline dressings and antibiotics were stopped, and granulation tissue appeared in 2 weeks. Within 12 month, the ulcers were fully resolved and did not recur.
Honey Part 2

Gastroenterology

Honey is helpful in preventing and treating disorders of the gastrointestinal tract such as gastritis and peptic ulcer. Honey is a potent inhibitor of the organism that causes these disorders, Helicobacter pylori (no, ulcers are not due to stress!) Honey works as a probiotic by increasing the number of "good" bacteria in the gastrointestinal tract.

Dental Health

Raw honey enhances dental health, and also helps to prevent cavities, likely due to its ability to prevent bacterial growth that contributes to cavities. Honey prevents dental plaque and gingivitis, and lessens pain associated with tooth extraction.

Mucositis is painful ulceration of the mucous membranes, usually an adverse effect or radiation and/or chemotherapy treatment for cancer. In a study of 60 patients divided in 3 groups, The first group was treated with natural honey applied directly to the affected area, the second group was treated with 0.15% benzydamine, and the third group was treated with normal saline. Notable reduction in mucositis in the honey-treated group was seen, leading to the conclusion that "pure, natural hone can be an effective agent in managing radiation induced oral mucositis, which is also an easily available, simple, potent and inexpensive agent."

Eye Disorders

The therapeutic use of natural honey to treat eye diseases is documented, and currently being studied further. In traditional medicine, natural honey was applied on the eyeball itself to prevent scarring due to corneal infections. Clinical trials involving over 100 subjects with eye disease including blepharitis, conjunctivitis and keratitis unresponsive to conventional treatment were treated with honey applied topically to the eyeball, resulting in "astounding successful healing."

Anti-inflammatory

Honey has anti-inflammatory activity not only on wounds, but even when taken internally. Ingestion of natural honey is associated with a decrease in prostaglandins, pain-causing substances. In one study examining the use of honey as an anti-inflammatory in colitis, honey was found to be as effective as the drug prednisolone. Honey has been found to promote wound healing, reduce swelling and drainage, stimulate tissue regeneration and reduce scarring.

How to test honey for purity

There are several ways to test honey. Here are a few of them. Place a drop of honey in the palm of your hand. Pure honey will stay intact, if the drop disperses, it is not pure. You can also add a spoonful of honey to a clear glass filled with water. If the honey dissolves, it is artificial, but pure honey will settle at the bottom of the glass. Pure honey is also flammable. To test this, dip a dry matchstick into the honey to be tested. Strike the match on the matchbox, and if it is coated with real honey, it will light and the flame will keep burning. Sometimes pure honey is mixed with other ingredients, if so; you could have mixed results on these tests. One local honey distributor is known to mix different batches of honey before placing in jars for sale.

The best way to ensure pure honey is to manage your own hives! We have many local experts willing to share their expertise. For an initial investment around $200, you can harvest your own honey, and contribute to the health of our local ecosystem.

Index

A

arthritis, 42, 68, 96, 107, 136, 233, 243
  rheumatoid, 68, 242–43
Asia, 59–60, 88, 102, 183, 189, 275
aspirin, 122, 132, 193, 231, 282
asthma, 79, 93, 148, 157, 163, 243, 253, 259, 306, 324
astringent, 71, 74, 76, 144, 211, 221
athlete's foot, 297
atrial fibrillation, 165
atropine, 103, 289

B

baking soda, 8, 82
barbiturates, 275–76
bark, 7, 17–20, 56, 88, 156, 173, 200–203, 240, 253, 259–60, 305–
  6
beans, green coffee, 25, 30
bees, 6, 31, 75, 225, 236, 299, 320, 323
beets, 38, 206
behavioral problems, 30
benzodiazepines, 138, 275–76
beta carotene, 19, 223
Bible, 4, 170
bitter, 226, 268, 295, 305
blackhead remover, 15
bleeding, 49–50, 74, 76, 170, 184, 211, 228
blepharitis, 326
blood, 29, 50, 125–26, 134, 157, 165, 177, 205, 209, 213, 215–16,
  234, 270
  oxygenated, 281, 283
blood cells
  red, 11, 134
  white, 4, 283
blood circulation, 219, 324
blood glucose levels, 90, 164
blood pressure, 10, 13, 17–18, 26–28, 82, 119, 123, 187, 209, 223,
  256, 260, 321
  treating high, 201
blood sugar, 14, 153, 234, 256, 323

D

energy, 151, 236
enzymes, 18, 63, 202, 243, 306
epilepsy, 132, 242
ergot, hazards of, 170–71
Esophageal Cancer, 100
esophagus, 35, 100, 103
estrogen, 39, 42, 180, 206, 250
etoposide, 67–68, 273
expectorant, 57, 71, 91, 122, 177, 201
extinct, 118, 249, 272
extract, 17–19, 39, 46, 76, 79–80, 89–90, 96–97, 111–12, 132–34,
    157–58, 272–73, 296–97, 300, 303, 314–16
eye, 29, 73, 113, 210–11, 283
eye diseases, 325–26

F

Familial adenomatous polyposis, 100
farmers, 107, 134, 143, 163, 184–85, 265–66
fast heart rate, 253, 291
fasting, 166, 262
fat, brown, 89
fat cells, 89, 296
fat content, 257, 306
fat metabolism, 72, 89
fatty acids, 45, 49, 53, 106, 151, 160, 204, 314
fatty liver, 136, 138
FDA, 36, 57, 148, 171, 194, 288
fermentation, 40, 163
fertility, 60, 127
fetus, 23, 191, 274
fever, 7, 42, 75, 78, 121, 130, 137, 144, 151, 177, 226, 259, 268,
    275, 306
fever reducer, 56, 75, 144
Fexofenadine, 80
fiber, dietary, 255–56
fibromyalgia, 19, 137
Flagyl, 182
flavonoids, 106, 134, 300, 311–12

J

K

L

lymphomas, 67–68, 201, 273

M

mad cow disease, 317
  contracted, 318
magnesium, 53, 71, 82, 106, 129, 144, 160, 240, 314, 323
malignant melanoma, 113
manganese, 71, 82, 106, 151, 299
Measles, 57
medicinal gargle, 315
melanin, 293, 301
melatonin, 19, 136–38
  natural, 137, 139
membranes, 84, 193
  mucous, 92, 157, 259, 261, 325
memory, 11, 60, 62, 175, 205, 225
menopausal, 44, 84
menopause, 42, 206
menstrual cramps, 22, 226
mercury, 35, 134, 195, 273
Meriweather, Lewis, 320
Meskwaki tribes, 148, 246
metals, heavy, 133, 218, 273, 313
methicillin, 109, 299, 317
migraine attacks, 79, 291
migraines, 78–80, 171–72, 290–91
Monarch Butterfly, 250–51
Monsanto, 264–65
mothers, nursing, 22, 80, 133, 142, 165, 191
mouthwash, 23, 214
MRSA, 109–10, 299, 317, 325
  acquired, 110
MRSA lesions, 300
mucus, 18, 80, 148
muscles, 180, 283, 323
  treating painful, 286
muscle spasms, smooth, 290, 324
mutations, 39, 219

P

R

Szechuan pepper, 202

T

Tamiflu, 57
Teething children, 123
Terminator Gene, 265
theobromine, 167
thirst quencher, 143–44
throat, 76, 97, 282, 297
thymol, 141, 178, 283
Thyroid Disease, 75
tincture, 44, 69, 284, 291
tongue, 35, 97
toothpaste, 34–35, 82, 84, 214
  homemade, 84
toxicity, 34, 97, 133, 142, 159, 178, 191, 208, 218, 244, 277
toxins, 103, 205, 214, 300
tract, intestinal, 65, 261
traditional medicine, 17, 50, 71, 147, 275, 300, 321, 324–25
Treating Infection, 116, 144
tremors, 22, 289, 318
triglycerides, 63, 100, 119, 262
tuberculosis, 66, 92, 163, 208
tumor effects, 113, 133, 137
tumors, 35, 50, 61, 133, 156, 161
Type II diabetes, 191, 324

U

ulcers, 23, 72, 76, 122, 132, 204, 227, 262, 286, 311, 324–25
United States, 31, 56, 59, 121, 125, 150, 173, 250, 252, 261, 289, 295, 306

V

vision loss, 210–11
Vitamin, 3–4, 19, 38, 45, 49–50, 64, 125–26, 144, 151, 160, 204, 223, 230, 261, 295

ABOUT THE AUTHOR

At the time this book is published, Marie Lasater has practiced nursing as a Registered Nurse for 38 years. Her passion for healing continues, as does her belief that our Heavenly Father has provided all the tools we need to heal illness in the form of native plants and holistic treatment.

www.ingramcontent.com/pod-product-compliance
Lightning Source LLC
Chambersburg PA
CBHW060233290526
45789CB00001B/33